IF LOVE COULD KILL

IF LOVE COULD KILL

The Myths and Truths of Women Who Commit Violence

ANNA MOTZ

ALFRED A. KNOPF   NEW YORK   2024

THIS IS A BORZOI BOOK
PUBLISHED BY ALFRED A. KNOPF

Copyright © 2023, 2024 by Anna Motz

All rights reserved.
Published in the United States by Alfred A. Knopf,
a division of Penguin Random House LLC, New York,
and distributed in Canada by Penguin Random House
Canada Limited, Toronto. Originally published in hardcover
in different form in Great Britain as *A Love That Kills*
by Weidenfeld & Nicolson, an imprint of
Orion Publishing Group, London, in 2023.

www.aaknopf.com

Knopf, Borzoi Books, and the colophon are
registered trademarks of Penguin Random House LLC.

Library of Congress Cataloging-in-Publication Data
Names: Motz, Anna, 1964– author.
Title: If love could kill: the myths and
truths of women who commit violence / Anna Motz.
Description: New York: Alfred A. Knopf, 2024. | Includes index.
Identifiers: LCCN 2023012367 | ISBN 9780593534151 (hardcover) |
ISBN 9780593534168 (ebook)
Subjects: LCSH: Female offenders—Psychology. | Violence in women. |
Female offenders—Mental health services.
Classification: LCC HV6046 .M638 2024 |
DDC 305.48/42—dc23/eng/20230330
LC record available at https://lccn.loc.gov/2023012367

Jacket image by undrey/Getty Images
Jacket design by Jenny Carrow

Manufactured in the United States of America
First American Edition

*To three women who, in different ways,
taught me much about the truth of maternal love:
my friend and mentor Estela Welldon,
my daughter, Hannah,
and my late mother, Lotte*

Contents

Introduction

In more than thirty years of working with women who span the extremes of psychological disturbance, I have been confronted with descriptions of extraordinary violence and fantasies of worse. These stay with me, yet my most vivid memories are not of what patients have done or dreamed about. Nor are they the moments of fear I have sometimes felt when sitting across the table from someone who has a violent history and may see me as their enemy.

Instead, the episodes that most readily come to mind are quiet ones in which little was said but much was communicated about a woman's trauma and torment: the life experiences and psychological damage that led her to commit an otherwise inexplicable crime. I think, for example, of Miriam, who had lived for fifteen years on the secure wing of a psychiatric hospital where I worked. She arrived at one session in an unusually frenzied state, so agitated that she was struggling to speak. Eventually, she was able to explain. Staff had searched and turned over her room, after reports that she was keeping items not allowed on the ward, including razor blades, lighters, and medicine. Her carefully maintained set of possessions, including photographs, trinkets, and clothing, was in disarray, and so, as a result, was she.

This might have seemed an overreaction, because having your

room "spun" is a routine part of life in any form of incarceration. But, for Miriam, I knew this was a particular torment. She had come to England as a refugee from Ethiopia, an unaccompanied child who had already known painful exploitation and neglect in her life. Having left her family and the horrors she had witnessed behind her, she encountered yet more difficulties as she grew up, living in hostels, in shelters, and on the streets. In a life that had known only instability, she hoarded and lovingly maintained her possessions in her room on the ward to create the closest thing to a stable home she had ever known. For her, having this room invaded and its contents plundered felt not far from the collapse of her entire world. Though the hospital staff were aware of the effect of disruption on a sensitive and traumatized person, the perceived threat to security trumped any such concerns. After the session I accompanied her back to her room and watched as she scrabbled on hands and knees, searching through the items that were strewn all over the floor. She seemed almost in physical pain as she surveyed and tried to repair the damage, facing the reawakening of a lifetime of trauma. She looked at me and asked if now I understood. I could only nod in silence.

Witnessing Miriam's torment, and that of so many women I have worked with in prisons, psychiatric hospitals, and specialist clinics, was a reminder of the human truths that accompany every criminal story. The women I work with may be convicted killers, sexual abusers, arsonists, stalkers, or child abusers and are largely considered only in that light. Yet the perpetrators of crimes that shock and appall us have also, almost always, experienced an extreme form of abuse or trauma in their own lives. They are victims as well as perpetrators. As a forensic psychotherapist, I try to understand the connection between the two aspects of their existence and to help my patients do the same. My job is to probe the roots and psychological geography of the crime, deriving insight that may then be used as evidence during a trial, as the basis for risk assessments concerning child custody, or as the starting point for a course of treatment.

The principle of forensic psychotherapy is that we look at the whole person, the factors that shaped them, and how experiences in one part of life ultimately prompted their development and actions in another. These links are not necessarily obvious, or conscious, and often only emerge after many hours of careful therapeutic work. That work must embrace complexity and contradiction, seeking to draw common threads out of chaotic lives: explanations that can offer a lifeline for people who might always have struggled to understand why they think or behave in a certain way. Together, we uncover and reconstruct the meaning of their offenses. Leading this process requires acceptance and equanimity, putting aside personal feelings about what a person might have done in order to help us both understand why.

For more than three decades I have worked in prisons, in secure units in hospitals, and in the community, acting in both assessment and treatment roles and working with female and male patients. I initially trained in clinical psychology, using treatment models including cognitive behavioral therapy (a talking therapy that focuses on identifying and altering harmful patterns of behavior and thinking patterns) and the psychodynamic approach, which seeks to help an individual access and then understand their unconscious thoughts and feelings. But the vast majority of my work has been in the field of forensic psychotherapy, which brings the psychoanalytic approach into the field of criminality, using psychodynamic techniques to probe the motivations and meaning of a person's criminal actions. Many years of this work have shown me that this can genuinely help people to recognize unconscious influences in their lives that explain their actions. Moreover, this understanding can provide a solid foundation from which to treat, and to some degree resolve, these issues. In the best case, this can allow people who had been suffering intolerable and overwhelming emotions to control previously untamed impulses and regain some stability in their lives.

In this forensic work, I have been most occupied by the crimes and violence of women. Female violence is a subject whose nature is frequently misunderstood and whose importance is too often disregarded. For many in society, from the media to some areas of the medical and legal professions, the reality of women's violence is a truth too uncomfortable to take seriously: a taboo that offends the idealized notion of women as sources of love, nurture, and care. That mothers sometimes harm, or even kill, their children is simply too shocking for many to engage with, as is the idea that women in caring roles could sexually assault or otherwise mistreat minors. Even to consider these things implicitly threatens our social fabric, bringing the shock of maternal abuse and female cruelty into comfortable lives in which the idea of the loving, caring family is so central.

Our preconceptions about female violence are deeply embedded in history and culture. Stereotypes of vengeful women fill the pages of our oldest literature: the dangerous seductress, exemplified by the biblical tale of Judith beheading the Assyrian general Holofernes while he sleeps in his tent; the spurned wife driven to murderous rage in Greek tragedy, from Clytemnestra stabbing a helpless Agamemnon in the bath to Medea, so blinded by anger at Jason's betrayal that she kills not only his new wife but her own children. Our depictions of violent women in the modern world are no less extreme. Women such as Dee Dee Blanchard, Lisa Montgomery, Aileen Wuornos, Myra Hindley, and Andrea Yates all became figures of tabloid revulsion, treated as outcasts not just from society but from womanhood itself. They were monsters, angels of death, manifestations of pure evil: made into demons who could be kept at a safe distance from the ideals they threatened. The indelible images of these women in the public mind, staring grimly from newspaper front pages, show that society has no villain like a woman who kills. Women involved with sexual offenders, like Ghislaine Maxwell, are also hate figures. They show how the idealization of womanhood in general, and motherhood in particular, can quickly turn to denigration and disgust against those who subvert it.

My work has consistently shown me that the truth is both more complex and more troubling than these caricatures allow. Some of the women who kill, abuse, and commit violent acts can be deemed sociopathic or psychopathic, but many are not. Often, they have been subjected to shocking abuse by their own parents, carers, partners, or family members. Many are suffering from severe mental illness or psychological harm as a result of that abuse. For some, the desperate search for the love and nurture that they have been denied their whole lives leads them toward violent partners, pregnancies in which they invest impossible hopes, and the revival of trauma manifested in acts of violence that mirror those they once suffered.

These women are not the inhuman monsters of tabloid myth. They are not a species apart, driven by a madness or evil we could never hope to understand. They are not, in fact, so different from the vast majority of us, for their crimes are often the cruel result of the emotions we all share—the longing to love and be loved, the frustration and fear of parenthood, the corrosion of shame and self-loathing—brutally twisted through the prism of personal experience of violence and abuse. The tragedy of these crimes is that in trying to escape the horror of their own childhoods, many are condemned to reenact and repeat what they themselves suffered. Others, their perspective shattered by mental illness, commit violent crimes in the belief that they are helping the person they will so brutally, even lethally, harm. But overwhelmingly, the violent women I have known are not beyond the pale of empathy or understanding, hard as this can sometimes be to achieve.

I have devoted much of my career to working with women who commit unspeakable acts of cruelty and abuse and studying the violence that women do—a subject that deserves and demands to be better understood. While only 5 percent of the prison population in the United Kingdom, and 10 percent in the United States, are women, and an even smaller percentage of those are violent, we know that female violence often goes underground, occurring in the private and domestic realm in ways that may never come to light. That lack of visibility is then compounded by the public attitude toward the women whose crimes are revealed, one that wishes either to vilify violent women or, just as dangerously, to patronize them by deeming them incapable of a crime considered outside the realm of womanhood and motherhood. Women, this attitude holds, will engage in violence, particularly sexual violence, only under male coercion. These stereotypes, which I have seen expressed by professionals in both the legal and the medical spheres, carry a human cost. Opportunities for rehabilitation are lost when violent and abusive women are regarded as evil villains and treated as criminals beyond help, while the chance to protect future victims is missed when their potential abusers pass unnoticed, because they fit no one's image of what a murderer or child abuser should look like. Our state of ignorance and denial about female violence is one that does harm to both its perpetrators and its victims.

My work has been motivated by both curiosity and, as my career has progressed, a sense of mission and a desire for compassion. I have seen how the women I work with are treated as less than fully human, not only in newspaper headlines but by those charged with determining their fate and overseeing their care. With fellow professionals from various disciplines, including medics, prison governors, politicians, nurses, and teachers, I have worked to undo and remake systems in prisons and psychiatric hospitals that have been the cause of re-traumatization for too many women: the lack of dignity and empathy conveyed by overuse of strip-searching; cell doors being harshly rapped on with keys; treasured possessions damaged or removed; inadequate consideration given to many women's roles as mothers and carers; and disregard for their cultural and spiritual needs. Too often, the women I have known in forensic work are both hypervisible in their status as violent offenders and almost invisible as human beings with human needs. The work to change that reality and correct that injustice has been a slow process that continues today.

Women's violence and criminality were subjects that fascinated me from an early age. Growing up in 1970s New York City, I was mesmerized by news coverage of Patty Hearst, the heiress who was kidnapped by the militant Symbionese Liberation Army (SLA) and held hostage for only fifty-eight days, before professing allegiance to the group and participating in its crimes, captured on security footage wielding an assault rifle during an SLA bank robbery. Was hers a case of what had recently been coined Stockholm syndrome, in which prisoners begin to identify with their captors, or had the opportunity to become a revolutionary unlocked her latent desires? Was she victim, perpetrator, or both?

The Hearst kidnapping was one of the most prominent stories of many swirling around the crime-ridden New York of my childhood. My grandmother, a Holocaust survivor, would regale me with every dramatic tabloid headline: the girl killed while babysitting, the high school student raped on the subway, the twins kidnapped in a bowling alley. The fear of abduction was real to me as I traveled daily on the subway from Queens to my school in Manhattan. Trauma was part of my family story. My parents were Viennese Jews, and my mother had lived under Nazi rule for three years as a teenager, seeing some of her best friends become fervent party members and take full part in the everyday cruelties against Jews and other minorities. Hearing their stories disabused me early in life of the idea that women are innately kind or that the maternal instinct is infinite. Those stories have stayed with me; at times they have lent me perspective on the traumas of the women I encounter and empathy to relate to them. As I watched Miriam desperately surveying the wreckage of her hospital room, I believe a part of me was subconsciously recognizing the vulnerability and shock that my mother had described after Nazis had arrived at the door of her childhood home on Vienna's Schönbrunner Strasse on Kristallnacht, the pogrom of 1938 that saw Jewish homes and businesses seized and, in many cases, destroyed. As her father had already died, there were no men in the household for the Nazis to take to camps, and so my mother, her younger brothers, and my grandmother were able to seek and eventually receive sanctuary in the United States, not waiting for Papa to return.

While my work as a psychologist now stretches thirty years, my association with psychiatric care has spanned my entire adult life. As an undergraduate in Connecticut in the early 1980s, I worked as a tutor in a psychiatric hospital for patients then labeled "criminally insane," helping people who had never completed high school to gain qualifications. I had my first encounters with the steel doors, barren hallways, and vacant faces of medicated patients that would become such familiar sights. After I had moved to the UK in 1984 to complete my degree, I worked as a nursing assistant at Littlemore, a psychiatric hospital on the outskirts of Oxford that had been a Victorian asylum. I washed and bathed patients, changed bedsheets, and, most important, spent time talking with the men and women who had, in many cases, been living there for decades. Here I was exposed for the first time to the realities of long-term trauma, indelibly imprinted on the minds and bodies of women trapped by its consequences. As I tried to help one patient in her late fifties undress to take a bath, she pulled away from me and sat down, knees held to her chest and arms locked around in protection. "Leave the little girl alone," she screamed repeatedly, through her sobs. Even at twenty-two, with only a fraction of my subsequent training, I knew in an instant what must have happened to her.

A year later I started my training in clinical psychology, the beginning of a career that has seen me work in various posts in different forensic settings, alongside frequent appearances as an expert witness in courtrooms. My role varies according to the circumstances of the case. Sometimes I am asked to conduct a psychological assessment that will determine a woman's suitability for treatment or form the basis of expert evidence in an ongoing trial. I may be required to assess whether a woman displays signs of psychological disturbance that would allow her to claim grounds of diminished responsibility for her actions, or if it is reasonable to allow a mother who has previously harmed her child to retain custody, with the support of psychological treatment and ongoing monitoring. In parallel with the assessment work, and sometimes with the same individuals, I provide treatment: therapy that typically occupies months if not years of regular sessions, in which I help patients to explore the moments, influences, and traumas that have defined their lives, how these have contributed to the overwhelming feelings they may experience today and the violence they have engaged in. This work is slow, sometimes painful, and fraught with an intrinsic, unavoidable conflict: uncovering the memories and experiences that present a path toward understanding and treatment is also a potentially traumatizing undertaking for people who are returning to the worst moments of their lives. Although a psychologist's purpose and training are to help patients navigate this process safely, allowing them to access the past without being consumed by it, the intensity of these memories means there may be a risk of destabilization, to which a clinician must be constantly attentive. Throughout this work, two objectives are paramount: to help the patient lead a safer and more fulfilling life while reducing the risk they pose to themselves and to other people. By helping patients move from the impulse of violent or perverse action toward calmer thought and reflection, the psychologist may limit the power of traumatic reenactments and reduce the risk of future offending.

However highly trained you may be, and however accustomed to hearing stomach-churning stories of abuse and violence, each patient's story affects you anew. I must first acknowledge and then process my personal feelings about a crime that may disturb or disgust me, letting my professionalism come to the surface and take control. I have to remain open, receptive, and accepting, mindful of the anger as well as the pain that is being communicated. Sometimes, my countertransference (the personal feelings and thoughts evoked by a patient) will take place viscerally, in the body, not the mind, and I will experience pain, fear, or a deep wish to cry or scream.

I continue to do work that sometimes leaves me disturbed, shocked, and angry because I believe that every woman I encounter deserves to be heard, however difficult her story. Only then can she find another way to express her pain and her anger; to change her behavior, and her life, for the better. I also believe that the totality of women's experience needs to be better acknowledged and understood within society. We need to recognize the particular dynamics of female violence: what drives women to acts of extreme and unusual brutality, and what can be done both to provide individuals with treatment and to draw collective lessons. To look away from violent women is also to look away from the abuse of women and girls, and the harmful attitudes of a society that wishes either to patronize women as helpless victims or to condemn them as heartless monsters. It is to deny women's agency, bury the trauma that drives violent women to appalling acts, and ignore the social context that enabled their original abusers. We need to break the taboo of women's violence, making it easier for those who are grappling with dark impulses and the legacies of abuse to seek support.

This book tells the stories of women within penal and mental health institutions in the UK and the United States, and those outside them, who have come to forensic psychology and psychiatry services as a result of violence, criminality, or alleged risk to their children. It summarizes the histories, experiences, and treatment of women I have worked with during my professional career. In order to protect my patients, I have changed important details in their stories. For this reason, the case studies do not identify my patients by race or ethnic background, but it is important to recognize the disparities faced by women of color both in society and in the criminal justice system and the greater prevalence of mental health issues among BAME (black, Asian, and minority ethnic) women, in part caused by their experience of racism and inequality and compounded by lower rates of diagnosis and insufficient health-care provision. Additionally, women from BAME backgrounds are criminalized at higher rates. They are more than twice as likely as white women to be arrested and, in the case of black women, 25 percent more likely to receive a custodial sentence following a criminal conviction.

The book is structured as a series of cases taken from the hundreds of women I have worked with, in many different settings. Each touches upon a different theme within the spectrum of women's violence, from the horrific cases of mothers who harm or kill their own children to the forces that motivate arson and self-harm, experiences of domestic abuse and intimate partner violence, and incidences of women who sexually abuse children in their care. Drawing on my work in prisons, hospitals, and court, I have chosen examples that typify the women with whom I continue to meet on a weekly basis and which also reflect the reality that female violence is most often domestic in nature and targeted in one or more of three directions: against the self, against a partner, and against children.

These are not pleasant or easy stories; many of the details are distressing or disturbing, something that cannot be avoided in presenting a realistic portrayal of patients as I have known them. But that truth contains light alongside the darkness and long shadows. As much as I have struggled sharing in the pain of my patients, I have been continually inspired by the inner strength of women who were able to overcome experiences after which most of us could not imagine to achieve a form of recovery, fashioning islands of stability out of legacies of relentless abuse and overwhelming trauma. Mine is a job that brings many moments of hope and humanity beyond the corridors of horror through which I accompany my patients. Perhaps surprisingly, there are also moments of humor and pleasure as women recount anecdotes of their daily lives or share their achievements with me. Supporting women whose lives have been scarred by trauma and abuse to find some happiness and stability is the greatest privilege of my job.

When I tell people about my work, the most common response is to ask whether I am afraid to sit in rooms alone with women who have committed some of the worst crimes imaginable. The honest answer is that moments of physical fear for my well-being have been extremely rare. I have not yet had reason to push the panic button that usually sits within close reach. Much more prevalent is the fear that I am failing in my work—not able to help a patient, not breaking down their walls of denial and suspicion, not sure whether I am gaining someone's trust or being perceived as either prey or predator by them.

It can be difficult to reconcile my feelings about women who embody the contradiction of being both a victim and a perpetrator of terrible abuse. Many are angry, aggressive, and intimidating, but in equal parts frightened, vulnerable, and traumatized. Some appear meek and mild, but have committed acts of extreme violence whose realities they at first deny. It is only by seeing the whole woman—the trauma and the pain that shaped the crime as well as the act itself—that it is possible first to help the individual and ultimately to develop a wider understanding. Our duty as a society should be to understand and treat these women, supporting them to overcome generational cycles of abuse and learning from their experiences so that others might avoid a similar fate. To do so, we must resist the urge to vilify, the impulse to categorize, and the habit of reaching for simple explanations. Only by accepting and living with the complex reality of female violence can we bring an under-acknowledged social problem into the light and ultimately address its causes and consequences.

IF LOVE COULD KILL

MARY

Extinguished, Aflame

Mary was a forty-five-year-old woman who had spent almost half of her life detained in a secure hospital, after being convicted of an arson attack on her own home. She was one of only a few women living in an institution designed for men. Mary had been driven to despair by losing custody of her one-year-old son, taken away from her after she proved unable to break off contact with her violent partner, who also posed a risk to the child. Meeting her many years after these events, I encountered a woman who had been left largely untreated, her pain, rage, and grief often suppressed but occasionally boiling over into self-harming or minor acts of arson, all of which bore hallmarks of the original crime. Mary's story showed the lifetime trauma imprinted by childhood sexual abuse, the impossibility of burying forever our deepest human feelings, and the agony of what it means for a mother to be separated from her child—a wound that may never be healed.

*

When I met Mary, I was new to forensic work, in my second professional role after qualifying in clinical psychology. By contrast, my patient was a veteran and had lived in this and other secure hospitals for the previous twenty-five years, trapped by the consequences of an arson she had committed more than half a lifetime earlier. In the Midlands area of England, a part of the country still bearing the scars of deindustrialization, the setting was an environment very different from the clinical standards of today: women lived alongside men on a mixed ward where they were heavily in the minority. The risks of mixed-sex living were ignored, if they were even considered at all.

The unit in which I was working, and Mary living, was largely founded on the principles of behavioral psychology. This holds that external, observed behavior should be the focus of study and treatment in preference to the inner workings of the mind. It emphasizes the indelible imprint of our early environment in conditioning learned behaviors: the ways we respond to punishment and reward, reactions that are often unconscious and can become habitual. Behavioral psychology is a systematic and highly structured approach to exploring and adjusting such responses, through treatment known as cognitive behavioral therapy. In accordance with this approach, therapy on the unit was "offense focused," and patients were identified mainly in terms of their crimes, with much emphasis on the distorted thinking patterns that led to their behaviors, but almost none on the symbolic and unconscious meanings they conveyed.

Already frustrated by the evident limitations of offending behavior programs, especially for female patients whose particular needs had been given little consideration, I was exploring alternative approaches. Most notably I began to train in forensic psychotherapy, at that point considered a radical method, but one that would come to define my career. Forensic psychotherapy holds that criminal behavior is symptomatic of an underlying conflict or set of emotions, which it is the job of the therapist to help the patient first to recognize and, over time, to understand and gain control over: to convert action to reflection and ultimately self-awareness. Rather than simply stopping or changing a behavior, the patient learns to understand its meaning and what motivates it. Unlike the behavioral method, this places a premium on the relationship between therapist and patient: a prism to expose the latter's template for attachment and understand the fears, motivations, and experiences that have led them to this point. It has no fixed agenda, but instead seeks to create a secure environment in which a patient can bring their dreams, memories, fears, and fantasies—the manifestations of the unconscious forces that can drive criminal behavior—to be explored and interpreted.

Alongside my work in the secure unit, I enrolled in a forensic psychotherapy course at the Portman Clinic in London. It had been developed by Dr. Estela Welldon, whose mentorship provided my introduction to a very different way of working with people the Portman called "offender-patients," one that does not simply observe behavior but seeks to deduce and deconstruct its meaning: what it expresses about a person's past, their life experiences, and their conscious and unconscious thoughts and fantasies. This was the approach I wanted to bring to the secure unit, one that I believed was failing its female patients on multiple fronts. First, and most obviously, the mixed-sex wards meant that women who had been sexually and physically abused were living in proximity to men, some of whom had a history of serious sexual offending—something that was as damaging then, almost thirty years ago, as it is unimaginable now. Second, while the ward I worked on was designed to serve as a modified therapeutic community, this milieu hardly existed outside group therapy sessions; the mixing of male and female patients again seemed to undermine clinical integrity and any sense of safety. Third, the particular histories of loss, trauma, and abuse the women had suffered were not fully acknowledged and no special provision was made for them.

Mary had fallen between the cracks of this flawed system, living an almost anonymous life in which she did not participate in the group sessions or seek help from the medical and nursing staff. Only through infrequent acts of self-harm, inflicting cuts and burns on herself, did she request and receive attention. These had habitually occurred when she was at the point of being discharged to a lower level of security and increased personal independence, representing a form of conscious or unconscious sabotage that had left her almost suspended: neither tangibly ill nor demonstrably well enough for her circumstances to be changed. In her mid-forties when we began working together, she had experienced more than two decades of intermittent and largely ineffective treatment: "offense-focused work" that sought to address her fire setting, and courses of medication prescribed by psychiatrists to alleviate her depression. She was also living in an environment where smoking was the norm, for both patients and staff, often together if a nurse deemed that the best way of calming an angry or anxious individual was to go outside for a cigarette. This meant that Mary, an arsonist who continued to self-harm through inflicting burns on herself, was in an environment constantly surrounded by cigarettes, matches, and lighters.

My proposal to offer Mary forensic psychotherapy was accepted, less because of any confidence in my abilities than the somewhat laissez-faire attitude that permeated the hospital: the mentality that the details didn't really matter "as long as the work gets done." My male boss was eager for a woman to look after the female patients, whom he had, by his own admission, mostly neglected, out of concern that seeing a man could intimidate them. In turn, I gladly took the opportunity to implement a course of treatment that I believed would, at worst, do no further harm to a woman who had already suffered so much and whose pain remained untreated. At best, I could help Mary understand the hidden function of the relentless cycle she was caught in, creating hope that there could be a way out of the stasis that had settled over her existence.

As we began our sessions, I was struck by how Mary's appearance reflected this atmosphere of neglect and quiet hopelessness. Her movements were slow and her voice soft. Often, she appeared for our meetings with both her hair and her clothes unwashed. Her entire bearing was flat: a personality and life force that appeared to be extinguished, a human being stuck in a system that she had resigned herself to never leave.

Her self-harm was the surest indicator of a furious rage and deep need for care that persisted beneath this inert exterior. The sense of her voice being silenced, her trauma overlooked, and her needs ignored was made manifest in the way she burned herself and set small, manageable fires to demand the attention of the hospital staff. These acts demonstrated that the emotions that had built to the peak of her original crime had not gone away. Nor, in the light of Mary's inconsistent and limited treatment, had they been properly addressed. I was taken aback when, in one of our first sessions, she commented that she had little concept of what therapy was or how it could help her.

The specified purpose of Mary's treatment was to address her depression and self-harming behavior. Through forensic psycho-therapy, I hoped we could give her a new understanding of her self-harming, its motivations, and its conscious and unconscious meanings. In time, I hoped we would also uncover the roots of her fire setting and reduce the risk of it recurring. It seemed to me that the fire had meaning and that it was my job to decode it with her. To begin with, progress was slow. Because she was a patient who had been living in secure facilities for almost as long as I had been alive, I knew Mary's walls would be built high: defense mechanisms against an existence she found intolerable, and a past she had never dared to confront. In the tentative, fledgling hours of our clinical relation-ship, sessions were marked by long periods of silence in which she would look down at the floor, before her eyes flicked back to me, as if I might have slipped out of the room without her noticing.

The sessions were a struggle for Mary, but she was not unwilling to share the story of her early life. One of the long silences was bro-ken with a sudden flash of self-knowledge: she could not stop dam-aging her body, she said, because to do so would be like losing her best friend. As our conversations gradually revealed, this accorded with a long-standing belief that her body was not valuable.

That idea had established itself and grown as the result of child-hood sexual abuse, perpetrated by her father. When she was four-teen, she returned home early from school one day, the same time at which he—a night-shift worker—was waking up. Alone in the house, with Mary's disabled mother in the hospital for respite care, he followed her into her bedroom and molested her, beginning a grim cycle of abuse reinforced by the threat that if she were ever to disclose it he would walk out, leaving the family penniless and consigning the children to care.

The abuse left Mary scarred in numerous ways. It had begun shortly after she had her first period, creating an indelible association with her development into womanhood. She came to despise her adult body, a symbol of her powerlessness and humiliation, something that was hers by right but claimed and owned by her father. Alongside the self-loathing was a deep well of guilt: the feeling that she had been complicit in the abuse, out of fear for what would happen to her four siblings, and the guilt that she had somehow displaced her mother's role, by virtue of her own youth and health. Too scared to tell her frail mother what was happening, she nevertheless intuited the rage and frustration that she might feel if she did know: the anger that the mothers of sexual abuse victims sometimes turn on their own children, blaming them for the horrors they have experienced as a way of protecting themselves from their own feelings of fury, helplessness, and betrayal.

Mary's rage and shame, her self-image of being dirty and damaged, only deepened in adulthood. One catalyst was the beginning of a serious relationship with Nathan, a janitor she met at work who seemed friendly, even gentle. When she became pregnant six months later, his behavior took a dark turn. He treated the pregnancy as a provocation, questioning if he was the father and openly speculating that Mary was using it to trap him into a marriage. His frustration grew when Mary, already uncomfortable with sex, shied away from it entirely, unable to cope with the feeling of her body being intruded upon. Nathan, who drifted into a form of unconscious rivalry with the unborn baby for her body, became violent. He started to beat her, accusing her of infidelity and deceit. So ashamed was Mary of her father's abuse that she never felt able to tell Nathan about it and reveal the real reason she found sex so unbearable.

Unlike her father, who never acknowledged his abuse, Nathan would be remorseful after attacking her, begging for forgiveness and attempting to make up for his assaults by taking her out to dinner or buying her flowers. In sessions, Mary said that she took some tiny comfort from this, from the fact that he seemed to know he had done wrong. But her illusion was shattered when, late in her pregnancy, he raped her. She fell into a state of deep depression: the feeling of powerlessness and belief that she lacked any sense of agency over her body and her life became almost total. Only the knowledge of the baby growing inside her could alleviate the crushing weight of abuse that seemed never-ending.

*

Pain, shame, and anger were the natural consequences of the years of trauma and sexual abuse that Mary had endured. The one thing that cut across this grain, that gave her something hopeful to hold on to, was her son, Tom, born healthy at full term. He was the first grandchild and her parents were proud of her, and delighted in him. While Mary spoke of her own body being contaminated, she saw the baby as a counterpoint—evidence that a part of her had once been good, pure, and worthy of love. She poured all of her love into him: protecting her son from a cruel world while he offered her a sense of being shielded from it and loved in return.

The tragedy of Mary's life, the trauma that overwhelmed even the horrifying abuses that preceded it, was having this one source of hope and love taken away from her. Nathan's violent attacks on her had continued after the baby was born as his sense of being usurped and displaced from her affections continued to grow. One of these assaults took place while she was holding Tom, inflicting bruises on him that eventually led to social services becoming involved in his care after being alerted by a family member.

Mary tried, desperately, to escape the cycle of abuse and preserve the one good thing in her life. She spent weeks away from Nathan, living in women's shelters with her son. But something always drew her back to the relationship, made her unable to resist her partner's pleas that they reconcile or to disregard his promises that this time he had changed. Even the knowledge that Nathan was having an affair proved insufficient to break the bond between them. Like many victims of partner abuse, Mary was unable to free herself from the man who had been violent to her and to their child. The combination of her residual feelings for Nathan, her belief that this time he really would change, and her low self-esteem and fear of being alone meant that on multiple occasions she decided to give him one last chance. By doing so, she not only exposed herself to the ongoing threat of violence but jeopardized her status as a mother. In search of one bond for which she longed, she put at risk the one that mattered to her above all else—being a mother to her son. It was a tragic choice, born of the many abuses she had suffered, that would reverberate through the rest of her life.

As it became clear that Mary was not distancing herself from a violent partner who posed a threat to the child, child services placed Tom on the at-risk register, mandating close attention and regular monitoring of his care. Step by step, they increased their pressure on Mary to give up either her partner or custody of her son. It was a choice she found herself unable to make, even in the knowledge that she risked losing Tom and her belief that life would be intolerable without him. The social workers involved felt that she was continuing to place the child at risk, and following reports by neighbors of another violent argument between Mary and Nathan, during which a baby could be heard continually crying, Tom was taken into foster care and Mary's access to him limited to supervised visits. This made her only more depressed and hopeless and weakened her resolve to stay away from Nathan. Eventually, child protective services persuaded a reluctant Mary that the best thing for the son she loved was to be adopted and for his care to be taken over by a family who could safely look after him. She finally agreed because she knew that he "deserved a better life," but that knowledge did not lessen the punishing agony of the decision, one that left her feeling helpless and broken in a way that not even the abuse of her father and partner had done.

A quarter of a century later, it was evident that this experience still haunted Mary. The decision she made—effectively a forced choice to give up her child—was one that did not sit in the past but continued to live with her in the present as she went over and over what she could have said or done differently. Although child protective services took understandable action, justified by the risk posed to Tom, it was impossible not to feel sympathy for Mary. The combination of a violent partner whose threats and behavior echoed those of her father and her own feeling of being worthless and having nowhere else to go left her trapped in an abusive relationship: unable to escape the attachment that was fated to separate her from the one thing in life she truly loved. It was a compounding cruelty of a life scarred by abuse that Mary was never given the chance to be the good and loving mother that she so wanted to be and could have become.

Losing custody of her son was the defining moment of her life, a decision that she continued to agonize over in our sessions. It was the point at which the glimmers of love and care in her life became totally extinguished by the weight of pain, guilt, and trauma, after which her inner rage could no longer be contained and nothing in her life restrained her from acting without care for the consequences. Mary's experience of sexual abuse at the hands of first a parent and then a partner is sadly not uncommon for the women I work with. The formative nature of our earliest and closest relationships can forge a template that unconsciously drives women to swap one abusive figure for another. Yet Mary's life, and the explosion of rage that had brought her to the hospital where we sat together each week, were particularly cruel examples of this tendency. She had experienced not only the despair of repeated physical and sexual assault from those whom she wished to love but the agony of being able to glimpse a better future that she could never realize. First Nathan had promised to be the caring protector for which she so longed, before revealing his true face. Then Tom had arrived as a very real source of love and nurture, before he too was snatched away from her. This constant twisting of the knife, deepening Mary's despair and eroding the last vestiges of hope, brought her to a threshold of pain that I believe made arson not just conceivable to her but inescapable.

The act that preceded twenty-five years of incarceration took place on a Sunday. The day before, she had seen Tom, by then in foster care, but the joy of time with him was swept aside when the social worker informed her that they would be seeking a permanent adoption, killing her last hope of regaining custody. On the Sunday, Mary sat alone in the small apartment where she was temporarily living apart from Nathan but which he nevertheless visited frequently. She had made plans to meet up with her sister, but had been let down at the last minute. From her window she watched women walking with prams in the nearby park, a taunting image of the motherhood that was about to be taken away from her forever. Mary later recalled that as the moment she felt she had lost everything. No one would listen to her, no one had protected her, and now they had declared that they were taking away the most precious thing in her life.

Early that evening, she set fire to the curtains in her apartment. She remembered sitting on the bed for a time, watching the flames creep up the fabric and the smoke filling the cramped room. In her mind was the thought of running away to a new life, in a new city, far from the empty and violated one that she was now seeking to torch. She told me that she just had to do something to get rid of the feelings of pain and anger inside her. She hadn't expected the fire to take in the way it did, or that it would pose a danger to anyone else.

When the firefighters arrived, called by a passerby who had seen smoke billowing through the window, they found Mary sitting on the steps outside the building. She denied any knowledge of the fire, but a lighter with her fingerprints confirmed that she had indeed set it. With other flats in the building having been occupied at the time, she was charged with arson with intent to endanger life and found guilty. The fire was not only symbolic, a communication of her rage, but an act, I believed, that expressed the unconscious wish to be caught and punished—as if she believed she were responsible for all the bad things that had happened to her.

The potential danger of the fire was tremendous, though Mary appeared unaware of this. She had set her curtains alight during the evening, in such a state of despair that she had not considered whether other residents were home. She later expressed shock that they were, and could have been badly harmed, even killed. Fortunately, because the fire brigade had been alerted quickly, the dozens of residents in the building were safely evacuated without harm.

Mary's resort to setting a fire was characteristic of how women sometimes use arson as an expression of extreme feelings for which they have no other outlet. Although women represent only a small minority of arsonists, studies have shown that they have typically experienced various forms of abuse as children, including being more likely than other female offenders to have reported childhood sexual abuse. Setting fires can be a means of expression for those who feel they have no alternative. Requiring no physical strength, it is a form of violence that both is accessible and can appear to hold the promise of purification: a desperate attempt by people who have suffered appalling abuse to not only communicate their repressed anger but destroy the evidence of their own pain. For Mary, fire was also a source of power, fascination, and excitement. She shared childhood memories of how teenagers in her housing complex had set fires in bins and on one occasion torched a car. She recalled watching awestruck at the blaze that night, the yellow flames raging and their contrast with the flashing blue lights of the police cars.

Mary found fire thrilling but also soothing, something that could relieve pain as well as express it. And on that fateful day, it screamed the pain of a woman who had long despaired at the impossibility of having her voice heard. After years of torment at the hands of an abusive parent and then partner, the only response from authority she had ever received was to tell her that she was regarded as an unfit mother. Trapped in her bleak room, her son about to be taken away from her permanently, and with her world seemingly collapsed around her, she responded by setting it alight. Symbolically, she chose to set fire to an object that represented the very domesticity that had been defiled throughout her life.

The fire she started that Sunday evening was an expression of every suppressed feeling that years of abuse and suffering had imprinted on her. It revealed all the things she could not say, or that she believed no one was willing to hear. It brought to life the truth of her plight, the depth of her rage, and the extent of the injustice she felt at how she had been treated by the people who should have protected her. It was, without any words needing to be spoken, a scalding act of truth telling.

*

Mary's long institutional experience, first in prison and then in secure hospitals, had done little to alleviate the pain that had brought her to such an extreme act. Initially, her state of depression went unnoticed by the prison staff, who regarded her neither as a threat to them nor a risk to herself. Only after she had cut her wrists several times was her cell searched, revealing that she had concealed shards of glass and matches. At this point she stopped communicating with staff and initiated a hunger strike that brought her to a dangerously low weight. A more serious suicide attempt, again slashing her wrists, led to the prison psychiatrist referring her for assessment by a psychiatric medium-secure service, where she was soon accepted as a resident.

This had all taken place more than two decades before we first met. In the intervening years, Mary had continued to harm herself, though not to the same, potentially fatal extent. Self-harm of this degree is characteristic of protest, an act that is both a private expression of deeply held emotions and a public display of despair and alienation. Mary wanted the world to know that she was furious at her treatment—what she had suffered at the hands not only of her abusers but of the institutional authorities that had forced her into giving up her son. Harming her own body, an entity she had long been accustomed to consider worthless, was the only way she knew to communicate her inner torment, a vortex of emotion too powerful to be contained within. Although Mary described herself as having been "defused" by the nursing staff and "burned out" by the accumulation of her experiences, her actions betrayed an unquiet soul still seething at her treatment and raking over the events that had brought so much pain into the life of this quiet, contemplative woman.

Ever since the day her father had first assaulted her sexually, she had found herself trapped: in abusive relationships that she could not escape, in a situation where she was effectively forced to surrender her child, in the single room that she had eventually felt compelled to set alight, and finally in an institutional system where she had fallen between the cracks, her needs never urgent enough to demand improved care nor sufficiently diminished to allow her release. Most distressingly, Mary was locked in a maze of her own agony, walking the same mental corridors of past decisions as if they might some-how lead to a different place and a better life than the one she knew.

As our sessions unfolded, the grim reality of Mary's predicament became clear. Her attachment to Tom, to the place and part of her that represented goodness, had become a false promise, a kind of psychic sanctuary where she dreamed of undoing the past, changing from a distance what she had hardly controlled in the first place. The impossibility of this hope had created the cruelest trap of all, one that had led her time and time again to overwhelming anger, with self-mutilation as its only outlet.

I knew that far from being burned out, Mary would continue to repeat this cycle unless she could be helped first to see and recognize it, a necessary precursor to detaching herself from its consequences. To succeed, the therapy had to free Mary from the relentless recrimi-nations of her own mind and grant her a permission she had never been willing to give herself: an acceptance that she was neither to blame for what had happened nor capable of retrospectively altering the outcome.

*

Sessions with Mary were a cautious, painstaking business. The psy-chological prison into which she had walled herself was built to keep others out. A woman who was understandably terrified of inti-macy and accustomed to betrayal treated all newcomers as potential sources of danger. Having been abused so badly by the two men in her life who were supposed to be her primary protectors, she was naturally ill-disposed to trusting anyone in a position of authority, or who claimed to be helping her. Although she was intrigued by my interest in her and my American accent, our early encounters demonstrated the guardedness of a patient who had known institutional settings far longer than I had been in the profession. At the same time, she longed for love and for the sense of fulfillment she had found so briefly with Tom. I was alert to this, looking for cracks in her defenses through which I could reach to make contact.

I had to absorb the thoughts and memories that a patient brings to the session, to reflect them back in digestible form, and at times act as a container for emotions that would otherwise be overwhelming. Coming so close to such powerful feelings can be a physical experience, projecting itself into the mind and body of the therapist. In sessions with Mary, I sometimes found myself feeling vacant, mindless, useless, and sleepy. This was, I think, a response to the violence Mary suppressed and an identification with her own sense of having a mind that had been destroyed by too much pain.

Despite the depth of pain that Mary had experienced, it never stopped her love for Tom and longing to be reunited with him from shining through, and much of our time together was spent discussing him. Always on her mind was the question of whether he might one day seek her out, a hope she held on to for the promise it represented: a chance to undo what she regarded as the worst day of her life, when he was taken away from her, and to fulfill some version of the loving maternal role she had always dreamed of. Mary was not alone in the world or without family. She had siblings and received a regular stream of updates about the progress of her nieces and nephews. But Tom's absence, a gaping wound in her psyche, meant that the moments of joy she took from being connected to her family would quickly dissipate in the face of her persistent, silent grief—a psychological drumbeat that no amount of good news from elsewhere could drown out for long.

The extent of Mary's attachment to Tom, even after so many years apart, became alarmingly apparent one afternoon when I went to collect her for our next session. Unusually, she was late, and the nursing staff had also made a note of her low mood during the intervening week, speaking and eating little. Out of concern I went to the door of her room on the wing and found her sitting on the floor, arms around her knees, rocking gently back and forth. She had tears pouring down her face and what appeared to be blisters on her skin. When the nurses quickly arrived, it became clear that she had burned her wrists by pouring boiling water over them and extinguishing a lit cigarette on them.

Mary sat on the floor being tended to by the nursing staff, her eyes flickering wildly around her immaculately well-kept room as if she had never seen it before. When our gazes met, I felt unable to move or look away as decades of stored-up pain, grief, and rage stared back at me.

Strict procedure would have dictated that we not meet until the following week's scheduled session, but the urgency of the situation compelled me to suggest that we do so the same day. She agreed to see me, and we sat down, her wounds bandaged and the familiar sense of muted calm restored. But, unlike in many of our previous sessions, Mary seemed in the mood to share. Almost before I had said anything, she handed me an envelope that was yellow with age, the adhesive long since worn away. Inside I found a photograph of a smiling young woman holding a baby boy. Both of them were looking at a cake bearing a single lit candle. She told me to turn the picture over, and I took in the full weight of what she wanted me to see—that the date, neatly noted on the back, was today's. It was Tom's birthday: the happiest day of her life that had now become its most painful anniversary. She began to cry as she told me about it—the one birthday they had shared together, how happy she had been and how beautiful her son was to her. It was hard not to join in with her tears as she shared her secret pain and the horror of how the joy of Tom's birth and early life had served only to make Nathan more and more abusive toward her.

For Mary, Tom's birthday was just one of the anniversaries that continued to haunt her, bringing her anger and despair bursting to the surface: the day he was born, the day she agreed to his adoption, the day she saw him for the last time. Over my career I have come to learn the importance of such markers for women living in institutions where significant dates are too easily forgotten. No patient's or prisoner's life began inside the walls of the place they are now compelled to stay. Making a plan for how to mark these most meaningful days—whether by lighting a candle for a child who has died or been taken from them, visiting a religious space, or simply spending time talking about their memories—is often an important part of therapy. It creates space for the grief and agony that women like Mary have been trying, impossibly, to contain.

Many patient-therapist relationships have an inflection point, a session or moment in which a trust that was fleeting or absent becomes mutually established. With Mary, we reached that point when she handed me the envelope containing Tom's photograph, extending the trust of her most treasured possession. By doing so, she reached out her hand for help in a way that might never have been achieved through words alone. She had brought me into her inner world, the sanctuary and torture chamber that had for so long been hers alone to navigate. She wanted someone else to witness the pain that, for so long, she had been carrying alone.

In the sessions that followed, we walked a path she knew so well: the long, sad trajectory of events that had led to Tom's adoption. By retracing the steps with another, someone who could counteract the inner voice that knew only self-recrimination, she began to see how these events could be seen differently, to recognize that she was not, and never had been, to blame; that so few of the actions that led to the defining tragedy of her life had truly been in her control. In the two subsequent years we worked together, Mary gradually acknowledged this new narrative without wholly accepting it. Her original version of events was too ingrained for her ever to surrender it entirely. But she became open to the alternative, less convinced of her own guilt, and more sympathetic toward herself.

Mary's life had been too traumatic to escape the legacies of the past. There was never any question of therapy wiping away the pain of the abuse she had suffered or the loss she had endured when her son was taken away forever. Nor did she ever, to my knowledge, stop harming herself. She said that she found it impossible to believe that she would never again burn her skin or set another fire. But what the therapy could and did achieve was to loosen the binds of a behavioral pattern that had left Mary trapped for decades, first blaming herself for every bad thing that had ever happened to her and then expressing that anger and self-recrimination through self-harm. Gently, we managed to separate her from that cycle, without ever breaking it entirely. By putting her feelings into words, she no longer felt compelled to communicate through the violent abuse of her body, or to punish herself in this way. The thought of freedom no longer became so intimidating that Mary had to sabotage it, as she had so many times before by harming herself when on the verge of being discharged. Released into the community, she adopted a dog and talked in our outpatient sessions about her happiness in its company and the sense of purpose the pet had given her. It proved, most importantly to Mary herself, that her capacity to love was real and had survived.

I still think of Mary, a woman whose life and struggles left me feeling humbled and at times helpless. She taught me about the power of unexpressed rage, the complex reality of women in incarceration dealing with the legacies of loss and grief, and how pain untreated threatens to overwhelm the soul. But she also showed the extraordinary endurance of hope: how the need for love and the ability to provide it can survive decades of overwhelming punishment, finding new expression with the right nurture and support. While the fire of anger and remorse that burned within Mary was never entirely extinguished, together we reduced its intensity so it lost the strength to consume. Such mitigation was the difference between an unbearable existence and one in which, tentatively, she was able to begin living again.

*

Mary was one of the first women I treated as a forensic psychotherapist. My work with her also revealed the power of the state to separate mother and child, ostensibly to protect the vulnerable, and

the painful aftermath. In clinical terms her story was one of arson
and self-harm, but the real lesson it taught me was about pain: how
it can be imprinted in childhood and spread slowly throughout a
person's life; the impossibility of hiding it away and burying it deep,
even though that is so often the human instinct; and how it can flare
to the surface through moments of acute violence, often targeted
inwardly, acts of self-recrimination for people who may bear little
responsibility for what has happened to them. Working with Mary,
I learned for the first time the connection between untreated, unac-
knowledged pain and violence, the shocking but inevitable consequence of a feeling that must find expression however much it is
ignored. She revealed how deep losses can be hidden away but are
still secretly mourned. This truth has remained with me throughout
the following years, and I have never forgotten how marks on the
skin can serve as memorials for hidden losses and secret pain. My
work with Skye further revealed that acts of self-harm speak with the
body, expressing what is not yet possible to put into words.

SKYE

Speaking Through the Skin

Skye, a twenty-three-year-old woman incarcerated after an assault conviction, was known by staff in the prison as its most prolific self-harmer. She craved not only the feeling that she got from tying ligatures to herself but the recognition and care that followed. Her experience was revealing about women's violence against the self, an often misunderstood phenomenon. Often seen as simply "attention-seeking" behavior, self-harm can also be a means of expression, an essential release of pain, and a trusted method for managing the mental anguish of trauma. For Skye, the routine of prison life and her own self-harming was, distressingly, the closest to a sense of safety she had ever known.

*

As we approached the cell, my new patient could not be seen; I could make out a shapeless mass under gray bedclothes, a body that, without looking carefully, you might not have noticed at all. As is protocol, I waited outside while the correctional officer knocked, entered, and called Skye's name. When there was no answer, he moved closer to the bed and put a hand under the blanket, not to wake the prisoner, but to examine her. The officer was checking

for one specific thing: a ligature around her neck of the kind that
Skye tied to herself repeatedly, often multiple times in the same day,
tight enough to bruise but usually loose enough that she could still
breathe. No words were spoken, but he quickly found what he was
looking for and reached into his back pocket for a device to cut away
the elastic bond she had tied tightly around her neck. Still partially
obscured by bedclothes, the patient I had not yet met responded
with a low cry of protest. This was a wordless dance of pain and procedure, a routine well-known to both parties that I would witness on
more than one future occasion.

It was a snapshot of the kind of scene I had often known during
my time working as a psychologist in a prison, a job I held at the
beginning of my career and have done again in my most recent post.
The combination of so many people suffering from mental illness or
psychological trauma living in proximity, in such tightly controlled
conditions, creates a distinctive and often troubling environment
for the women I work with. Being surrounded by others with similar
or worse conditions, and knowing how the machinery of authority
will respond to different triggers, my patients experience not just
the reality of their own illness or distress but living conditions that
can actively exacerbate it. An act of self-harm might be the only way
they know to express themselves and solicit the care they crave. It
could be provoked by the action of a cellmate or fellow prisoner that
feels to them like competition or emulation. Within prison walls,
the nature of the environment can be as significant as individual
trauma and psychology.

Once Skye had been untied and untangled, and we had moved
to the meeting room for our session, I was able to see her properly
for the first time, although she had soon scrunched herself into a
human ball on the chair, face turned away and de-laced sneakers
pointing toward me. I had to check my notes to see that she was
actually twenty-three, for this waiflike figure could easily have been
a young teenage girl. She had been homeless before the aggravated
assault that led to her imprisonment, and still gave the impression
of a runaway who might have been sleeping on the streets. Her pale

skin only accentuated the dark bruising around her neck from her frequent self-harming. Even when she was denied access to obvious ligature materials like shoelaces, Skye would find ways to fashion them from anything she could—underwear elastic, or torn bits of bedsheet.

My work in the prison as a consultant psychologist is primarily focused on those considered the highest-risk offenders, women whose complex cases and histories require an intensive psychological approach. In parallel, I work with the staff who tend to them daily. I also support prisoners deemed to be of significant risk to themselves, and Skye was one of the women referred to me under the prison's newly instituted Self-Harm Strategy, a program that sought to understand the meaning and motivation of the behavior, not simply to treat incidents as they arose. Skye, of course, knew that she was a test case for this new approach, the latest in a series of interventions that her constant self-harming had earned her. While her initial posture toward me was defensive, her notes suggested that she had enjoyed and happily participated in work with other medical and pastoral staff at the prison. Though I wanted to help address the forces that drove her to self-injure, I also worried that rather than helping Skye to break the cycle of cutting and tying cords around her neck, our work might actually achieve the opposite. It could reinforce in her mind the connection between self-harm and care, the idea that only the acts of self-harm could give her status and earn the attention she craved.

*

Accepting a full-time position in a prison had brought my career full circle, recalling one of the first jobs I did in the field, within HMP Belmarsh, one of the UK's most notorious maximum-security prisons. In many ways Belmarsh provided the foundations of my career. It taught me about the intensely difficult life experiences that so often underlie violent or unstable behavior, the legacy of childhood abuse and how it can unspool throughout a person's life, and the strangely intimate, caring relationships that are such an important feature of the outwardly brutal and unforgiving prison environment. I never forgot the expression of the twenty-one-year-old patient who calmly said of Belmarsh that "it's just a grown-up children's home." Like so many of his fellow prisoners, he had been in care, and this was simply the latest institution in a life dominated by them. He helped me to understand that prisons are not simply detainment centers for those being punished by the law but often the only secure places for people who find themselves unwanted and uncared for anywhere else in society. For many, prison is the container that they have never known in the form of a loving home, parent, or guardian—"a brick mother," as the psychoanalyst Henri Rey described a psychiatric hospital.

The reality of prison work was confounding my somewhat simplistic preconceptions, but even as I began to accustom myself to the environment, it was still an overstimulating place to be, one where noise and movement were constants and there was always a detectable tension. This carried over into the waiting area of our clinic, a goldfish bowl of transparent walls in which everyone could see who was in session and who was waiting to be seen. Although the details of patient conversations remained confidential, it was strange to conduct therapy in an environment without any of the privacy that normally surrounds clinical encounters. Nor did I ever fully get used to the odd cocktail of power and responsibility that came with eventually being given my own set of keys, allowing me to shout ahead for others to leave gates open for me or to steer my own way through the maze of corridors.

Part of my clinical remit in Belmarsh was to work not just with prisoners but also with prison officers, exploring the psychological challenges they faced and what it meant to be surrounded by people who had committed such serious crimes and be responsible for their welfare. I ran groups for staff working with prisoners classed as vulnerable, mainly sex offenders who were in a separate wing for their own protection. In one poignant session, an officer broke down as he began to relate the sexual abuse he had suffered as a child. It was a reminder of the fragile humanity that pervades an environment and a workplace in which everyone is wearing a uniform of one sort or another and projecting a defiant face to the world. With prisoners, glimpses of this vulnerability would peek through the visage of tattoos, muscles, and swagger, while I was struck by the almost tender relationships between these usually young men and the staff who were both their captors and their protectors: an intimacy that was unspoken as orders were barked through cell hatches and the prison echoed to the clattering of "bang-up."

Returning to the prison environment three decades later, and specifically to a facility for women, has opened my eyes to the huge challenges that still remain to support patients with high levels of trauma and significant requirements for social and psychological care. In addition, for every patient I see, I know there are so many more I cannot, who need the help but in a place of limited resources are not considered a high enough risk to receive it. Imprinted on my mind are the comments called out through closed cell doors as I walk through the prison. "Are you a doctor, miss? Can I see you?" It can be hard to depart at the end of a day with a clear conscience, knowing exactly how much unmet need for care and contact you are leaving behind, with women in distress and captivity while the gates close safely behind you. As most patients waste no time in pointing out to me, only one of us gets to go home at the end of the day. Nor is it ever possible to forget that in a women's prison the majority of those incarcerated are not violent offenders and are also much more likely than male prisoners to be sole carers of children. More often than not, imprisonment means not just the denial of personal liberty but a traumatic separation from children, a partner, and a home—a dislocation that only adds to the burden of trauma that so many of the women carry.

*

In order to help the people within an institution, it is important to treat the institution itself. This fundamental principle in working within complex organizations emerges from the work of Isabel Menzies Lyth, the psychoanalyst and preeminent expert on the interplay between institutions and patient behavior. She showed how the social defenses created by an institution reflect the unconscious anxieties of those who work within it. According to this logic, those working in a prison will unwittingly develop systems and procedures designed to limit their contact with prisoners, reducing their exposure to challenging experiences that can awaken feelings of anger, desperation, or even the legacies of their own past traumas. Hence the organization itself needs to be treated before the individuals it purports to serve can be properly helped, with these social defenses being first uncovered and then deconstructed. This "whole system" approach guides the current UK government strategy for improving conditions in women's prisons.

One of Menzies Lyth's most important arguments was that the staff working in an institution must understand the meaning of its systemic behavior in order to address it and must also become aware of their own feelings and thoughts—how they respond to the people being kept in the institution. That may sound obvious, but the sometimes necessary bureaucracy of a prison can too easily flatten such perception, turning every woman into a number and every behavior into a metric to be observed rather than a problem to be unpacked and treated. There are so many ways in which institutions create structures to minimize contact between workers and inhabitants—nurses and patients, officers and prisoners. Together, these build unconscious defenses against the anxiety of making emotional contact and can obscure clear thinking about the underlying meaning and function of behavior. Our new approach sought to counter this, creating spaces for staff to come together and talk about their work and the personal effect it had on them and to think about the women they worked with outside the strict confines of official processes.

Nevertheless, the heavy hand of procedure still hangs over such work. Part of this is a process whereby every prisoner who self-harms will have it recorded in their ACCT (Assessment, Care in Custody, and Teamwork) book, a document that staff carry wherever the women go, so it accompanies them at work, in classes, in the gym, or in the health-care center. Important in many ways, the book is also a symbol of the prevalent mindset toward treatment: that the record in itself effectively represents care, and the process of tracking how a prisoner behaves is paramount. The book is manageable precisely because it is minimizing, reducing the complexity of individual histories, thoughts, and moods into a series of observable statistics. Because everyone who sees the woman at risk of self-harm or suicide is required to record their interactions with her, she is reassured that she will not drop out of their minds and be forgotten.

Some of the women begin to locate their sense of identity in the book, treating its record as a badge of honor akin to the scars they bear from cutting or ligating their bodies. They become reliant on the care and vigilance that come with being observed for evidence of self-harming: in their minds, being checked on twelve times in a day might represent care, while only half as many will start to feel like neglect. The very system that is meant to be addressing the problem can end up, inadvertently, helping to reinforce it. There is an unerring certainty, a concreteness and rigidity, to this system of observation that closely mirrors the internal logic of self-harm itself. On both sides, interactions and conversations are valued primarily as a unit of supply, to be rationed and counted out like pills. Prisoners might sometimes be talked about as being "on" two or three conversations a day. This competition for care between already vulnerable prisoners is clearly destructive, because self-harm can become the currency for interactions with each other and with the staff who, in turn, sometimes grow exhausted and despair at their inability to make progress.

Skye's experience at the prison had demonstrated the limitations of attempting to address behavior without probing its underlying causes. By the time we met, she had already been subject to numerous interventions from different levels of the prison hierarchy, ranging from the promise of a certificate signed by a governor to recognize when she stopped self-harming for a week, to a stuffed animal toy to mitigate the absence of the pets she loved so much, to a job she had requested working in the prison library. Yet all these were ephemeral compared with her animating need, which was to express her trauma and solicit care in the best way she knew: by tying ribbons of whatever she could find around her neck until the skin became welted and bruised. The very attempts to wean Skye off this behavior ended up driving her back to it, because she saw her "improvement" reflected in a diminishing return of care and attention and became frantic when other self-harming prisoners assumed the status she believed was rightfully hers. Inevitably, this meant that any reduction in her self-harming and associated reward was simply the precursor to the same behavior ramping back up again.

Our meetings were often fitful encounters, and she seemed to consider me yet another person whom her self-harming entitled her to sit and talk to, and to whom she could complain about perceived neglect. Religiously, she would remind me to bring her ACCT book to sessions and to record my observations in it. She was eager to learn how many observations she was "on" per day, a fact that was not disclosed to her officially but one she valued and would use as a means to compare herself with others.

In parallel, she would present me with a "to-do" list of her complaints and requests about her prison life. In the early sessions of our six months working together, these meetings seemed to become another cog in the wheel of her confined existence, one she had honed to a minor art form and whose dangerous realities she showed little intention of escaping. When I tried to turn the conversation toward why Skye felt the need to harm herself, she retorted that the past was too painful for her to want to discuss, more than once saying that it "messed with her mind." She had little appetite to probe her self-harming because she saw it not as a problem but as a way of transmitting the pain she felt, getting it out of her system, and calling for help. She was more open about the crime that had seen her imprisoned in the first place: an assault on a couple, like her, sleeping on the streets, who she said had stolen from her. With some relish, she described kicking the man and hitting him around the head with a bottle. For her this was proof that she was not some timid or frail girl but a dogged survivor, one who had been fighting in different ways her whole life.

Yet on the central issue she remained frustratingly reticent. After several sessions, and when she arrived for another clutching the customary list, I decided to challenge her on this. These meetings, I said, had become no different from any other part of her day. Everything was the same to her and no one person distinguishable from another. In an attempt to get under her defenses, I remarked that she seemed to value me as little as she did herself. It was this last comment that seemed to break through her diffidence. The look I received in return was unlike anything I had seen from Skye in several hours of previous contact. It was as if she were seeing me, actually taking in my face and noticing my features, for the first time. Until this point she had been reluctant to talk in any detail about her self-harm, let alone her inner thoughts or past life. Her flat demeanor suggested a resignation that this was simply an irreducible part of her life, as if the ligatures she tied around her neck were akin to a morning exercise routine or an afternoon snack. But now, whether out of curiosity, frustration, or the feeling of having been provoked, she finally began to share something of her life and how she had come to be in prison.

Having grown up in care from the age of nine, she had first been institutionalized at fifteen, convicted of grievous bodily harm against a caregiver in her group home, and committed to a young offenders' institute. She had lived a disrupted life alongside her younger brother, Jacob, with both children eventually removed from a family home in which both parents were long-term drug users and the siblings had witnessed repeated episodes of domestic violence. The anger that stemmed from these experiences led to the breakdown of several placements with foster families, requiring both siblings to return on each occasion to a children's home. Her sense of abandonment only grew when Jacob, who was withdrawn and sometimes mute in his behavior while Skye raged outwardly, was adopted by a family who had initially considered taking both children but considered her too much of a "burden." Alongside the aggression, like many traumatized children she wet the bed at a later-than-normal age and was sometimes doubly incontinent. The shame she felt at this simply compounded her behavioral problems, because she would try to hide the mess, lie to foster parents, and act out in response by stealing.

As she told me all this, I was struck by her description of feeling "inside out," unable to contain either feelings or bodily functions. It brought to mind Freud's notion of the ego as something that is first expressed through the body rather than the mind: "The first ego is the body ego." Whereas the baby that is nurtured learns the boundaries of its bodily ego through being contained by the parent who holds it and meets its needs, a young child like Skye was uncontained, leaving her vulnerable to being entirely overtaken by her bodily sensations, emotional or otherwise. She had very little sense of herself as an integrated being that could hold the needs of body and mind in balance. Rather, she lived in a collapsed state of uncontrollable feelings that were internalized within and identified with her body, then finally expressed through it—as a child in the form of incontinence, and as an adult through self-harm. Her skin had become an emotional battleground, both a weapon and a canvas for self-expression. Later Skye made clear, credibly so, that she was not suicidal and in fact used the ligatures to stay alive, to combat feelings of being invisible, neglected, and stressed.

In this Skye was typical of women in prison, who are disproportionately affected by different forms of childhood abuse (53 percent of all female prisoners in the UK, compared with 27 percent of men) and much more likely on average to harm themselves (a third of female prisoners, compared with 15 percent of men), a finding also replicated in studies of female prisoners in the United States. Self-harm is a defensive, life-preserving act for those who use it, although not necessarily consciously chosen. It is a way of reclaiming ownership of the body, now under one's own will and not used and abused by another. As is commonly understood, self-harm can be recognized as a combination of needs not expressed through other means: a cry for help and a call for care, an articulation of pain and trauma, a manifestation of the guilt that many abuse survivors feel, believing they were somehow responsible for what was done to them.

Yet self-harm is often interpreted simplistically, even in settings such as the prison, where it is frequently encountered. Routinely it is characterized as a function of inarticulacy, when in fact the women who slash, burn, and bruise their skin are often eloquent about what they do and why. Skye was one of many self-harm patients in my career who had kept a written record of their harming, in her case a journal, while others have included drawings and poems. The common theme from these women is that their harming is a mode of expression they choose rather than one they feel forced into for lack of any alternative. There is an expressiveness, a visceral directness, and a rewarding urgency to marking and maiming the skin, conveying truths about grief, shame, pain, and trauma that the spoken or written word cannot. It can be painful and distressing to hear patients talk about the harm they inflict on themselves and to witness the labyrinthine scar patterns that they carry with them, sometimes on every visible limb. But I cannot let that obscure the message that so many women have tried to convey to me in their own way: that self-harm is not always a hopeless and formless cry, but can be a deliberate and chosen expression of a person's deepest emotions. Self-harm can also be a compulsion, an addiction to a method of release that is very hard to give up. And it is not always a public expression or call for help. As many patients I have worked with in my private practice have disclosed to me, it is not uncommon for women to have secret rituals of self-harming with no outward signs of disturbance or violence, but no less compulsive as a result. Though this is often shameful for them, it can feel like their only lifeline.

Now that we had made real, though brief, emotional contact, Skye began to tell me more about the beginnings of her self-harm during her adolescence in care. She had no one to turn to, no one she trusted, and when she confided to a residential caregiver that his colleague had handled her roughly and called her names, she was not believed. When another child sexually assaulted her, she tried to tell staff and was told that she had exaggerated. She felt she was going crazy and wanted to tell her mother, but, perhaps predictably, her mother did not visit her as she had promised to, so she was left silent. Out of desperation at having been so roundly ignored, she cut herself on the leg with a razor blade, her way of proving that something bad had in fact happened. At that time she told no one and tended to the wound herself. Her pain was unspoken, but this wound was real. She recalled that even having the blood come out felt good, like a release of tension and a feeling of poison being drained. Skye looked as if she were in a trance as she remembered this, then peered up at me, her expression scared: "Do you think I'm nuts? Should I be in a mental hospital?" I shook my head and acknowledged that it had been a language that made sense to her when spoken words had achieved nothing and she was left alone, in pain. She had marked onto her skin a truth that no one else had been willing to hear, let alone believe.

This confession was a turning point in our therapeutic relationship. She began to use the sessions to trace the history of her self-harming and revealed that it was not just the currency of communication with others, crying out for care, but also a kind of "memory map" for herself, a way of ensuring that she marked significant events. She painted a picture of a little girl, alone in brutal institutions, who became both the perpetrator of her own abuse and its nurse as she tended to the wounds she had just caused. She would use anything she could get hold of to cut herself: shards of glass, coat hangers, bra wires. Skye felt in control of her own body when she cut herself, as though proving it was hers and hers alone. She didn't like her scars, showing me how they went all the way up her arms, but respected them because they proved her pain and validated her experiences. Although I found it hard to look at these scars, I understood that she needed me to bear witness to them.

I was increasingly moved and impressed by her insight and maturity, so different from the outer self she presented, the wild girl who seemed to collapse unless contained and confined. She had this private, secret way of relating to herself, of keeping her memories alive, encoded on her body. At the same time, cutting was becoming too violent, and when she was fifteen or so, she wanted to replace it with something that was less "ugly." At sixteen Skye had a bird tattooed on her wrist, a delicate image in soft grays and mauves that she said she would touch whenever she wanted to cut, imploring the pain to "fly away." This was almost unbearable to hear, conjuring up an image of her loneliness and desperation, even as I felt admiration that a girl with so little meaningful support had found a creative way to try to alleviate such damaging behavior.

At eighteen she found herself out of care and "sofa surfing," variously with friends, in hostels, with a father who kept kicking her out and on the streets. She no longer carried razors, but began to tie ligatures whenever she felt overwhelmed by memories or feelings. There was always enough material to create these, whether from plastic bags, shoelaces, or elastic. Over time she became less secretive about her harming, and the bruises on her neck were obvious. Her mother, whom she now saw regularly, would see these marks and worry about her, which is when Skye realized that showing people her physical wounds was one way of asking for help. The psychoanalyst Betty Joseph talks about patients who are "addicted to near-death" and who seem to thrive on acts of self-destruction, not wanting to die, but equally feeling unable to trust life and to embrace it. I felt that Skye was caught up in this addiction and that the question facing us was how to release her from its grip. Talking to me more openly about her past, despite her shame and sense of being unwanted and unloved, was part of her gradual escape.

Helping patients who have reached a point where self-harm has become routine and even treasured is a gradual, uncertain process. For Skye, the recognition of how little she truly saw the people around her, and her inability to perceive or relate to them as whole people, was the first step. Her early deprivation meant that she was "insecurely attached," never believing that someone else could protect or look after her, but also indiscriminately seeking people to depend upon, as if they were all interchangeable. Acknowledging her inability to perceive other people as individual human beings brought home the reality that she regarded herself as nothing more than a body and helped her to recognize the total dominance of her bodily ego. There was a notable change in her after that conversation. She carried on bringing the lists and reminding me to carry the ACCT book, but also began to describe what she had felt before tying her latest ligature and what the triggers had been. Having spent so many years trapped by her body ego, and her sense of being only a body without a mind, Skye began to be able to reflect on her inner world of thoughts and feelings, stepping outside her torment to analyze some of the forces driving it. By seeing others more clearly as individuals, not just a faceless mass of "officers" and "helpers," she became for the first time able to see herself. She was beginning to truly see herself as others saw her, and to perceive them from the inside, as people separate from one another with minds and feelings of their own.

I knew there was no magic solution to such a deeply ingrained and meaningful pattern of behavior, but I was equally certain that there would be no resolution of any kind unless we challenged the institutional regime that had surrounded her self-harm and inadvertently served to canonize it. Skye herself was still attached to these routines and comforts. I found it significant that even though she had the "enhanced" status that would have allowed her to wear her own clothes, she continued to don the prison-issue sweats. In many ways this was the only stable home she had ever known, and she was unwilling to relinquish one of the most visible expressions of that. I believed she was keeping herself in a state of neglect and need, unconsciously requesting that we, the staff, dress and care for her.

My work with Skye encompassed the final months of her prison sentence. In many ways our progress was faltering. She continued to tie things around her neck, in attempted strangulation. There is a Russian roulette aspect to this because women can and have died, having mistimed the anticipated observations or misjudged the tightness of their nooses. Part of my work was with her prison officers, helping them deal with the frustration and anxiety they felt about the risk she posed to herself. Their widespread compassion and concern for Skye's welfare were remarkable, and it was hard for them to bear their charge's relentless assaults on herself. She seemed childlike to them, a perception that prompted care but also impatience. At the same time, the focus on building relationships with her outside the old template started to bear fruit. She began to bring hopes, fears, and secrets to our meetings, including the fact that she had a crush on one of the older female prison officers, as well as talking to me for the first time about a different form of her harming, very occasional instances where she would cut herself on the inner thigh where no one could see. To do this required her to store up objects she could use to cut into her skin, including razor blades taken from her weekly shave. At other times she had taken staples from the stapler she used in the library. Like other women who self-harmed, she had a wide repertoire of self-harming methods and was able to fashion weaponry in ways I could not imagine. Even when the last ligature was taken away, she would always find another way to self-harm.

As she told me about her secret stash of weapons—shards of glass from perfume bottles she had broken, staples taken from the art room, a secret razor blade, and some cloths that could easily be used to strangle herself—and how she both obtained and hid them, I felt Skye had a sense of triumph as well as relief: she knew that if things got too bad in her mind, she could still evacuate the pain onto the surface of her body. If she felt too neglected and unseen, she could do something visible and tangible that she could show to the officers and then to the nurse who would be called. Unlike her inner pain, the wounds she bore couldn't be ignored. By letting me into her world of secrecy, ritual, and the bodily expression of psychic pain, Skye, I felt, was getting closer to a resolution of her inner conflicts and demonstrated gradual shifts in her ability to think about her mind, her feelings, and me.

In her daily prison life she was also beginning to form relationships with other prisoners, another novel development. One of the prison officers designed a program in which she was guaranteed a walk outside each day with a consistent group of women, some of whom were older, in their forties or even fifties, and began to mother her and enjoy her company. Rather than being connected to whether she had ligated or not that day, it would happen as a matter of routine—shifting focus away from the self-harm and onto the regularity of having meaningful contact with the same people, being part of the community of women in the prison. The friendships she formed might have been short-lived, but they were important in two ways. They were based on a different template from the relationships centered on harming she had previously craved, and they represented a form of assimilation to life following her release. They gave Skye hope that people other than paid workers could be interested in her and see her as funny, creative, and kind, as she was underneath the layers of need and despair.

Given that the prison had been the most meaningful home of her short life, Skye's departure from it represented an even greater risk than her self-harming. Freedom would leave her bereft not just of her brick mother but of the routine of care and attention it offered and that she had come to rely on. I knew that Skye would never completely stop harming herself. It was simply too great a part of her, too reliable an ally against the traumas of her life, to ever relinquish entirely. But I nevertheless saw that she had made progress through the combination of psychotherapy and the diligent, sympathetic work of her prison officers. Together, this combination of interventions had helped Skye to see that underneath her behavior was a deep need to relate to others. She had begun to understand how her self-harm was in so many ways an attempt to reach out a hand, in the hope that it would be reciprocated. Knowing this, and being exposed to a new template for attachment and relationship building, gave her a different lens through which to see the world and perceive herself. Self-harm was still a fundamental part of her, but it was no longer the totality, an overwhelming appetite that eclipsed her every emotion and human need. Skye would always feel the need to speak through the skin, but she had also begun to learn other ways to communicate. It gave me hope that outside the institutional environment she might slowly continue to emerge from self-harm's long shadow.

A few months after her release Skye wrote to me, telling me she was settled in the community, though it had been scary to leave prison. She still thought of self-harming at times and saw it as a "last resort," a sanctuary from unbearable pain, but had been able to resist its pull so far. Since leaving, she had found a part-time job volunteering in an animal shelter and was in close touch with two old friends. Skye said she still traced her tattoo when she had urges to self-harm, and also replayed our conversations, imagining I was in the room with her, listening. She remembered telling me how she felt that without visible marks she was invisible, and that I had said that with time she would be able to find other ways to be seen and heard and to trust that others cared about her even if they weren't tending to her wounds. Now, she wrote, she had learned to rely on her voice to speak and wanted her body to heal.

*

Accessing the causes of pain and helping a patient to understand them—the raison d'être of psychotherapy—mean breaking down the barriers that she has built primarily to protect herself. It is essential to understand the meaning of these and reach the fears that lie beneath. The art of forensic psychotherapy is to become the ally of a person who may initially perceive you as an intrusive force, seeking to undermine them or colluding with others they believe are against them (a particularly common belief for women such as Skye who have been criminalized). This dynamic is always present to some degree, but in certain cases it can become extreme, defining months or even years of a therapeutic relationship. My work with Paula addressed self-destructive behavior of a different kind, and from a woman several decades older than Skye. Her aggression was palpable, her vulnerability hidden. Her defensive walls were also built several times higher. It was one of the most challenging relationships I have had with a patient, dominated by paranoia and aggression that were not merely aspects of Paula's personality but seemed to engulf the entire person.

PAULA

The Volcano and the Void

A patient with a long history of threatening and committing acts of violence against medical professionals, Paula was a terrified, terrifying woman who managed her own fear by making others afraid. A middle-aged mother, she presented an aggressive and volatile face to the world, with threatening and controlling behavior that was designed to keep those who cared for her—including her husband and adult children—at a distance. So great was Paula's fear of abandonment that she actively sought to provoke their rejection, to her a safer feeling than living in a frightening state of uncertainty. It was a constant challenge trying to form a clinical relationship with a woman whose primary aim was to drive people off and who believed anyone claiming to offer help actually wished to demean and degrade her.

*

For thirty years, I have seen patients behave in many strange, disturbing, and provocative ways during consultations. Some desperately want to withhold the memories and emotions that it is the business of therapy to reveal. Others believe the therapist is an opponent to be defeated and pounce on the opportunity to turn the tables, even as they look to her as a potential source of love and understanding.

In all that time, Paula was the only woman who refused to let me see her face. For the first few weeks we met, she would sit sullenly behind huge dark glasses, rejecting invitations to remove them. The glasses were the first of numerous barriers that this violent, traumatized, and deeply suspicious woman sought to erect between herself and a world in which she saw disdain or mockery in every comment, gesture, and facial expression. As I searched for the first clues of a new patient's personality, and the first glimmers of a relationship, darkness stared back at me.

I knew how much pain, anger, and aggression lurked behind this barrier. Violent records are the norm in those referred to a forensic service, but as I read the letter summarizing Paula's case, I felt more trepidation than normal. She had a history of violent and threatening behavior toward the medical professionals who were trying to help her, especially if she sensed that they would reject her. At this time I was still based in the Midlands and had some autonomy over selecting the patients I could work with. As ever, the female forensic patients, though in the minority and generally not a risk to others, were considered "harder work" than the men, emotionally more draining than the vast majority of our referrals—men with long histories of violent crime.

Paula had been referred for forensic psychotherapy by a community mental health team who felt overwhelmed by her increasingly threatening behavior, considering her too dangerous for them to manage. They represented the second layer of the medical system who had found her a patient too hot to handle; her previous treatment with her local doctor had been terminated after she was so consistently abusive toward the surgery's staff that they no longer felt able to admit her. In response, she had held the doctor hostage with a knife, an attack she would later recall with laughter, glorifying the details of how she had also smashed a glass window, kicked desks, and pulled signs off the doors as she was forcibly removed from the facility. After initial charges for criminal damage were dropped, she wrote threatening letters to the GP that included death threats, which led to further charges of threats to kill, to which she pleaded guilty. It was this that brought her to the attention of forensic services and ultimately to my clinic, with the treatment being a condition of her probation order. This psychological treatment would run alongside the cocktail of psychotropic medication she was taking: antidepressants, mood stabilizers, and antipsychotics that seemed to do little to contain her disturbance.

Although no physical harm to the doctor was done on the day Paula held them hostage, I would come to learn that aggression was characteristic behavior for a woman whose vulnerability and volatility were deeply entwined. Suffering from borderline personality disorder with antisocial traits, Paula could not stop herself from alternating between the two extremes, which I thought of as the volcano and the void: outbursts of violent anger that would lead to depressive periods of isolation, introspection, and self-loathing, which left her feeling hollow and empty. The confident, defiant, and aggressive mask that she wore so well concealed deeply held frailties, the legacy of childhood abuse from a violent mother and an alcoholic, often absent, father. Recognizing that the aggression was in fact a mask helped me not to walk away, as so many people and even professionals would, upon meeting this unambiguously frightening woman. Rejection was what Paula both feared and craved: the trigger and the excuse to launch into another violent episode. This was a satisfaction that I knew I had to deny her as an essential precursor to treatment.

Paula had known difficulty in her life from an early age, being treated by her mother, who suffered from what appears to have been postnatal depression, with a degree of contempt and cruelty verging on sadism. She blamed Paula, her first child, for having cut short her successful career as a dancer and focused the full force of her rage and despair on her while lavishing affection on the other children. Paula's father, loving and attentive when sober, was a violent man when drunk, who would lash out at her and her mother, prompting Paula to offer herself as a scapegoat to protect her siblings.

With two troubled parents, Paula was often left alone to look after her three sisters or in the care of deeply unsuitable adults: the root cause of her persistent and crippling fear of abandonment. From the age of six she was sexually abused by one of those carers, an older male relative, a persecution that continued until the age of eleven. He had groomed Paula—who confused his predatory behavior with love—into sexual activity, enforcing her silence through threats and bribery. The abuse only stopped when the man was arrested for assaulting another child, but Paula's parents never asked if he had hurt her, and she never told them out of fear that he would carry out his threat to kill her. Her teenage years spiraled into a cycle of aggression, sexual promiscuity, substance abuse, and, at times of desperation, cruelty to animals. The last was a crime I found particularly distressing, indicating as it did a degree of sadism and contempt for weakness. At sixteen she met the man who would become her husband, and at eighteen she became pregnant with their daughter.

Even before I met Paula, it was clear that the consistent violence and invalidation of her early life lay at the heart of her personality disorder, a condition that affects someone's self-image, emotional stability, and ability to form relationships with others. Like so many abused children, Paula had internalized a sense of guilt and shame about the physical and sexual abuse that had been inflicted on her. These deep-rooted feelings competed with the desire to be loved and cared for, which had gone so cruelly unmet during her childhood. Being neglected by those who were supposed to care for her, and abused by those who had shown interest in her, had shaped the self-image of a woman who craved affection as strongly as she fought those who offered it. These experiences had formed a personality so raw and open that it could be bruised by the gentlest touch, and a sense of self so fragile that it could be shattered by the shadow of a perceived slight or the first, faint inkling of rejection. Characteristic of those classified with borderline personality disorder, often born of early trauma, Paula's relationships unfolded as a series of conflicts and contradictions: searching for care, only to reject it when offered; fearing abandonment while often attempting to provoke it; seeking love but then perceiving it as an invasive force to be resisted.

In her late forties and a grandmother by the time we started working together, Paula had a sense of worthlessness and being unlovable that had metastasized over the course of decades. It had corrupted almost every important relationship in her life, most critically that with her husband, Reuben, and the two children whose childhoods she had terrorized with coercive control of their behavior, relentless verbal abuse, and episodes of physical violence that alternated with moments of remorse and affection. She was especially aggressive toward her family either when they wanted to leave home and see other people or when they tried to stop her from harming herself, attacking them as they tried to restrain her or remove the razor blades and ligatures she used to self-harm. Only through this intoxicating violence toward herself or others could she evacuate terrible feelings or fill up the void inside her. Having vowed never to treat her own children as she had herself been treated, Paula was distraught as she found herself inexorably drawn to repeating the abuse and volatile environment she had experienced. Her story was a reminder of how the embers of childhood abuse, which for some survivors may simply be buried, can be rekindled when their circumstances are mirrored in adult life. Paula's violence was a product not just of what she had suffered as a young girl but of how her family life with Reuben had confronted her with a similar set of scenarios, leading her toward reprising the role played by her own distant, angry mother. Paula found herself repeating parts of the abuse she had herself been subjected to, often the fate of those who seek out family life as an escape from an abusive past, only to inadvertently set the scene for its revival. Her abusive childhood did not condemn her to becoming a violent and aggressive adult, but it had created the template for this behavior and made it harder to avoid embracing it when triggered.

Paula came to me with her vulnerability in a heightened state; she was now awake nights worrying that her family would abandon her as her parents so frequently had. She knew she had tortured them with her threats, assaults, and suicide attempts and now felt retribution was near. Even this knowledge could not contain her from continuing to abuse herself and those closest to her. She was now self-harming most days and tracking her husband on their shared phone. The circumstances that had brought us together had heightened her fear and accentuated her destructive behavior: she felt in a state of exile, persecuted by having had her previous clinical arrangements withdrawn against her will. She rationalized the actions that had led to this decision: the reception staff at the GP's office had been incompetent and deserving of her abuse; the doctor had merited her revenge for choosing to abandon her. In Paula's eyes, she alone remained the victim. Because she was angry and afraid, her feelings of vulnerability were exacerbated still further by the fact of having to attend my clinic as an outpatient. The need to ask for help felt like a humiliation in itself, an admission that the vulnerability she so consistently sought to mask with violent behavior was real.

The dark glasses she hid behind in those early meetings symbolized a woman who had become a prisoner, both of the body she loathed—concealing her skin, scarred with self-harm marks, behind long, loose clothing—and of her emotions, her longing to be loved interwoven with paranoid suspicion of anyone who showed care toward her. The internalized certainty that people were on the verge of abandoning her liberated Paula to push them away aggressively. Her behavior epitomized the contradictions that can twist around the minds of those who have survived childhood abuse: desperate to feel love, but disdaining that need as a sign of weakness; terrified of being abandoned, but constantly provoking and testing people in the hope and expectation that they too would leave. This offers a sense of control, preempting the inevitable abandonment. Her need to be cared for vied constantly with her conviction that she was unworthy of it. In our sessions she would talk both of her corrosive fear that her husband was about to leave her and of moments when she wished he would go so that she could at last have the peace and certainty of being alone. The finality of being abandoned often seemed a more palatable prospect than the constant dread of waiting for it to happen, so much so that she would actively create her own rejection through aggression and violence. Only by resisting the role she was asking you to play in this, and denying the behavior its intended climax, would this vicious cycle be disrupted.

*

An abiding legacy of her childhood traumas was that Paula clung
to controlling behavior as her primary source of stability and
strength. For her partner and children, this had led to misery. She
made Reuben—who cared deeply for her but had his own problems
with depression and substance abuse—the principal target. Paula
obsessed over his every waking moment, seeking to prevent him
from working late, seeing friends independently, or being apart from
her for any length of time. She would unleash barrages of questions
and text messages onto her husband, demanding to know where he
was, whom he was about to see, or when he would be home. In person, these inquisitions would quickly escalate to shouting, finger-
pointing, and shoving when, inevitably, she was displeased with his
responses and refused to accept his mollifications. Such hypervigi-
lance is common to those, like Paula, who were the children of unreliable or unsuitable carers. They remain constantly on the lookout,
scanning the environment for harm, studying the face of the one
they depend upon for every sign of anger, sadness, or tenderness.
Not able to trust that carer, they insist on keeping them close at all
times. For Paula, any unplanned absence on Reuben's part was taken
as irrefutable evidence that he must be having an affair and punished
accordingly. Even his snoring was taken and treated as an intense
provocation, an indication of his contentment while she lay awake
anxious and agonizing.

The sexual abuse she had suffered as a child left her with conflicting feelings about her femininity. Part of her wished to be soft and
pretty as her mother had been, but the trauma had engendered the
indelible feeling of being dirty and unworthy, internalizing guilt and
shame in her physical being. Conflating femininity with weakness,
Paula ultimately adopted habits, behaviors, and appearances she
regarded as masculine. She spoke harshly, resorted quickly to pro-
fanity and violence, and found it hard to cuddle or speak lovingly to
those around her—something she could not bring herself to do for
fear of being seen as soft or weak, the same reason she hated pets and

would shout at her neighbor's cats. She pursued what she regarded as male hobbies, including golf and shooting, and was contemptuous of those she deemed feminine, like crafting or knitting. And she spoke about sex in crude terms, a middle-aged mother who openly engaged in locker room talk in front of her friends and family, hoping to shock and unsettle them. While in reality sex terrified her, she hid this under a macho facade, mocking men with "small cocks" and describing them as "pathetic queers" while boasting about Reuben's sexual prowess as if to somehow assume it as her own.

In Reuben she found a partner who could fit into this construction of herself: he could fulfill the role of the submissive wife to her abusive, hypermasculine husband. It was a reversal of stereotypical gender roles that suited both partners. Outwardly a conventional middle-class couple—on a comfortable income, driving good cars, and enjoying regular holidays—within the marriage Paula was the dominant, stereotypically male figure, exerting control over all aspects of her husband's life. Although he would sometimes respond with violence, mostly he seemed to take her physical assaults with a kind of masochistic acceptance. While Paula raged that Reuben was about to leave, he constantly reassured her of his love and fidelity. When she withdrew from their children or shouted at them, threatening to hit them and telling them they were "little shits," he took on the role of carer. Like many intimate partner terrorists who exercise coercive control over their spouse through acts and threats of violence, Paula was acting primarily from a place of fear: unable to stop herself from lashing out at him, but even more terrified as a result that he would become the latest person to abandon her. As with other such abusers, the thrill of successfully exerting power over her family members fed Paula's toxic behavior, reinforcing her imposition of demands, threats, and harsh restrictions on their lives. As if under a spell, her husband and children accommodated themselves to her unreasonable and frightening regime.

Paula's uncontained anger often spilled onto those around her, whether her close family or simply people she encountered in her daily life. But the most consistent victim of this violence was Paula herself.

As well as cutting herself with both knives and razors, deep into her skin, creating marks that were painful to see and bear, she inflicted psychological damage on herself. There was a self-sabotaging intent behind the unpredictable and tyrannical behavior, ensuring that she constantly undermined her most important relationships and met offers of love with displays of aggression. She pushed away those who loved or wanted to help her because she could not trust or accept their expressions of care and kindness. Because she suffered terrible abuse as a child, her constant desire to protect herself from more pain led to the grim compromise of becoming her own abuser, as well as a source of fear and concern to those around her. Becoming the perpetrator of her own pain offered Paula, ironically, a sense of power and control: she was in charge of meting out injury and punishment, a process that she might not enjoy but that at least she could trust. This was no less a form of self-harm to mediate overwhelming feelings than Skye's cutting and ligating had been. It was notable that Paula was generally only violent toward her family at the times when they tried to physically restrain her from self-harming. She was an example of what psychologists call "dual harm," where violence toward the self and others can coexist, particularly in prisons and other institutional settings.

Despite this blinkered and contradictory approach to life, a part of her knew that she risked losing the people she most cared about. This need to control a situation that filled her with dread followed Paula into the outpatient clinic where we met weekly. For her, the moment of peak tension was not sitting with me in a consultation but in the waiting room, where she routinely lashed out verbally at reception staff. While she permitted herself to accept that the time spent with me was justifiable, everything that preceded it was a torture for her: passing through the building security, announcing her name at the intercom, then being asked to wait after she had overcome all her fear and anxiety to attend in the first place. All were barriers that stood between her and what she wanted and became the targets of her furious displaced aggression. Even worse were the fellow patients she had to sit alongside in the waiting room: people with problems not unlike her own, but whom Paula could see only as "perverts," "muppets," or "psychos," as she called them, waiting to see if I would agree or reproach her. In these moments, waiting for me to collect her, she was akin to a baby waiting to be fed, in a high state of arousal, at peak sensitivity, needing only a whisper of inferred provocation to tip into a violent outburst. Like an infant, she was incapable of self-soothing, unable to do anything with her rage and frustration except to unleash it on the nearest available person. In these moments, being made to wait was intolerable for her. Having people look at her was intolerable. Having to sit with her own thoughts even for a few minutes was more than she could bear.

As a consequence, by the time we met, she had often passed through her state of intense anxiety and had become relatively calm. Like many patients of similar disposition, she would talk of the intense feeling of emptiness that followed a cathartic outburst of anger or an attack on her own body. With the frustration voided, there was nothing left except the fear, anxiety, and self-loathing that had built it up to unsustainable levels in the first place. Paula knew at these moments of reflection that she was out of control. But, like an addict, she could not break the cycle of thoughts and feelings rising to a pinnacle when the release was needed, prompting a bout of self-loathing that would begin the sequence once again.

Nor was her behavior predictable, and small alterations in the environment could prompt a volcanic response. This was true both in the clinic and at home. In one session an administrator absent-mindedly walked into my room while the session was in progress, handing me a letter to sign, before quickly excusing herself when she saw a patient sitting there. Paula said nothing about it while the session continued, but I could see the tension had overtaken her: her whole body had stiffened into a rictus and the red-rimmed eyes—glasses now relegated to their case—glared back at me. Afterward she spotted the woman in the corridor as we were walking out. In a moment she was in her face, screaming that she had been spying and trying to humiliate her. The force of her rage was shocking, but I ensured the therapy continued, not rewarding Paula with rejection for her outburst.

A childhood marked by cruelty meant that Paula read malevolent intentions into every interaction, however minor. She was a frightened person whose main defense was to make herself as frightening as possible, leaving her ever more isolated. Violence, her safeguard against the humiliation of having her vulnerability exposed to the world, her instinctive response to the unbearable fears of exile and rejection, simply left her feeling even more vulnerable than before.

*

Paula was trapped in a complex maze of problems characteristic of women whose lives have been marked by abuse. This was manifested in her volatile behavior, her extreme mood swings, and, most important, her almost magnetic attraction to toxic relationships. The latter is an especially destructive tendency for those who have grown up in an abusive home, witnessing or experiencing violence. Research has consistently shown that our earliest exposure to relationships is defining. The patterns of behavior that children witness in their parents' relationship, and the way they are treated, form a template for the attachments they will seek out as adults. Abused or neglected children are more likely not only to develop personality disorders but to replicate the toxic patterns of attachment that led to their abuse and suffering in the first place. The experience of trauma can be as restrictive as it is harmful. It means children have grown up seeing adults fight but not resolve conflict, controlling and persecuting each other in the name of love. If a child has experienced no other form of relationship firsthand, they have nothing else on which to base their own future relationships. What would seem to the objective observer a safe and secure alternative can feel dangerously, undesirably unfamiliar to the victim of abuse.

All our attempts to form relationships are at some level a search for the familiar, and early exposure to domestic violence increases the risk that children will enter into similarly abusive relationships when they become adults. I have worked with numerous women who were the children, and later victims, of abusive relationships but who said that the violence and coercive control initially felt like markers of care to them. While they did not want this abuse, nor consciously choose it, at some level it felt "normal," showing they mattered and that their partners needed them. Only after years of abuse and tyranny at the hands of their partners were many able to see the coercive control for what it was, not the proof of love that they had initially assumed it to be. For other women, like Paula, the pattern may be different, in that the woman becomes the perpetrator of aggression or coercive controller. This subverts the traditional notion of the male as the abuser and can appear more shocking because it threatens stereotypical ideas about women as victims.

Paula had grown up in a home where constant conflict was the norm. In therapy she relayed vivid memories of the emotional and physical violence that had passed between her parents: a psychological bruise that remained livid even decades after the event. She could not help herself from perpetuating the same cycle in her own marriage. As frequently occurs in a toxic partnership, the couple's conflict fed off itself: Paula's rage would compel Reuben to drink and abuse drugs, to which she would respond by physically assaulting him. Feeling lonely and unwanted, he formed platonic friendships with other women, fueling her sense of rage and jealousy and contributing further to the animating fear of abandonment. The coercive control that she sought to exercise as a result became the keynote of their relationship, which was more than twenty years old by the time we started working together.

Many of the same dynamics existed between Paula and her children. Pregnancy had been a torture for her, provoking feelings of discomfort, nausea, and heaviness so extreme that she spoke of feeling as if an alien had invaded her body. After giving birth, she felt both that her body had been irreparably broken and that her freedom had been stolen forever, much as her own mother had felt. Her daughter's constant need to be fed and cared for disgusted her—an unavoidable reminder of the vulnerability that she so despised in herself and had worked to bury as deep as possible. All through the months of a pregnancy she had loathed, the one comforting thought was that the baby she was suffering so much to bring into the world might make her feel whole and beloved. Yet when her daughter, Jana, was born, she could not see the baby as anything but a huge, devouring monster—one that seemed to suck up all her energy and care but that still cried in apparent reproach, leaving her feeling inadequate and unwanted. Like many reluctant or accidental mothers, Paula pushed her infant child away at the same time as feeling deeply rejected by her. She saw the baby's anxious outbursts not only as a further form of persecution but as an implicit judgment on her: evidence that she was exactly the kind of "unfit mother" she had known in her own upbringing. Jana, it seemed to her mother's paranoid mind, had looked into her soul and found it wanting.

She later gave birth to a son, Alexander, and, as the children grew up, repeated the pattern of alternating abuse and neglect of their emotional needs that had been her own mother's hallmark. She found it hard to soothe or cuddle them, instead leaving them to entertain themselves for long periods of time, and sometimes forgot to give them breakfast and so sent them to school hungry. It was not clear if this neglect arose from intentional cruelty or simply a lack of care and attention to her responsibilities as a parent, so preoccupied was she by her own fears and self-loathing. The bond with her second child was more loving, the sense of identification with a son less strong and traumatic than it had been with her daughter—mirroring the contrasting treatment she and her brother had received from their mother. She was kinder and more maternal with her son, holding his hand in busy streets and sitting down to watch his favorite TV programs, something that she would have found too stressful with Jana. As he grew up, however, she sought to control him as much as anyone else—responding angrily to things that threatened her, like a new girlfriend or time spent away from the family home.

By the time we met, Paula's children were in their early and mid-twenties, living independently with nascent families of their own. The intensity of her abuse toward the three members of her close family had faded, but the core of her controlling behavior remained. In calmer moments she felt guilty about her actions, but her fear of abandonment and sense of self-loathing—the factors that continued to motivate that behavior—were as powerful and painful as ever.

*

My problems as Paula's therapist extended beyond the difficulty of getting her into the consulting room in the first place. I was far from the first clinical professional she had worked with, and had to deal not only with the deep-seated problems of a complex patient history but with the legacies of previous attempts to help her and Paula's feelings about therapy as a result. Our sessions would often be filled with pointed asides from her about the efficacy of the work we were undertaking together and veiled threats about the harm she would like to inflict on the doctors and therapists she felt had failed or abandoned her.

As a woman who had spent decades seeking to control those around her, Paula was unlikely to treat me any differently. She knew that I was fully aware of her past threats and attacks on people in my position; indeed, she made a point of relating the stories and let me know how amusing she had found the incident when she had held her doctor captive. She frequently found opportunities to make it clear that while I might be in her good books for now, this could easily and quickly change.

As she did with everyone else important in her life, Paula sought to make me her emotional hostage, someone she could control with flashes of anger or threats of what might follow. From the way she would enter the room, stiffly and without greeting, to the less-than-subtle threats she would drop into the conversation, she constantly communicated that her guard was up and our sessions were proceeding at her sole discretion, a permission that could be withdrawn at any moment. Sometimes she would challenge and find fault with everything I said, while at other points she would be flattering and try to co-opt me into her imaginary wars with the staff at the clinic: the classic abuser's pattern of positive and negative reinforcement combined in ways I could not predict. She would continually seek to probe my vulnerabilities at the same time as being acutely self-conscious of her own. "Why should I tell you anything when you tell me fuck all?" was her standard riposte to a question that displeased her. She was frustrated that as a professional matter of course

I would not share any details about my life, my marriage, and my children. Part of her wanted to build up a picture of me, a knowledge bank that she could weaponize. This fought against an equally powerful instinct to protect herself from what this knowledge might reveal: that I had been loved by my mother, had not suffered from postnatal depression, and had a stable relationship with my children. As ever with Paula, belligerence went hand in hand with self-doubt. She clung to aggressive behavior as desperately as she feared its consequences.

With Paula, the greatest risk was that our professional relationship would become another of the toxic partnerships that were her default template. Experienced patients like Paula understand and utilize the geography of therapeutic spaces to their advantage. They know that you are sitting near a panic button that can be pressed in cases of emergency, and their eyes will follow you after making a threat to see how you react. Are you about to call for help? Have they rattled you? Who is in control? At times, it was definitely Paula. More than once her behavior succeeded in making me feel like the child who is watching their parents fight for the fourth time that week: looking on, feeling helpless, and wondering if I were somehow to blame.

One particular session, halfway through the eighteen months in which we worked together, was more than usually disturbing. It took place after a hiatus of three weeks during which I had returned to New York to take my winter break and visit family. Given her perennial fear of abandonment, the sessions immediately preceding and following periods of separation were always the most challenging for both of us. Even with ample warning and explanation of the reasons, and discussion of how the temporary separation might make her feel, she would react with cold fury to the feeling of being cast aside. As we walked from the reception to my office for the first session after this break, her glasses stayed on and she lingered a step behind me, saying almost nothing. Still a little jet-lagged from my flight, I entered the room feeling unsettled and with a sense of foreboding I could not pinpoint.

It was the same room we had been meeting in for the past nine months, yet on entering it, Paula looked around as if seeing it for the first time, scanning the walls and ceilings as if she thought the place had been bugged. She commented that she had not wanted to come, but Reuben had insisted due to her "weird" behavior and growing sense of agitation around him and their son, with whom she was usually most patient and caring. The glasses were removed without suggestion, but I startled when she snapped them loudly into their plastic case with a discordant crack that could have been a bone breaking—an ugly noise she seemed to relish.

Seeking to calm her, I asked what she thought had been unsettling her and causing the recent change in behavior. She sighed and then laughed. "You're the expert, not me. How the fuck should I know?" Had it been, I suggested, the fact we had not been able to meet for the previous three weeks? Did it feel as if I had abandoned her? Her eyes, which had been darting around the room, now met mine directly. "You did, didn't you? Fucking off to your own perfect life."

She softened a little as we began to delve into the reasons for her recent troubles. Her son, Alexander, his partner, and their infant children were staying with them, occupying the spare bedroom where she would often retreat when unable to sleep due to her husband's snoring. Instead, she found herself going downstairs to the living room and turning on the television—anything to distract herself from the anxiety of having to play host, worrying about what meals to cook and about the dirt and dust that was accumulating because she thought that vacuuming would wake up the children. I nodded for her to continue, but here she paused. She didn't know if she could tell me about the programs she'd got into the habit of watching during these lonely nighttime sessions. At this, my mind started racing through the possibilities: it couldn't be porn, because sex repulsed her; it wouldn't be a cookery show, because that risked making her feel inadequate. And I was sure that she would be far too embarrassed to reveal if she had been watching children's cartoons, with all the associations of vulnerability that would bring with it.

I prompted her to continue, reminding her that I was there to help and not judge and that we did our most important work by discussing things that made her uncomfortable. At which point she relented and explained. Her new interest was a documentary series about the Third Reich. She'd been not just interested but excited to learn about how Hitler operated, how charismatic he seemed to her, and how much good the Nazis appeared to do for Germany. She'd started doing her own research in addition, learning about David Irving and his disproven theories about the extent and nature of concentration camps. She agreed with him that the Holocaust had almost certainly been exaggerated.

As Paula talked, with a mounting excitement, I could feel my heart racing as I battled to keep my face composed and my voice calm. Did she know—perhaps from more internet searching—that I was Jewish and that my parents were Austrians who had escaped from Nazi rule? Was she deliberately using one of the most sensitive and deeply personal topics she could have raised as another attempt to unsettle me and to exact punishment for the previous weeks of perceived neglect? Was this the honest testimony of an anxious patient seeking help, or the ploy of a manipulator and abuser who had chanced upon her most potent weapon yet? Instinctively, the rebuttals to her denial formed in my mind, and I had to stop myself from voicing them. The stories my grandmother and mother had told me about life under the Nazis flashed in front of me. I had rarely felt more personally exposed and vulnerable sitting in a room with a patient. It was hard not to feel overwhelmed by what seemed a targeted attack.

I forced myself to halt this spiraling internal monologue and start again. Whatever my personal feelings, the purpose of our time together was to attend to Paula's needs. However provocative and disturbing I found the conversation, my duty as a therapist was to probe what I was being told for its meaning and importance, not to judge it against my own needs and feelings. I waited for her to stop, which took several minutes as she expounded upon what she had been watching and reading over the Christmas weeks while I was in

New York, eating potato latkes with my elderly relatives and feeling more connected than usual to my Jewish heritage.

I was curious, I finally said, to understand what had attracted Paula to these programs and why she had become so interested in the subject. Was it perhaps her lifetime obsession with expunging perceived weakness and vulnerability—exactly what Hitler had purported to achieve through genocide and the creation of the Aryan master race? Was this gross abstraction and magnification of her own fears and convictions somehow the cause of excitement and arousal for her? She agreed. Her ideal world, she smilingly asserted, was a strong white society in which Jews and other minorities would not exist.

Although I had seen Paula behave in a racist way toward some members of the clinic's staff and had found much of this behavior hard to bear, I did not think that she was actually a eugenicist or white supremacist. I batted aside what felt like a blatant attempt at provocation and pressed on. Was this really what she believed, or had all this been the product of a period when she felt even more scared, lonely, and fragile than normal: an exile in her own home, denied the weekly therapy sessions that had become an important part of her routine? My revulsion at her admiration of Nazis and sense of persecution started to subside as I pictured a frightened woman, alone in her living room in the middle of the night, able to find comfort only in conspiracy theories that comforted her and fed her paranoia, keeping her own feelings of sadness and helplessness at bay.

I realized that the unspoken sparring match the conversation had represented was at an end as Paula smiled with what seemed like relief and admitted that she had scared herself by her reaction to the material, keeping it secret from her family. The last few weeks had been difficult. She was aggrieved at being denied her support system and constantly anxious about not being able to provide adequately for her extended family. I became certain that there had been deliberate intent behind her words, a retaliation for the punishment she considered my recent absence to be. But, more important, I saw that she also wanted to move beyond this. Whereas the woman I had first encountered would have pushed an area of weakness to the point of mutually assured destruction, now it was equally important to her that we could salvage the conversation and maintain our relationship. She had wanted to punish me, but now she sought to limit the damage. She was angry, but her outburst had not been uncontrolled. Her desire to fix the behaviors that had blighted her life was beginning to outgrow the need to control and terrorize everyone around her. At the end of this enervating session I felt as if we had survived a storm, and hopeful that we were beginning to make progress.

*

Paula's history meant that one of the most challenging parts of her therapy was successfully bringing it to an end. I dreaded this from day one, worrying that it could prompt a verbal or even physical attack, though we both knew that the weekly therapy would eventually need to stop. Ensuring Paula was aware of this from the start was crucial so she had a sense of control, but it did not mitigate the fear of actually telling her I would be leaving the clinic. This became necessary when I changed jobs, but was ultimately a process she took ownership over, deciding to end our sessions two weeks before they were due to come to a close. That this transition was managed successfully indicated how much progress had been made over the eighteen months of working together. As she stood up to leave the room for the last time, she turned to me, and I noticed that her eyes, now fully visible, seemed tearful. She reached out to take my hand and, still holding my gaze, thanked me, saying she would miss me. I was surprised and moved by this unexpected moment of honesty and intimacy. Our parting—something that in the past had been the cause of threats and recriminations—passed almost without incident. Paula was still affected by the same fears as ever, but by this point she had become interested in understanding them, their origins, and why they continued to exercise such a strong pull over her. A personality that had been entirely closed off began, in small ways, to open up. In the final months we had conversations about things that could never have been broached in the initial period. She told me about the long-running hatred of her body, appearance, and sexual desires. She talked about women whose looks she longed to emulate, even intimating that she felt some sense of attraction to them and referring to poems she had written expressing these feelings. Alongside the fear and self-hatred that had always been apparent in Paula, an impression of confusion and frustrated longings, hidden deep inside, started to make itself known. Even allusively, these were remarkable confessions: secrets she would once have jealously and aggressively guarded as evidence of weakness.

She had always been a patient in whom an inner battle raged between the need for change and fears about its consequences. After eighteen months there was no decisive result, but the balance of power had shifted. The side to Paula that desperately wanted to overcome her fears and escape the recurring trap of abusive behavior was getting stronger. She was coming to recognize that what she hated above all was her persistent compulsion to hate herself and project that sense of loathing onto everyone around her.

That evolution was partly the product of therapy, but equally important were changes in Paula's family life. One was the worsening health of her mother, a figure who had loomed as an unpredictable and monstrous presence her whole life but whose implied power inevitably became less as she became a frail and helpless elderly woman who gradually became a less potent source of fear. More meaningful still was the close relationship Paula developed with her grandson, Benjamin, a nine-month-old who had become severely ill, to the point where she and her husband acted as regular respite carers for her overwhelmed daughter. As a mother Paula had been so consistently abusive that I initially questioned the appropriateness of this arrangement, but in doing so, I could not have been more wrong. In the event, she offered much as a grandmother that she had been unable to do for her own children, demonstrating that she could be tender, caring, and above all patient. The same cries for help that had prompted anger and self-loathing when coming from her daughter filled her only with fear and concern when caring for her grandson, who was often in pain and therefore in even greater need of attention than most babies. Whereas she had seen her own infant children essentially as predators, feeding first on her body and then on every waking minute of her life, she was able to recognize her grandchildren as the innocently vulnerable beings that they were. In one session she described to me how Benjamin's illness had "shaken her world," a remarkable admission of vulnerability for someone who had spent an entire lifetime trying to conceal any evidence of it.

This was not a Damascene conversion: the old fears and jealousies remained, and by occupying the role of attentive grandmother, she was in part making yet another attempt to exercise control and supremacy over her daughter, who was struggling with the painful task of raising a sick child. But much of the change was meaningful. Paula and Reuben, who had so often argued when raising their own children, worked as an effective team almost for the first time in caring for their grandchildren, discovering a different kind of relationship from the one they had so often known. For Paula, the child's predicament finally brought her face-to-face with an even greater fear than that of being exposed to the world as someone vulnerable and in need. She was able to subsume a part of her own pain to the cause of trying to soothe someone else's, an infant who could not possibly be the source of judgment and disdain of which she had constantly lived in fear. Paula was able to bring these feelings to sessions and reflect on them within the safety of our therapeutic relationship, articulating what had for so long been untouchable and unspeakable.

It was moving seeing these changes in Paula at the end of our work together. I watched a woman who had, out of fear, fashioned herself into a tyrant learn how to be patient and maternal and to trust in another person—me. I saw someone who had nurtured the self-loathing image of being unwanted discover a role in which she was both wanted and truly needed. And I observed a person whose entire concept of relationships had been distorted by abuse finally discover what unconditional love looked and felt like.

Paula's life revealed the destructive consequences of trauma and how it can feed an addiction to abusive and violent behavior. But she also proved that these legacies do not have to be lifelong. People are capable of change, especially when circumstances in their life draw it out of them, providing the opportunity to reflect on hidden fears and wishes. The templates that circumscribe our relationships are strong but not unbreakable; the habits that form our behavior are ingrained but not indelible. No one was more surprised than Paula at the remarkable effect that a helpless baby had on the fears that had haunted her since childhood, within the context of a safe therapeutic relationship, where she could feel that she too was being seen and heard by another. Reaching this point helped her to recognize and grasp a defining need. To have what she wanted more than anything in the world—the love of her family—she first had to accept what she feared more than anything: the depth of her own vulnerability.

*

The cases of Mary, Skye, and Paula help to illustrate the breadth and complexity of women's violence against themselves and how this can easily spill over onto others around them. Unable to express anger within a public forum, as men are readily able to, in a society still wedded to stereotypes of femininity that deny acts of aggression, no matter how justifiable, women turn their anger inward. Self-harming behavior in all its forms is especially characteristic of female violence: the expression of hidden rage and despair, targeting the body or the home, to manifest pain that was often done against that body or within that home. As their stories show, the agony that expresses itself in these acts may stem from either violence that has been perpetrated against them or the terrible feelings of rejection that come from being ignored or discarded—as Mary had been as a mother, and Skye had been by her own parents and a succession of foster families. Women who carve open their skin or set fire to their bedrooms have looked for help and support and found it lacking. They have cried out in pain and not been heard or believed. Violence becomes the last resort for pain that can find no other outlet.

Such violence cannot be minimized, but it should also be

understood as the expression of a desire to feel something other than hopeless despair. The inner clarity and external care that Skye achieved through self-harming, and the thrill of intimidating others that Paula realized through her threatening behavior, allowed them to experience some sense of power and control, however fleetingly. These behaviors were ultimately attempts to create connection by people whose relationship templates had been forged in rejection and abuse. As so many women in similar situations have shown me, meaningful treatment comes through demonstrating that there are other, better ways to form attachments, not by the therapist identifying and punishing the offending behavior.

Self-harming is an essential starting point for understanding female violence, not just because of the inward dimension that reflects the domestic nature of much abuse, but due to its relationship to violence against others. As Paula showed, this violence can be a direct consequence of self-loathing, self-destructive behavior. While Mary's case could so easily have become one in which an act of private protest became a destructive event that harmed or killed others.

Women's violence against others is often driven by the same combination of factors that drives them to harm themselves: the experience of abuse, toxic partnerships that stem from early relationship templates, and life experiences that present feelings they cannot control. For the violent women I have worked with, motherhood has often been the most challenging of these experiences: something that many have longed for but that also has the ability to imbue feelings of worthlessness and powerlessness, as well as reviving past traumas. The emotional torrent that comes with being pregnant, giving birth, and caring for a vulnerable infant can be especially forceful for women whose own experiences of being mothered were troubled, or who lacked a maternal figure altogether. In a society where motherhood is still devalued as an occupation and where idealizations of "maternal instinct" can be oppressive and blinding, there may be few places for women who are struggling with its demands to turn with safety.

The idea that a mother would deliberately harm her own child may be unpalatable, but it is an unfortunate reality that I have often encountered in my work. Sometimes mothers become overwhelmed by the demands of a small child and lash out in desperation or frustration, a response to feeling worthless and incapable. Some had such difficult experiences of pregnancy and childbirth that they see their child not as a beloved being but as a hostile invader occupying their life. Others cannot avoid seeing their child as an avatar for their own childhood self, to be made to suffer the same shocking abuse that they once did. In the case of Amber, which I cover in chapter 7, this can lead to a chilling indifference toward the vulnerability of children that allows women and mothers to commit abuse that is shocking in its callousness.

The link between motherhood and female violence is one of the most challenging and important dimensions of the subject. Recognizing it is necessary to understand the breadth of emotional pressures that can lead women to violence, and how motherhood can sometimes be a lightning rod for these. My work with mothers who have harmed their children—often acting as an expert witness in a care proceeding or custody hearing—has exposed me both to the existence of female violence against children and to wider perceptions surrounding motherhood in the medical and justice systems. These cases have brought me face-to-face with motherhood as one of society's most sacred ideals and contested realities. And they have presented what feel like impossible questions: How could a mother harm the most precious thing she could create, and how do you decide whether a woman who has caused harm to her child can ever be trusted with their care again?

4

SAFFIRE AND JACKIE

Motherhood on Trial

Some of the most difficult work for a forensic psychologist is to assess mothers who have been deemed a potential risk to their children. It demands that you answer two questions: What harm has been done to the child in the past, and, crucially, what risk of harm in the future still remains? Is it safe to leave the child in their mother's care? The need both to safeguard the child and to resist easy condemnation of the mother, who may credibly claim to love and wish to care for them, can be an excruciating balancing act.

Saffire was a twenty-four-year-old woman who had neglected her two young sons, prioritizing her party lifestyle to the point where both boys were found unattended and wandering the streets unfed. She was also prone to fits of rage that could explode into violence against her children: in the most serious incident she had caused a hairline fracture of the older boy's arm. Yet she was intelligent and empathetic, fully aware of the harm she had done and apparently determined to turn her life around.

Jackie was thirty-one, mother both to a baby daughter, now aged fourteen months, and to a daughter from a previous relationship whom she had abandoned. At ten months, the baby had been seriously injured in a presumed assault, which she denied either perpetrating or covering up on behalf of her partner. Both in sessions with me and later in court, when her custody was formally considered, she continued to deny that she was prioritizing her relationship over her child and presented an image of concerned motherhood that seemed to me at distinct odds with the reality.

Saffire

Although a psychologist should never prejudge a patient, it is only human to have certain expectations of a person you have read so much about before first meeting her. In the case of Saffire, whom I had been asked to assess after her two young sons had suffered both neglect and physical injury at her hands, my assumption was that I would be meeting the kind of guarded, defensive, and disengaged figure who is typical of many younger women I have evaluated. I have sat across from so many women in these situations who are accused of serious crimes or breaches of parental responsibility, but who themselves seem like scared girls. Unable to flee the room, they seem to be trying to retreat back inside their own bodies, or under the layers of heavy clothing that are a typical first line of defense.

Saffire confounded every element of this archetype. Her large, athletic frame was matched by an apparently generous and big-hearted personality. She radiated emotional availability, with an unusually direct gaze and clear, focused eyes that did not attempt to mask an impression of sadness and shame. She responded quickly, animatedly even, to my initial questions—the kinds of inquiries that so often land on the stony ground of an uncooperative and apprehensive patient. I knew it was possible that I was being manipulated—early in our conversation she made a point of saying that she could tell I was a good listener and that I cared—but found it hard to discount my first impression that this warmth and engagement were part of Saffire's authentic self.

That was further reinforced by the way she spoke about her children, four-year-old Owen and two-year-old Joel. Typically, parents involved in care proceedings will describe their children in one of two ways: either in highly negative terms that accentuate the troublesome behavior that they blame for their own subsequent actions, or as an idealized account of children who never cry, complain, or wake up in the middle of the night, who are "good as gold," and whom they "love to bits." Both approaches betray a parent who, for whatever reason, refuses to be honest with me about what has transpired, presenting an unrealistic, sentimental vision of their children and their parenting or a complete denial of how they have projected malevolent power onto an innocent child, viewing them as a persecutor. Saffire defaulted to neither of these extremes. She lit up when I asked as open a question as one can of a mother whose children have been found outside in the cold, dressed in dirty clothes, apparently underfed, and with bruises on their skinny bodies: "Tell me about your boys, what they're like and what you do best with them."

Her response was a lengthy answer that spanned the personalities, needs, and contrasts of both children. Owen, she told me, was lively, sociable, and energetic, an adventurer who loved to play, a boy who was "into everything" and liked nothing more than to run around or play football. His brother, Joel, was quieter, a "dreamer" who loved having stories read to him and watching the family's cats play. Each had a favorite toy that went with him everywhere. Both could be temperamental at bath time if the water was even slightly too hot or cold. She worried that Joel, the more cerebral of the pair, might find kindergarten too hectic, even intimidating. His older brother had thrived there and was just about to begin elementary school.

Saffire was speaking much as any loving mother might, the woman who will never find herself in a courtroom pleading to retain custody of her children. Like that of any caring parent, her love was apparent from the deep knowledge she demonstrated of her children, her attentiveness to the nuances of their personalities, concern for what might challenge them, and affection for their foibles. Yet Saffire was not a straightforwardly loving or safe parent. She had inflicted injuries on the boys that were deemed "non-accidental" and confessed to hitting Owen when she had lost control in the past. Social services were treating Joel, whose slow growth suggested developmental problems, as being at risk of neglect. She had admitted neglect when visited by the police after a neighbor had found the boys shut out of their home, wandering the street in distress.

However much I had warmed to Saffire in our initial exchanges, and however touched I might have been by her attentive description of the two children, these boys had nonetheless come to serious harm. One had suffered a broken bone; both were covered in bruises and had obvious signs of dangerous neglect: their school reported they had turned up hungry and in inadequate clothing on several occasions. Both the proximate reasons and the underlying causes of this mistreatment needed to be brought to the surface before we could begin to broach the question of whether Saffire could ever be considered a safe and suitable parent.

The facts of the case combined Saffire's neglect for the boys, as she prioritized her social life, with moments of violence that had arisen from the challenging situations that any parent of young children should calmly navigate. Saffire enjoyed hosting the kinds of long, loud parties that attracted the concern of her neighbors, not just because of the disturbance, but when it became clear that Owen and Joel were frequently left out in the garden for long periods to fend for themselves, with their mother preoccupied and apparently oblivious to their needs. In addition to this neglect, Saffire attacked her sons on multiple occasions, in outbursts of aggression when she found their behavior impossible to handle. She described to me how the boys could "turn," becoming "monsters" and going "from Jekyll to Hyde." To most parents these are ordinary, predictable temper tantrums: a fact of life for children that age. For Saffire they were unbearable. She would herself descend into fits of panic, rage, and hysteria, willing to try anything to silence them. She described one occasion where she "lost it" and reached for something to threaten them with, picking up a metal spoon that she had just been using to stir hot soup for their tea. In her rage she began hitting them with it, leaving minor burn marks on their arms. She also related an incident when she had twisted Owen's arms so hard that it caused a hairline fracture of his arm, requiring hospital treatment.

The thread connecting this chain of disturbing incidents was Saffire's volatility: her tendency to snap in and out of moments of extreme anger characterized by outbursts of violence. These explosions of abuse were shocking but also fleeting. As soon as she realized what she had done, and the consequences of her actions, she would revert to the role of caring parent: shocked at the burn marks she had inflicted on her sons' arms, and quickly taking Owen to the emergency room once she realized she had caused him a serious injury. It was not the boys who acted as Jekyll and Hyde but their mother, who could not control her sometimes wild oscillations between attentive care and volcanic rage.

To better understand Saffire's behavior and her distorted views of her children, I returned to the work of Melanie Klein, the Austro-British psychoanalyst who did much to influence the development of the profession in the first half of the twentieth century. Klein was famous for her work with children, around whom she formed one of her foundational theories of development, that of the paranoid-schizoid position. This describes the presumed psychology of infants during their first few months of life. Babies are, according to Kleinian theory, unable to recognize that both good and bad can exist within the same entity. Rather than seeing that the mother who feeds them can also be the one who sometimes deprives or frustrates them, they "split" these experiences, perceiving a "good" breast that provides and a "bad" one that withholds, feeling persecuted by the ongoing contrast. In typical development, Klein held that the paranoid-schizoid position develops (around the age of six months) into the depressive position, in which infants begin to perceive that the good and the bad can exist within the same entity.

The ability to move beyond the paranoid-schizoid position, to perceive ambivalence and ambiguity, is a critical stage in our development as human beings with empathy, social skills, and the ability to form healthy relationships, where we accept that the person we love can also be the person we sometimes hate. Good and bad coexist in the same person; in us, and in others. This same development is also a critical part of psychotherapy, with the patient learning afresh through their relationship with the therapist that the good and the bad, the supportive and the critical, must coexist. Yet this evolution is not always clear-cut, nor do we necessarily shed every vestige of the urge to see what Klein termed "objects" as wholly good or bad. As she wrote, "Love and hate are struggling together in the baby's mind; and this struggle to a certain extent persists throughout life and is liable to become a source of danger in human relationships." At times of anxiety all of us can revert to the polarized and rigid mindset of the paranoid-schizoid position, collapsing again into an infantile state in which things are either all good or all bad. If all badness exists outside us, the world is terrifying; if it is located inside us, we hate ourselves.

I came to believe that this way of relating to others, and herself, was at the heart of Saffire's shortcomings as a parent. Often she was in a state of mind akin to the paranoid-schizoid position, veering dangerously between seeing her sons as the source of everything positive in her life and perceiving them as unmitigated sources of strife and distress—"monsters," to use her word. Her inability to hold the good and the bad in mind, balancing as any parent must the moments of love and joy with those of exhaustion and frustration, meant that she could not self-soothe at the times when the boys were descending into tantrums of their own. Instead, she would become locked in a battle, her offspring as the bad object, violence her only escape from the temporary spiral.

This pattern of conceptualizing others as entirely good or bad also helped to explain her unusually positive, even effusive, attitude toward me at the beginning of our time together. Rather than the guarded reception to which I was accustomed, as a new patient considers whether I might be of help to them, she had rushed to praise and welcome me—to place me on a pedestal and venerate me as a "good" object, the nurturing, feeding breast. Which is not to say that Saffire behaved entirely innocently in our meetings as I prepared my psychological risk assessment. Like many in her position, she at times sought to turn the tables, on one occasion asking me if I had children myself and how I would feel if, like her, I had been declared an "unfit mother," one who could not put her children's needs before her own. While it is often tempting to engage with these questions, whether to reject a provocative suggestion or share something of your life with a patient to whom you feel a personal connection, it is important to resist this. Self-disclosure moves into the realm of friendship and can carry the risk that it is prompted by the therapist's needs and not the patient's. As far as possible, the therapist should exist as a blank slate onto whom a patient can project their own perceptions and needs, leaving the space for transference and minimizing the scope for distortion and suspicion. Confirming that you are actually a mother can evoke envy, longing, or hatred, while revealing that you are happily married or recently divorced introduces a reality that can undermine the purpose and integrity of the therapy. But these questions are important to consider, if not to answer. They remind me that there is a continuum of human experience. The patient and I are not worlds apart; I could be sitting in her place, feeling her pain.

As I began to prepare the conclusions of my report, I knew it was not a simple case, nor one that would be decided on paper. Saffire's abuse and neglect of her two sons were clear and demanded action. Her account of how rage would burn up inside her, transforming her into a monstrous creature who could only see her beloved sons as beasts needing to be tamed, was as extreme as the acts she then described. Yet in dynamic risk terms, it was by no means clear that she was a lost cause as a parent. Despite her episodes of terrifying impulsive anger and violence, Saffire evidently had the capacity to care for, empathize with, and respond to her sons, and also the desire to. She wanted treatment and did not dispute that child protective services had become involved in her children's care, nor the purpose of the assessment. She acknowledged and accepted responsibility for what she had done and emphasized that she would do "whatever it took" to address her behavior, subdue her worst impulses, and become a parent who could provide consistent, safe, and reliable care for her children. When I suggested that this might involve a long-term course of therapy focusing on her anger, its roots and consequences, including delving deep into her childhood, she indicated that she was eager to participate. I was cautiously optimistic that it would be possible to alter the one dynamic risk factor that posed the greatest danger to Saffire's two sons: her own volatile behavior and the intense fluctuations in mood that drove it.

The risk assessment I prepared reflected the dualities that ran through Saffire's life and her case. She was a perpetrator of violence but had also been a victim of it, with more than one abusive relationship in her past and a childhood that had been entirely spent in the care system. In her worst moments, those lightning strikes of uncontrollable emotion, she was clearly an unsafe mother, yet for the majority of her parenting she was as loving, attentive, and concerned as you could hope anyone to be. And she had been guilty of neglect, but was also a parent closely attuned to her children, their personalities and inner lives. She desperately needed and wanted help to manage her angry outbursts, which had seen her lose control in a dangerous way. She knew she had to offer her sons the kind of calm, responsive care that she had not known in her own early life.

Assessing a case such as this, a psychologist must fully recognize both the good and the bad contained within the same person and make sense of their contradictory behavior. As I so often did in these cases, I worried about veering too far in one direction or the other, that I would underplay the ongoing risk to children or excessively discount the opportunity that a mother like Saffire had to modify her behavior sufficiently to become what the child psychoanalyst and pediatrician Donald Winnicott terms a "good enough" mother. The final report outlined all of this, detailing the factors that could lead to harm in the future, and also how treatment and protective elements could limit these risks—potentially to the point where Saffire could be trusted to retain care of her children without the involvement of child protective services. As I added the final sentence to my report, the one that states I believe the contents to be true and understand that they may be put before the court, I was almost certain that my part in this case was not yet over.

Jackie

If I had found Saffire a disarming presence, Jackie put me on the defensive in the first few moments of our meeting. She could not have made it clearer that she did not want to be having this conversation. Indeed, she believed the entire assessment process and everything it was predicated on to be an outrage, an insult to her, and a waste of time. She glared at me, bristling with bright-blond short hair, an oversize fake-fur jacket, and military-style boots: an incongruous presence in the drab office that was the venue for our session.

The case was a serious one. Jackie's daughter Amy, then aged ten months, had been taken into care following serious injuries that were deemed non-accidental. These included bleeding in the brain, which could have been the result of being shaken, a direct blow, or a fall onto a hard surface. She also had cuts and bruises on the sides of her face, suggestive of having been hit or scratched. Only Jackie and her partner, Leon, who together had care of Amy, were being considered her potential assailants—what is known as a "pool of perpetrators." Amy had recovered while she was placed in foster care, and a series of assessments of Jackie with and without her began. Beyond the physical evidence of mistreatment, Jackie and Amy had undergone a psychological evaluation known as the "strange situation" test, in which a baby is successively put in a room with its parent, a stranger, and alone (and different sequences of the same people), to determine levels of attachment between parent and child. It was noted that Amy had shown little concern when Jackie left the room during the assessment, continuing to play with the toys provided, and then crawled away from her mother when she returned.

Despite the shocking abuse that had been inflicted on her daughter, Jackie presented as if she herself were the primary victim. She was furious that Amy had been taken away from her and made clear her disgust at social services and me personally. Neither her demeanor nor her explanation of events was convincing. She maintained that Leon could not have caused the injuries without her seeing, and that she had not noticed evidence of the scratching and bruising or any changes in Amy's behavior until just before she took her to the hospital. When I pressed her on how these injuries had indeed happened, if not inflicted by either her or Leon, she told me that all she knew was that she had left Amy in her crib for a nap and that she was lively and protested. She was trying to stand up and must have fallen as Jackie heard her unusual, piercing cry. When she came back in, she saw Amy lying, facedown, with her head against the crib bars, suggesting that this could have been what caused the major head injuries. She thought the scratches on her face were caused by Amy's own fingernails, which she had since cut short. She was adamant that only after that "accident" had she noticed her baby "acting funny" and "whining," looking pale and seeming dizzy, and had taken her to the hospital in the next few hours. This was not just an improbable story but one that failed to square with the medical record. By the time Amy was admitted, her bruises were already fading and the pronounced swelling on her head indicated that the relevant injuries had occurred at least twenty-four hours earlier.

In my role as psychologist and forensic psychotherapist it is generally incumbent on me to remain calm, curious, and compassionate, to suspend judgment, and to listen. But the task of risk assessment is in stark contrast to this, later, stage of psychotherapy and makes different demands. You have a mandate to arrive as close as possible to the truth of a serious and concerning matter and little time in which to do so. You do not have the luxury of a long series of sessions stretching over the course of months, which allow a skilled therapist to ease patients gently out of conscious or unconscious rabbit holes. This urgency can make an assessment session a tense affair, and I felt frustration and despair rising within me as I believed that a mother who had either participated in or ignored the horrific abuse of a baby girl was trying to deceive me with a blatant and absurd lie.

Yet I also had to put this feeling aside and deal with the other half of my brief, to understand what had led Jackie to this point, the psychology that underlay her behavior as a mother, and the possibility that she could be helped to become a safe parent. She had already been diagnosed with personality disorder, of both a histrionic and a borderline type, with antisocial traits and also had a history of postnatal depression. Her criminal record included shoplifting and theft. Her diagnosis indicated impulsivity, difficulty in sustaining relationships, and a tendency to drama. That was reinforced by what I viewed as one of the most significant parts of her history: that she had suddenly and permanently left behind an older child after beginning her relationship with Leon. After leaving her eight-year-old daughter in her father's care two years earlier, the two had had minimal contact. Jackie described how bored and dissatisfied she had been in her former family life, living in a suburban home and working part-time in a pub. It was at work that she had met Leon, whom she described in contrasting terms as someone who was cool and sexy and made her feel alive again.

Swept up in this excitement, she appeared to leave her old life behind without regret or hesitation. She was irritated, even bored, when I asked about the effect that her walking away might have had on her older daughter. Along with the evidence of the "strange situation" test, it gave me serious cause for concern about her ability to form and sustain relationships that would allow her children a secure attachment to her. Unlike her glowing and engaged portrait of Leon, her description of both Amy and her older daughter was flat and generic, almost as if she were talking about children she hardly knew or had heard about from someone else. There was none of the texture, the loving tone, and the attention to small details that Saffire had demonstrated when describing her boys. Had we been talking about children in general rather than hers in particular, I would have guessed that Jackie had never been a parent.

I was painfully aware that in assessing Jackie as a mother, I was at risk of putting greater emphasis on this abandonment than if she had been a man. Assessing the capacity of mothers to care for their children without falling prey to tropes about motherhood is a constant challenge, as I struggle *not* to betray either my own feminism or my duty as a psychologist to the court, which may rely on my evidence in determining the future of vulnerable children. In this case, I reassured myself that I was not overreacting to any single incident but recognizing a trend: that of a volatile and impulsive parent who had more than once demonstrated that the well-being of her children was not her abiding priority.

Jackie being mostly unwilling or unable to talk in detail about her daughters, I shifted the focus of our conversation to her early life and her experiences of being parented. Quickly it became apparent that her uneven temperament and volatile decision-making were grounded in a childhood that had been scarred by instability. With a father working in diplomatic service, stationed overseas with the family, she narrated how her early life had frequently seen her moving from town to town and forever being the new girl at school who struggled to make friends. She appreciated her stay-at-home mother but idolized her father, who doted on her when present but was more often preoccupied with work or drink. Although she described herself as a "Daddy's girl," Jackie also related how his drinking and mood swings meant the entire family would be walking on eggshells around him, adding to the feeling of persistent unease. She had been well educated despite the disruption in her early years, and this was to show later, in her capacity to present her evidence in court.

In many ways, Jackie's subsequent life choices could be characterized as a repudiation of her loving mother and a continued pursuit of her idealized, unpredictable father. When she found herself in what most would describe as a safe and stable lifestyle, working part-time and married to Toby, a "solid" partner with whom to raise her child, she chafed against its limitations and ran away, in pursuit of a man who offered danger and excitement. Leon had a history of violence and had spent two years in juvenile detention after being convicted of wounding with intent. Jackie found him a magnetic presence and swapped her calm suburban life for one of clubbing, partying, and drug use—drinking deeply of a lifestyle she felt she had missed out on by being diligent at school and marrying early to Toby. While Jackie gave up much of this after Amy was born, Leon did not. For him the late nights, the drugs, and the fighting continued. This created tension in the family home, because he would regularly be disturbed by the baby's crying while trying to sleep off the previous night's excesses during the day.

From the available evidence, it was not difficult to surmise the most likely explanation for Amy's injuries. Only one or the other of her parents could have inflicted them, and she had a father with a history of violence, a habit of drug use, and a tendency to find her behavior disruptive. Yet to establish this for certain would have required either his admission or Jackie's testimony, and she refused to say that Leon had been responsible. She had been reluctant even to entertain the idea that he could have been. It created a stalemate whereby neither parent could be conclusively identified as the perpetrator of Amy's abuse, a kind of prisoner's dilemma.

It also brought to the fore an idea that is almost as challenging as maternal harm itself: that a mother might simply choose to prioritize something or someone ahead of her children. The case of Susan Smith, the South Carolina mother who killed her two young sons in 1994 by driving her car into a lake and letting them drown, was notable in this regard. A week before the murder, she had received a Dear Jane letter from a man with whom she had been pursuing a relationship. One of his reasons for dumping her was that he wanted no children of his own, nor to be responsible for anyone else's. Prosecutors in her trial argued that she had in effect killed her own children to clear the path for that relationship. Although the case in front of me was far less dramatic, and thankfully the harm had been relatively minor, the dynamic carried an echo. Jackie was a mother who—I strongly believed—was putting her romantic relationship ahead of her daughter, to the point that she worried more about protecting her abusive partner than her vulnerable child. There were factors in Jackie's life that had brought her to this point, but perhaps none as significant as the reality that she had been bored in a dead-end relationship and decided that she wanted to be Leon's girlfriend more than she did anyone's mother. The things that drive people to become perpetrators or enablers of violence can indeed be banal rather than complex or innate. This is something I must remind myself of as I strive to break down a patient's actions and life experiences, probing for any relation between the two. Much as these connections are often fundamental to understanding patterns of behavior and advancing treatment, occasionally a psychologist can find themselves searching in vain for a deeper meaning or nuance that does not exist.

Whatever the realities of this case, my job was simply to assess Jackie's suitability as a parent. Here the conclusion could be more unambiguous. While I considered it only an outside possibility that she had inflicted the injuries herself, even in the most generous interpretation she had willfully blinded herself to the likely culpability of her partner and was trying harder to protect him than to safeguard the best interests of her infant daughter. It seemed to me that she had fabricated an explanation to cover up Leon's violence to which she stubbornly clung despite its evident lack of credibility. Another possibility was that she had inflicted the injuries herself, in a one-off loss of control for which she felt too scared and guilty ever to confess. I was in little doubt that neither Jackie nor Leon was close to being a safe parent for Amy. But, as I was to discover in court, what appears clear to one psychologist can seem questionable to another. My conclusion was far from the sole interpretation of the mother's psychological state, and the evidence I was to provide in Jackie's case would not go uncontested.

To Court

Child-care proceedings, during which the future placement of the child is ultimately at stake, are complex affairs in the United Kingdom, in which multiple parties are being represented in parallel. There are child services, which must go to court to secure the various types of orders that give it authority to take a child into care or closely supervise its parental care. There is the guardian *ad litem,* an official appointed by the court to represent the interests of the child. And there are the parents, who will often be represented individually by separate lawyers. As an expert witness, I can be commissioned to conduct an assessment and then to appear in court by any one of these parties. But my role is to be an independent authority, ultimately responsible to the court itself, and with the welfare of the child or children involved paramount. That independence is enshrined by several provisions: my instructions must be agreed to by all parties and my conclusions made available to all in parallel. Furthermore, and unlike in a criminal case, the report cannot be disregarded even if unfavorable to the party that commissioned it.

Giving evidence in court and being cross-examined are taxing experiences, demanding of the expert witness that they demonstrate an independence and detachment from cases in which the material is often shocking and deeply personal. The interrogative style of lawyers in a UK courtroom, in some cases spinning eloquent webs that seek to mold, or discredit, witness testimony, is an additional challenge to neutrality and equanimity. Above all, the gravity of the moment when you take the witness stand and swear the oath to tell the truth does not diminish, even after numerous cases and court appearances. Nor should it.

In Saffire's case I appeared at the interim hearing, one that determines immediate arrangements for care of a child, short of a final decision about custody being reached. For ninety minutes I was cross-examined on the findings of my evaluation and risk assessment: that, although Saffire's abuse and neglect of her sons was serious, her acknowledgment of the harm she had caused, her advanced understanding of their needs, and her willingness to engage with a course of treatment should all be considered as factors in her favor. She was no longer in the volatile relationship that had been going on at the time she had caused the fracture on Owen's arm and had agreed to submit to regular drug testing. I believed that Saffire would benefit from treatment and there was a good chance that this could result (within twelve to eighteen months) in a material improvement in her psychological stability, ability to emotionally self-regulate, and understanding of how to respond to the changing needs of her young sons.

Not unusually, the lawyers asking questions pressed consistently for the kind of certainty that is almost impossible to offer when dealing with the vagaries of treatment, the complexity of human behavior, and the strength of psychological resistance to change. How long would the treatment take? What likelihood was there of a change in Saffire's temperament and ability to handle stress? When would we know that the treatment had succeeded? As an expert witness, I find it uncomfortable to be vague and to keep underlining what I do not know, but it is important not to attach certainty to matters that are by their nature unpredictable.

One of the most pertinent questions was the last one, put by the judge, who asked whether Saffire's psychological treatment could be done while she retained care of the children. Would it be destabilizing for her to be caring for Owen and Joel while she underwent treatment that would be delving deep into her former abuse of them, or would it in fact help her to be with them? My answer favored the second view: therapy is not a panacea and should generally be used as part of a package of support for a parent such as Saffire. In my opinion, it was better that she receive regular supervision to support her parenting in parallel with the psychological treatment rather than simply undertake the therapy in isolation, to be returned into a role to which, when the time came, both she and the boys would have become unaccustomed. I also continued to believe that Saffire was a dedicated mother who cared deeply for her children, and that their best interests would be served by remaining in her (closely supervised) care, rather than the instability of shuttling between different arrangements. I saw her beaming, clearly hopeful, as I confirmed my opinion that she could take care of her sons while undergoing treatment, which I was willing and able to provide within the outpatient clinic where I then worked, supported by colleagues.

Saffire's case was an example of where the difficulty arises from balancing different needs, rather than trying to reconcile opposing views. In their various ways, all parties agreed that the question was how to support Saffire to become a safe parent: the guardian *ad litem* agreed with me about her capacity for growth and change, while the boys' father was also content that they should stay in her care provided safeguards could be put in place. At the final hearing, a care plan was approved that saw the local authority provide close supervision of Saffire as she retained custody of her sons and embarked on a course of therapy with me. In the fourteen months that followed, a combination of progress with her treatment and the greater involve-

ment of the boys' father in their care had the positive effect that all
involved in her case had hoped for. Saffire gradually gained greater
awareness, self-control, and a sense of calm in her role as a mother.
She was able to subdue her wild temper and enhance her empathy
for the boys and their perspective on the world. Ultimately, with the
right help and support, she grew into the safe and secure parent that
I had always hoped she was capable of being. It was a joy to see and
hear her as she talked with pride about the boys, their development,
and her bond with them.

By contrast, the hearing at which Jackie's custody of her daughter was determined could not have been more adversarial. This was a
final hearing, at which she and Leon were opposing the local authority's care plan for Amy, which would have meant her being removed
from their custody permanently and placed in an alternative home
(at the time of the hearing she was temporarily in foster care). A
further complication was that Jackie's parents had also lodged an
application to become Amy's carers if their daughter failed in her
own attempt to regain custody. Jackie also opposed this and continued to insist that not only should she be Amy's guardian but Leon
should also remain involved in her care.

My report had strongly recommended that Amy not be returned
into the care of either parent, but that the local authority be granted
what is known as a full care order, giving them the power to place
her permanently with alternative guardians. Jackie's lawyer, who
had initially approached and commissioned me, not only disagreed
with this but took the unusual step of obtaining a second assessment from another expert. They also summoned me to the hearing
for cross-examination as a hostile witness. The proceeding became
even more combative when my professional colleague and I were
asked to be present to hear each other's evidence and comment upon
it during cross-examination. The lawyers had not, as is sometimes
the case, convened an earlier professionals' meeting in order to try
to forge a consensus expert opinion and avoid a contested hearing.
Nor does the law permit expert witnesses to converse or discuss dis-
crepancies in our reports at this stage—an act that would be deemed
contempt of court.

What we did have was access to each other's reports prior to the trial, and I was surprised by both the methodology and the conclusions of my colleague's work. Our findings were dramatically at odds, with marked differences in emphasis on key elements of Jackie's case. Whereas I had found and assessed her to be an able, self-possessed, and independent woman, my colleague presented her as a manipulated young woman who had fallen under the spell of a controlling, violent partner. While my primary concerns were about the injuries that had been inflicted on Amy and the inadequate explanations for this near-fatal assault, my colleague's assessment focused more on the potential trauma for Jackie of having her baby daughter removed, emphasizing the role that postnatal depression had played in her life and troubles. In this report little attention was given to Jackie leaving her older daughter, while there was much discussion of the significance of Jackie's having given up smoking and drinking when she fell pregnant with Amy, and that she had been breast-feeding her until they were separated. Jackie was portrayed as a devoted mother, with a close bond to Amy that had suddenly been interrupted.

Presented with an identical case history and subject, we had reached remarkably discordant conclusions. In my assessment, Jackie was suffering from personality disorder, had demonstrated a tendency for volatile and impulsive behavior, struggled to form stable attachments with either of her two children, and was more concerned with her relationship with Leon than the welfare of her baby. By contrast, my colleague presented her as a tragic figure, a victim of injustice, and a devoted mother who should not be separated from her child. No attention was given to the "strange situation" test that showed Amy did not appear securely attached to Jackie. Although this alternative interpretation in no way undermined my confidence in the assessment I had made, and both the local authority and the guardian *ad litem* favored my conclusion, I was taken aback by the yawning gap between our two opinions. It was a reminder that there can be no such thing as a totally objective assessment and of how different weighting of identical evidence by experienced professionals can lead to dramatically alternative viewpoints.

Those contrasts would continue to be felt during the five-day hearing, four days of which I attended either to give my own evidence or to hear that of others. My professional counterpart and Jackie both took the stand before me, allowing them to set the scene and implicitly positioning me as the voice of negativity, a thought that I found concerning as I sat silently through the early part of the hearing. That sense only grew as I watched my fellow expert give an emotional account, arguing for Amy and Jackie to be reunited and citing breast-feeding as a point of evidence for their bond. Jackie's sacrifices, stopping smoking and drinking in pregnancy and beyond, showed she was "turning her life around" out of love for her child. Jackie herself was calm, composed, and eloquent. Although Leon had been seen entering and leaving her home, she denied that they remained in a relationship. She also indicated that unlike during our meeting she had now begun to accept the possibility that he might have caused their baby's shocking injuries. Her account both disturbed and impressed me, contradictory as I found it in places, and it seemed to confirm my perception of her as a woman with independence and agency, not the helpless victim portrayed by the second expert.

When I eventually took the stand, setting out the various risks that I believed Jackie's continued custody of Amy would pose, I quickly got the impression that my testimony was falling on deaf ears. While the judge had listened attentively, even indulgently, to my fellow professional and to Jackie, he seemed distracted as I spoke. Then, as I touched on my concern about her relationship with Leon and the likelihood that this was ongoing, he interrupted me.

"Miss Motz, have you never heard of a woman loving a man?"

Even now, more than two decades later and after countless meetings with violent and disturbed patients, this still ranks as one of the most breathtaking things that anyone has said to me in a professional setting.

"Miss Motz, do you have children?"

The meaning of these interventions could not have been clearer. As a (then) young, unmarried, and childless woman, I found that my evidence and professional opinion seemed to be discounted to the point of being disregarded because of one man's assessment of my life experience. To that judge, I appeared a naive girl who did not understand romantic or maternal love. Based on that alone, he had little interest in what I had to say about Jackie, her capabilities as a mother, and the risks she posed to her daughter's welfare. Hours and hours of careful work to develop a psychological portrait and rounded risk assessment seemed to be cast aside with a single, sweeping arm of prejudice and prejudgment.

Those two sharp, jolting interventions told me everything I needed to know about how the case would be decided. Had a judge, who held the future of a vulnerable infant in his hands, been seduced by a narrative of female victimhood and maternal love? He certainly seemed to be making a decision that would define multiple lives based more on idealized preconceptions about womanhood and motherhood than on a reasonable appraisal of the evidence and professional opinion. Against this backdrop, my professional counterpart's repeated emphasis on Jackie's breast-feeding of her daughter had been an inadvertent masterstroke of courtroom advocacy. Moreover, when he was called back to the witness stand to comment on my evidence, he argued that I had wholly underestimated the influence Leon exerted on Jackie and the fact of her postnatal depression. He was categorical in his evidence, outlining the traumatic effects of separation on a young baby, adamant in his view that Jackie and Leon had genuinely separated and that she was in a position to protect herself and Amy from harm. The effect of maternal abandonment on Jackie's other daughter, who had been only eight years old when she left, was ignored.

I was far from a voice in the wilderness as far as Jackie's parental risk was concerned. Social workers and representatives from the local authority testified that she and Leon had been uncooperative with them and identified deficiencies in their parenting—both individually and as a couple. The evidence of the guardian *ad litem,* and of a pediatrician who had examined Amy in the emergency room—who described the potential long-term ramifications of her injuries—was also compelling. Yet the judge remained unmoved. He rejected the plan that recommended Amy be removed from her parents, and said that the minimum he would be prepared to accept was an arrangement with shared responsibility for Amy that incorporated a plan for her to be returned to Jackie's care. The social services could not approve this, because they did not want to share responsibility with a mother they considered dangerous. They were left with the option of reapplying for a "supervision order," one that would give them no power to remove Amy from her mother's care unless a time came when she was thought to reach the threshold criteria for sustaining harm, meaning that, unless that happened, she might fall under the radar.

Maternal abuse of children is difficult for a society to bear and sometimes difficult to see, even when it happens in plain sight. In the UK the case of Arthur Labinjo-Hughes, a six-year-old boy murdered in the care of an apparently sadistic stepmother and abusive father in 2020, was widely reported, causing outcry and shock, as if this were a highly unusual case, when sadly it is not. According to the National Society for the Prevention of Cruelty to Children (NSPCC), at least one child is killed a week on average in the UK, with children under the age of one the most likely to be killed by another person, and parents or stepparents the most frequent perpetrators. In the United States, in 2020, a total of 255 child fatalities due to abuse or maltreatment occurred in Texas alone, the most out of any state. In that year, California, New York, Illinois, and Florida rounded out the five leading states for child abuse deaths. It is all too easy to see how children at risk remain in dangerous situations, despite multiple opportunities for intervention.

It is no accident that most of these stories go untold, barring the occasional exception that will be presented as a tragic outlier. The reluctance to acknowledge these deaths stems from a widespread unwillingness to confront violence that happens close to home, in recognizable domestic situations. The novelist Siri Hustvedt identified this tendency, in her essay on the case of the American teenager Sylvia Likens, tortured and murdered in 1965 by the woman in whose care she had been left, Gertrude Banisewski, and a group of the other children living under the same roof. As she wrote, "The lone gunman who 'snaps' and begins firing his weapon in a church, synagogue, or school, and the sadistic psychopath who secretly stalks his prey are easier to keep at a comfortable distance by reason of mental illness than any group, small or large in number, that turns on its victim(s) with rabid fury."

We do not acknowledge the full extent of maternal violence against children, because it is countercultural: too challenging to our preconceptions of family and motherhood, and too threatening to that "comfortable distance" we wish to maintain between ourselves and the possibility of serious violence. Jackie's case showed me that this myopia extended to the justice system and the authority figures who determine the course of children's lives. It remains one of the most troubling examples in my career of a child being returned to the care of a mother I thought an unsafe and untrustworthy parent and potential danger to their welfare. It revealed to me the power of preconceptions and of our cherished images of motherhood. No less concerning was how this outcome limited transparency. Unless child services found Amy had come to serious harm, through their visits under the supervision order, I would not be able to follow her case, her guardian *ad litem* would have no future contact, and, once the order ended, Jackie would be free to reunite with Leon or any other partner who might pose a risk to Amy. In this case no such harm was determined during the supervision period, and the long-term outcome for Amy remains a troubling mystery.

*

Jackie's case has stayed with me, because I continue to wonder if the decision would have been different had it happened today—now I am a wife and mother of adult children—or if I had been giving expert testimony as a man. It also taught me a lesson that I believe has endured regardless of any change in personal circumstances or social attitudes in more than twenty years since. Cases involving a mother's custody of her children are uniquely emotive events. They provoke strong feelings in all concerned, regardless of their life experience and whatever measures they take to maintain a professional distance. Almost everyone involved in such cases, in whatever capacity, has some experience of the mother's unique bond with her child. Most of us know what it means to have or to have lost a mother, whatever kind of parent she might have been and whatever our relationship with her may be today. Motherhood exists not just as a state of being but as an idea in people's minds. No discussion of it can ever happen in neutral territory, free from personal experience, sentimental attachments, and cherished ideals. As Jackie's case showed, in proceedings like these you are dealing not just with legal norms and clinical assessments but with layers of our most deep-seated social conditioning and prejudices. Society is deeply invested in such idealizations and largely blind to their dangers. Women are seen through a distorting lens—judged not as the parents that they actually are but as the mothers that society either wishes or believes them to be.

This is not just a British quirk but a tendency seen around the world. The sentimentality surrounding ideas of motherhood crosses cultures. This can put children at risk when mothers are not considered likely perpetrators of abuse. But it can also lead to the vilification of women who appear to contravene these ideals.

The tragic story of Lisa Montgomery and Bobbie Jo Stinnett is a case in point. In 2004, aged thirty-six, Montgomery killed the heavily pregnant Bobbie Jo Stinnett, strangling her and cutting the baby out of her stomach. The child would survive and later be returned to her family. This was a deeply shocking crime, to which Montgomery immediately confessed, describing herself as a monster. Yet the way her case was handled, up to the point in 2021 where she became the first woman to be executed in America in sixty-seven years, also demonstrates the distorting effect of crimes involving and violating motherhood.

Montgomery's life had been scarred with abuse from the moment she had been born, with fetal alcohol syndrome brought about by her mother's heavy drinking while pregnant. As a child she experienced psychical, psychological, and sexual abuse—routinely raped from the age of eleven by her stepfather and often confined to a dungeon-style room. She was reportedly also trafficked by her mother, who traded her for sex to help her pay men for handiwork. Her crime may be understood in the context of these appalling traumas—a proxy assault on her own mother and even an attempt, through removing the baby, to save a version of herself.

Yet law enforcement and the justice system proceeded as if Lisa Montgomery had been of sound mind when she killed Bobbie Jo. The local sheriff insisted that the planning Montgomery had undertaken—befriending her victim online under a false identity and researching how to perform a cesarean—proved she was sane, ignoring the reality that a delusional mind can also be a logical one and psychosis does not prohibit calculation. Notably, he also made a point of highlighting that Bobbie Jo had been discovered by her own mother.

The upshot was that rather than being treated by the justice system as the deeply damaged individual that she was, Montgomery was simply decried as the devil, a pitiless psychopath who deserved no mercy and received none even after numerous pleas for clemency. For society to protect the ideal of motherhood, it was easier to vilify a woman who had killed a pregnant mother as outside all human norms, rather than to recognize her as the victim she was of a life of pitiless abuse and consequent mental illness. Bobbie Jo's status as a tragic heroine and idealized mother figure simply cemented the idea that Montgomery was inhuman, a monster.

In my career I have seen how ideals of motherhood affect so many lives—whether protecting women who are themselves abusers or leading others to be unreasonably denounced and misunderstood. As I was later to discover when assessing Grace, a mother who had deliberately faked and induced illness in her daughter, these ideals are not just a form of idle prejudice but beliefs that shape professional decision-making and can put the lives of children at risk.

GRACE

Under Cover of Care

A mother of one, Grace came to the attention of child services after her daughter, Alyssa, was brought into the hospital experiencing a life-threatening allergic reaction—one it transpired Grace had deliberately caused herself. This incident unraveled a years-long pattern of hidden abuse in which Grace had fabricated a series of illnesses in Alyssa, constantly presenting her for medical attention that was not in fact required. Her own childhood experiences of medical care had led to her becoming addicted to hospital treatment and the sense of safety it represented—a need that she fulfilled by abusing her daughter. Now expecting their second child, she and her husband had to be assessed to establish if they could ever be safe parents.

*

The notorious case of Gypsy Rose Blanchard, convicted of murdering the mother who had for years falsely presented her as being seriously ill, brought to wide attention the rare phenomenon of parents who fabricate or induce illness in their own children. For almost all parents, the greatest fear is that their child will become unwell; the small subset like Dee Dee Blanchard, Gypsy Rose's mother, behave oppositely. They invent or actively cause problems that require med-

ical intervention, whether because they crave and enjoy that attention or wish to be perceived as the devoted caregiver coming to their
child's aid. As the Missouri case of the Blanchards showed, this is
a pattern of abuse that can have deadly consequences. Sometimes
those are visited upon the children themselves. In the UK, the nurse
Beverley Allitt was convicted of murdering four babies at a hospital
in 1991, attempting to kill three others, and causing serious harm
to a further six: she was in the habit of injecting her patients with
insulin so that she could be seen rushing to their bedsides to help.
Known as the "Angel of Death," Allitt was eventually sentenced to
thirteen concurrent terms of life imprisonment.

Perpetrators such as Allitt and Blanchard are guilty of what is
now termed FDIA, formerly known as factitious disorder by proxy,
or factitious disorder (which may be imposed upon another or the
self: Allitt also had a history of feigning illness in herself, including
persuading doctors to perform an unnecessary surgery to remove her
healthy appendix). In the past this has been more widely known as
Munchausen's syndrome by proxy (MSBP). Most perpetrators are
mothers while some work in medical professions, reinforcing that
this is a form of abuse routinely hidden under the guise of a maternal and caring role. The combination of real and implied authority
over a child's care makes detection of these cases extremely challenging, as do the deception that can be involved in the fabrication
of illness and the ingrained belief that a mother would not wish to
harm her own child, nor a nurse their own patient.

Such cases therefore present essential questions for any psychologist working with women who have harmed children. How
could those who were charged to protect become perpetrators? How
could individuals who vowed—professionally or implicitly—to do
no harm become the agents of such cruel abuse? What is it that
turns someone in a position of care and responsibility into a danger to vulnerable young children who rely on and completely trust
them?

*

Grace was attentive, articulate, and sophisticated about medical matters. No one meeting her without the benefit of her file notes would have guessed that she was suspected of having harmed her six-year-old daughter, Alyssa, and was now being assessed for the threat she may pose to her second, unborn child. No one could have initially known that this seemingly concerned, caring mother was also someone with a narcissistic personality, so addicted to doctors and medical attention that she would put her own daughter in harm's way to feed that need.

As the Allitt case showed, incidences of FDIA can lead to serious harm or even death. The ten or so I have encountered in my career included one in which a mother had inflicted a severe cranial injury on her son during a hospital stay that she was apparently seeking to prolong, so much did she enjoy the attention associated with her role as dedicated mother and the drama of medical interventions. But this level of harm is an uncommon feature of an already unusual situation. In typical FDIA cases the harm is relatively moderate. Children are presented to doctors or hospitals with either invented conditions that do not stand up to medical scrutiny (such as rashes painted on the skin) or actual illnesses or issues that have been induced but could easily have arisen in the natural course of a young life. It is the lightness of these fingerprints that can make FDIA such a difficult problem to identify. Usually, a pattern of false alarms or suspicious circumstances needs to be established before the possibility of a carer being responsible can be seriously considered. The upshot is that children are exposed to harm for longer, while the role or status of those abusing them, at least for a time, shields them from suspicion.

Grace had sought excessive medical attention from the very beginning of her daughter's life, including during her pregnancy. She often presented to her GP with fears that the baby was not moving, requiring scans and examinations to calm her until her next bout of anxiety. She frequently insisted that she had developed preeclampsia, a potentially serious condition that can affect women in the second half of their term, even though her doctors repeatedly reassured her that she was not experiencing any relevant symptoms after testing her urine and, at her insistence, taking blood samples to ensure she showed no signs of diabetes or iron deficiency. Surgery staff became familiar with her: she telephoned so often that they knew her by voice before she had even given her name.

After Alyssa was born, Grace soon began to express concerns about her development. Her husband, Marcus, recalled how she would ring him at work, sometimes several times a day, in a state of intense agitation, to complain that the baby had not fed properly, was bringing up food, or had a high temperature. At least three times in the first six months of Alyssa's life, Grace said that her daughter had experienced what appeared to be a seizure, and wondered aloud that she may be epileptic. By the time Marcus returned home, he would invariably find nothing wrong with Alyssa and Grace claiming to have successfully calmed and soothed her, the crisis averted.

As well as the distress calls during the day, Grace would often wake her partner up during the night and insist that they take Alyssa to the emergency room. On one of these occasions the baby was unusually drowsy and hard to wake, with Grace saying that she had heard her struggling to breathe and seen signs of seizures. By the time they arrived at the hospital, Grace had switched from a high peak of anxiety to a state of alert and animated confidence. She relayed at length her daughter's apparent symptoms, seemed familiar with every condition and medication that the doctors mentioned, and argued repeatedly that Alyssa should be admitted for more detailed examination. This duly happened, and the doctors tested Alyssa thoroughly for the epileptic seizures her mother believed she was suffering from, finding nothing to concern them. This neither calmed Grace nor stopped her from making repeated calls to her GP in the months that followed, reporting further epileptic episodes and requesting more tests.

Cases such as Grace's underline the complexity of recognizing when a mother may be fabricating symptoms or inducing illness in their child. There is nothing uncommon or unreasonable about stress and anxiety during pregnancy, or concern from first-time parents regarding the well-being of their baby that can appear to be bordering on paranoia. No doctor is surprised when a mother or father asks for another test to be done just to be sure, or questions what they are being told because it does not match the diagnosis they had assumed or that they found online. It is this echo of the legitimately worried parent that makes FDIA cases so distressing and challenging to identify. In the early stages of diagnosis, any doctor relies to a significant extent on patient testimony; when that patient is a young child and cannot speak for themselves, they rely on what the parent or carer says on their behalf. In the frenzied context of a young child being presented for emergency care, manipulative, self-serving, and abusive behavior dresses itself in the clothes of reasonable concern and any parent's worst fear. Adding to the confusion, not all of Alyssa's medical issues were false. After she had been brought to the hospital on account of apparent breathing difficulties, tests showed that she did indeed have a severe milk allergy. With this mix of real and apparently imagined medical problems, Grace seemed to be simply another anxious, overprotective young mother who had spent too much time searching for medical answers on the internet. The truth was much less benign. Far from looking after her daughter, she was in fact co-opting her, a prop in her favorite play, one that allowed her to take center stage as the indispensable savior.

That reality only dawned gradually as fragments of evidence formed a picture that left no other explanation. Some of that evidence was medical, including a routine urine test that found traces of diazepam, a prescription drug that can be given to children suffering muscle spasms and seizures but had never been prescribed to Alyssa. Grace explained this away by saying that she had given her the medication to treat her epilepsy, a condition that repeated examinations had shown she did not have. Other evidence was circumstantial, but hard to ignore. When Marcus was later interviewed by his daughter's GP, who had by now begun to suspect FDIA, he was asked whether he had ever witnessed any of the seizures Grace frequently claimed, or seen his daughter be given excessive medication. He recalled that on the occasion of the first ER visit he had noticed an empty children's Tylenol bottle in Alyssa's bedroom that he was almost certain had been half-full the day before. She had been sick and brought up a thick red-colored vomit. Although he had a "weird thought" that his partner might have overdosed the baby on Tylenol, he dismissed it, especially when she later insisted to the doctors that no medication had been given.

Gentle suspicions began to harden into serious concerns as Alyssa became older and her mother continued to present her for an array of supposed problems. Grace had consistently lobbied for her daughter to be tested for suspected autism and ADHD, which led to an assessment by a child psychiatrist. He did not identify features of either condition, much to her surprise and disappointment, but he did note concerning aspects of the relationship between the two. Alyssa, he thought, appeared hypervigilant to her mother's mood and statements, relieved when she was pleased and constantly looking to her before answering questions. When asked about her frequent health episodes, she said only that she felt tired a lot, which her mother told her was natural after seizures. She also said that she hated it when her mummy put her in a wheelchair, as she sometimes did when taking her out for "a walk," and stopped other children from coming over to the house to play, to protect her from getting too tired or becoming ill.

In parallel with the panoply of medical conditions for which Alyssa was presented, few of which appeared to have any basis in reality, was the growing divergence between how Grace perceived her daughter and how professionals encountered her. While the mother described her as cognitively impaired, physically clumsy, and hazy in her memory of events that had happened just hours earlier, her school reported that she was able, well coordinated, and alert. Doctors noted that while Alyssa would sometimes show symptoms of her alleged conditions in her mother's presence, she appeared better when separated from her for examination.

It became clear that an essentially healthy child was being routinely presented with illnesses or conditions that she did not have, and subjected to a barrage of unnecessary medical testing as a result. The only question was if Grace was a hyperactive, hypervigilant mother who needed help to be more rational about her daughter's health or whether under the mask of fear, care, and concern she was an abuser, recklessly manipulating Alyssa and the health-care system for her own gratification. If so, her elaborate deception was also damaging to the health care professionals themselves, as she lured them into inflicting harm on her daughter, performing procedures that were invasive and unnecessary.

The answer came when Alyssa was six and the subject of yet another hospital visit. This time she was not brought in by her mother but driven in an ambulance. The breathing difficulties that had previously been minor were on this occasion severe. An allergic reaction had sent her into anaphylactic shock, and without the emergency administration of epinephrine (adrenaline) she could have died. As the nurses tried to calm a distraught Grace, they were disturbed when she revealed what had led to this crisis. Grace had watched a documentary about experimental approaches to treating severe allergies in children that had promoted a micro-dosing approach: administering tiny amounts of the allergen, under the (false) premise that this would create a tolerance. Frustrated by what she described as doctors' unwillingness to take her seriously, she had been attempting this so-called treatment unsupervised, deliberately feeding Alyssa dairy even though she knew her to be allergic. She stated that this was a radical attempt to cure her of the allergy, with a scientific underpinning. Even though her daughter had just received lifesaving treatment, Grace seemed unaware of the danger of her actions. She also seemed more concerned with her own sense of injustice about how doctors had treated her than with her daughter's urgent medical condition.

Such a severe incident triggered a series of institutional responses. Child protective services, hospital pediatricians, and the police all became involved. Official eyes were on the family, with Grace now in the second trimester of her pregnancy. Alyssa's medical records were reexamined and the presumption that Grace was merely a highly anxious mother questioned. Despite her indignant response to the suggestion that she had deliberately harmed her child, the team involved began to seriously consider FDIA as a possible and even likely explanation for the troubling series of events. Child services commissioned a risk assessment produced by a specialist family and child clinic, which expressed deep concerns about Grace's psychological functioning, noting her denial of having fabricated symptoms, inability to perceive the harm she was doing to her daughter, and constant badgering of health and emergency services. The conclusion was that Alyssa should be considered seriously at risk and Grace and Marcus's custody of her, and the unborn baby, be placed under urgent review. This was the point at which the case landed on my desk. I was asked to conduct an evaluation of Grace's suitability for psychological treatment, the precursor to deciding if the underlying causes of her behavior could be addressed, and whether this would allow her in time to be deemed a suitable parent. It was clear from the outset that this treatment had not been freely chosen by Grace, but it was nevertheless a prerequisite if she was to prove herself safe enough to be granted custody of her children.

*

My early sessions with Grace were complex, distressing, and sometimes confrontational. I did my best to put her at ease, reassuring her that I was there not to judge her but to try to help her understand what had led child services to become so concerned and what a path forward might look like. But she remained on edge throughout the first hours of our work together, clearly desperate to get away. Although she began her version of events confidently, reciting the circumstances of Alyssa's medical crisis with almost robotic familiarity, this veneer soon wore away, revealing the true face of a woman who was simultaneously angry, paranoid, and afraid.

When I began our second meeting as I normally do, by asking what she had thought or felt following the first, I received a look of terror and disgust. "I think you hate me. You want to take my children away." For a time she ranted about what she believed to be a "stitch-up." I was not independent, just doing the bidding of social services, part of a coordinated effort to persecute her. My attempts at reassurance did little to dent this certainty, and she ended the fifty minutes almost as anxious as she had begun them. Grace's response to me was extreme, but by no means unusual. Like many forensic psychotherapy patients, she was seeing me because she felt she had to rather than because she wanted to—in her case as part of her fight to retain custody of her children, while others are seeking to avoid prison or save their relationship. But the upshot is that the patient can feel coerced into engaging in therapy and suspicious if not out-wardly hostile toward the process as a result.

We did not meet for a third time until a fortnight later, after she canceled the interim session, blaming exhaustion and a migraine and saying that it clashed with a meeting at Alyssa's school. She again looked pale and distressed and was soon in tears, saying that she had been awake since 4:00 a.m., worrying about having to meet me and feeling as if she were falling apart. It was at this point that I took an unusual step, agreeing to her standing request that Marcus, sitting outside in the waiting room, be allowed to join us in session. Her face immediately lightened. "Really? You would see me with him?" This turn in mood felt telling. I felt compassion for a woman who seemed terrified to be alone, even with me.

In this instance, the risk assessment had made it clear that while Grace was the primary instigator in Alyssa's abuse, there was also a shared problem of understanding in her relationship with Marcus. If Grace and Marcus were to be deemed appropriate parents for Alyssa and their as-yet-unborn son, it was necessary not only to unpack the personal history that had led Grace to fabricate and induce illness in her child but to address the distance between the pair that had contributed to a mutual failure to support each other in raising their daughter.

Her husband's presence at her side also visibly relaxed Grace, helping us to move the conversation on to the more productive ter-ritory of her early life. As we did so, some of the key motivators of her behavior as a mother quickly became apparent. Before she became pregnant with Alyssa in her mid-twenties, many of her most meaningful life experiences had happened in the context of health care and doctors. She recalled that her own mother had been in the habit of regularly taking her to the GP, citing asthma attacks, allergies, slow growth, and a supposed nut allergy. She would be dressed specially for these trips, as if going to church or visiting grandparents, and remembered that the level of care and attention she received made her feel special. During the GP visits her mother seemed more animated and articulate than normal, less preoccupied with her work or inclined to lavish attention on Grace's younger sibling. Foreshadowing the way she would later parent her own daughter, Grace experienced an isolated childhood, with her mother limiting her contact outside school with other children. She would be asked to "babysit" her sister and resented this. She said that the places she felt safe as a child were at home, on the couch with her mother watching TV, or at the hospital, where she was surrounded by so many caring professionals, many of whom gave her special attention.

We were starting to get closer to the truth of her behavior, and my initial sense of despair at the prospect of making any progress was abating. In particular I was struck by Grace's description of the connection between medical attention and care, one that is often cited by those experiencing Munchausen's syndrome or engaged in MSBP/FDIA. As one woman with this diagnosis explained, "It's about receiving attention and tenderness. When I'm being lifted into an ambulance there is that feeling of being carried and of being loved and looked after—I feel comforted and peaceful; it's a very powerful feeling."

In parallel with her own frequent, seemingly unnecessary medical visits as a child, Grace's outlook on health and care was shaped by her mother's own medical problems. She suffered from legitimate seizures, the first of which happened while Grace was in the room, aged eight. She acted quickly in calling an ambulance and luxuriated in the praise and attention that was showered on her for having been such a bright girl, calm in a crisis and looking after her mum. At an impressionable age, and deprived of important parts of her childhood, Grace clung to this experience. It became her template for how to access the care and attention that she felt had been denied her, including by her adored father, after he walked out on the family and moved abroad several years earlier. She had rarely felt as loved as on the day of her mother's seizure, with all the paramedics and nurses telling her what a little angel she had been. As a young child, adolescent, and then mother, she continued to crave this feeling and invariably turned in the same direction while searching for it. Although this later manifested itself in her treatment of Alyssa, fabricating and inducing illness in order to receive the comfort of medical attention, Grace aspired to be a care provider as well as a patient. As a teenager she volunteered with St. John's Ambulance, where she started to make proper friends for the first time, including romantic partners. In turn she nurtured a career ambition to become a paramedic, one that she still held on to at the time of our sessions.

This childhood conditioning did much to shape the parent that she would become. It imprinted on Grace a fear of the isolation that had been imposed by her father's abandonment and her mother's overprotective cocooning, and a belief that the surest means to find love and care was through seeking medical attention, or positioning herself as a central actor within a caregiving setting. Now Grace did not seem monstrous so much as lonely: a woman desperate for affirmation at any cost, urgent to assume the familiar role of patient or carer.

These fears and wishes intensified during her unplanned pregnancy and then the birth of her daughter. On one level, the arrival of a baby offered hope of the unquestioning love for which Grace had been searching her entire life. It was a chance to immerse herself in the kind of caregiving role that so excited her. But as the psychoanalyst Dinora Pines explains, the gap between a woman's expectations of a loving infant during pregnancy and the reality of the needy, hungry creature that emerges can be extreme. For Grace, this bifurcation was especially jarring. The passage from being an expectant mother, the center of attention with her pregnancy and baby bump, to an isolated parent faced with the very real demands of a vulnerable infant was overwhelming for her. Rather than finally achieving the love and adoration she sought, she was left in charge of what felt to her like a willful and demanding creature whose needs she struggled to meet. With Marcus often absent due to work, she was frequently required to confront this challenge alone. Soon this led to her reaching for the one constant in her life, finding any reason to make her way to the hospital—a reliable refuge from the feelings of estrangement and insignificance that stalked her and a sanctuary that she felt compelled to seek out by any means necessary.

*

Grace's case illustrates one end of the spectrum that FDIA encompasses, where abuse continues undetected for what seems an unthinkable length of time. A UK study found that the median time between presentation and identification of cases was more than two years when symptoms were being induced (by means other than poisoning or suffocation), and more than four years in instances of verbal fabrication with no illness induced. It is not simply the natural bias toward the parent as a concerned carer that impedes FDIA cases from being detected. Abusers in this mold are sophisticated, more medically literate than the typical parent, and more willing to challenge a doctor's diagnosis. They are knowledgeable about the health-care system and how to manipulate its sometimes unwieldy machinery, with referrals to specialists, second opinions, and demands for further examinations creating procedural mazes that can eat up months or years. Carers in these cases may also attempt to falsify medical records or interfere with tests (for example by doctoring samples), further delaying the ability of medical professionals to find answers and reveal the true source of the problem.

This combination of preconceptions about a mother's legitimacy and artful navigation of the medical system's many corridors can allow parents like Grace to feed their addiction to medical attention at the expense of their own children for intolerably long periods. The abuse may be far more subtle than when a parent is physically wounding or actively poisoning their child (both of which can also be features of FDIA), but the harm is no less real. Even in cases where physical harm is limited or nonexistent, the psychological damage of convincing a healthy child that they are ill, isolating them from their peers, and subjecting them to invasive medical procedures can be profound. The child can internalize the role of the invalid and start to see themselves as weak, frail, and unsteady, doubting their own capacities. They may also experience real confusion, feeling perfectly well while the person they trust most is telling them that they are not.

For medical professionals, the young victims of FDIA can present puzzles that are solved only slowly: patients who appear well and then unaccountably become sick, whose test results and reported or apparent symptoms do not tally, or who present a confusing combination of fictitious episodes and legitimate ones. Doctors have to guard against becoming actors in this dangerous performance, unwittingly inflicting harm. The deliberate frustration of normal diagnostic methods, added to the difficulty of unreliable input from a manipulative parent and a child too young to advocate for themself, makes evidence trails complex and often contradictory. In some cases, extraordinary methods such as video surveillance have been used to try to establish whether a child is actually experiencing seizures, although this has become less common. I have seen shocking footage of apparently concerned mothers taking pillows and smothering their peacefully sleeping children, then calling for help to say they are struggling to breathe. This was back in the 1990s, and the clinician who showed this footage at an international conference was himself subjected to an angry audience who felt they had unwittingly taken part in something illicit. Contemporary guidance encourages clinicians to be aware of what are defined as medically unexplained symptoms or perplexing presentations as possible first indications of FDIA.

The complexity and controversy of FDIA do not end with the difficulty of identifying and then proving a case. At the opposite end of the spectrum are parents who have been falsely accused of harming their children, with MSBP (then the common description) cited and used in evidence for murder convictions that would later be overturned. In particular, a series of cases in the late 1990s and early years of the twenty-first century brought into question diagnoses of MSBP. There were concerns that a climate of suspicion and reliance on flimsy evidence were being used to demonize parents who had already suffered the agony of losing their children through no fault of their own. This spotlight was intensified by the identity of the key witness in a succession of trials that produced wrongful convictions: Professor Roy Meadow, the pediatrician who had first defined MSBP as a condition in 1977 and subsequently became its leading expert. His evidence was later discredited after misleading use of statistics in the trial of Sally Clark, a mother whose initial conviction for murdering her two infant sons was subsequently quashed. He had suggested that the chance of two children suffering sudden infant death syndrome (crib death) in the same family was one in seventy-three million—a sum reached by taking the figure for one child dying in this way in a family such as the Clarks and squaring it, a calculation later denounced by the Royal Statistical Society as a "serious error of logic." Notoriously, he had also authored the mantra "One sudden infant death is a tragedy, two is suspicious and three is murder until proved otherwise," which he defined as "a crude aphorism but a sensible working rule for anyone encountering these tragedies."

In the years since, the controversy has lessened around MSBP/ FDIA, which is widely regarded in medical circles as a real and also very rare form of child abuse. Cases in which parents are actively harming children to induce illness, as opposed to verbally fabricating a condition, are a smaller subset still. Yet the tangled web that surrounds FDIA can make its perpetrators as hard to treat as they are to identify in the first place. As a forensic psychologist, you are treading ground that is at once unfamiliar, scarred with controversy, and littered with the potential traps of siding too decisively with either the child or the mother. You are faced with a particular form of denial that is wrapped up with the patient's own conviction that they were providing love and care to their child. And you are trying to judge whether an individual with a track record of manipulating medical experts should ever be allowed to care for children again, even more unsure than normal whether to place your trust in anything you are being told or your own judgment of the evidence.

Despite the clear evidence that Alyssa was not suffering from any of the conditions that she had supposed, Grace continued to reject the suggestion that she was fabricating her illnesses. She flatly denied that she had ever harmed her daughter to induce symptoms and, at least initially, that she had ever used inappropriate medication for whatever reason. While such defensive postures from patients are a stock-in-trade of my work, I was also aware of my inexperience in cases of this nature. Identified examples of FDIA are exceptionally rare, even when the possibility of underreporting is taken into account: a decade-old study in Italy found that it had been a factor in only 0.53 percent of referrals to a pediatric unit.

With Grace, I was struggling to retain my professional neutrality and resist the feelings of hopelessness that naturally accompanied work with a woman who continued to lie in the face of strong evidence, or my impulse to identify with the child victim. As I listened to Grace denying evident reality, it felt as if I were being invited to share in her deception and collude in the narrative of harm cloaked in care. Her denial of harm and facade of being the innocent victim evoked anger in me at some moments, and shock and confusion at others. In managing these feelings, I was helped by the forensic psychotherapy axiom that underneath any act of offending there is a wish to be caught, stopped, and punished. My role is not to punish but to understand, to confront offenders with the truth without condemning them in the process. I could not allow personal feelings to interfere with the therapeutic work of dealing with a parent who might have abused her child but was also herself ill and in need of treatment.

I also recognized that as a result of that illness Grace was not fully in control of what she thought and believed. As well as evidence of somatization disorder—the distress caused by extreme

focus on symptoms of pain or illness—Grace had traits of histrionic and borderline disorder, the combination of which gave her
an almost delusional quality of conviction in her own falsehoods.
These classifications are often the result of traumatic early-life events
and disrupted care, making it difficult for women to feel secure in
their own skin or to trust others to meet their needs. Like other
women with somatization disorder, she believed her own lies and
would often present herself for the unnecessary medical treatment
she craved without recognizing the deceit involved.

Because she had conflated medical care with love, to her it was
a contradiction that her treatment of Alyssa could ever be considered abuse. It shocked me that there appeared to be no limits to the
risks she had been willing to take with her daughter's body, from
the diazepam she had given her without prescription to the lactose
micro-dosing that had put her life in danger. Isolated and lonely,
she had little sense of the world outside the bubble that she had created, shuttling from home to hospital appointment and back again.
I was struck by how confidently she could reel off Alyssa's supposed
list of physical conditions, but how vague she was in describing her
personality and character. She treated her own daughter not as a
beloved child in need of nurture but as a patient: a mind and body
to be twisted until it fitted the shape of her ill-formed notions of
love and caregiving. The balm of medical attention, and the familiar
hospital stage, were at once Grace's preferred method of demonstrating love and the only way she knew how to receive it. This need had
been in her since the day she had shone as the little angel saving
her mother, but the isolation of motherhood had driven it to new
heights, making it an all-consuming part of her life.

Because loneliness was so clearly an exacerbating factor for
Grace, I wanted to use the couple's sessions to understand the fault
lines in her and Marcus's relationship and how these had affected
their parenting of Alyssa. During these meetings, two things gradually became clear. The first was that Marcus had emotional trauma
of his own that affected how he related to both his partner and his
daughter. Having been sent to boarding school at a young age, he

had developed a coping mechanism that took the form of exaggerated independence, relying on himself to the point where he repressed all dependency needs and had little trust in other people. Whereas Grace's answer to loneliness was to seek medical attention, his was to disappear into his work. The result was that their partnership was ill-equipped for the challenges of parenting: Grace housebound and lonely, Marcus often absent and consciously taking a backseat in terms of decision-making about Alyssa, deferring to his partner's greater knowledge both of their daughter's day-to-day condition and of medical matters. While he saw Grace as highly competent and was wary of challenging her pronouncements about their daughter's health, she was jealous of his "other" life at work, which she believed gave him a status and role that she was lacking. He was frightened of disturbing his wife's equilibrium and devoted to her, but also described her as "high maintenance" in a way that revealed his fear of her displays of emotional intensity and his tendency to withdraw as she became more anxious and distressed.

To make progress, these joint sessions needed to address the physical and emotional distance between the couple. Hearing each other talk about themselves in new ways, with unaccustomed vulnerability, was eye-opening for both. Having previously regarded Grace as difficult but ultimately competent, Marcus was able to see the true nature of her suffering and appreciate the level of disturbance that had corrupted their daughter's care. He recognized the panic that Grace felt when he would leave the house, and the sensation that accompanied this of being cast into a terrifying darkness. In turn she heard him talk for the first time about his own feelings of isolation and anxiety and realized that she could benefit from his care by inviting and encouraging it. Each began to see the other in a fuller, truer light, one that revealed their flaws and underlined their needs. Most important, the beginnings of this stronger relationship were the basis on which the couple were ultimately allowed to keep custody of Alyssa and their unborn son, Jason—under regular monitoring from child protective services, alongside regular assessments with me, health visitors, and other support agencies in the eighteen months after his birth. Alyssa's progress was also to remain under close surveillance.

Decisions in court cases where a child has been harmed are always complex, and the outcomes can appear counterintuitive—especially when seen through the lens of past actions rather than future risk, which must be the primary consideration for those making the decision. I wondered if a couple who were not so middle class would have been treated similarly, and whether they would also have received the benefit of the doubt and been given so much opportunity to show they could change.

I continued to work with Grace, now in individual sessions, after she had given birth to Jason. Over the first year of her second motherhood, I observed a gradual but unmistakable improvement in Grace as her family circumstances changed. Marcus was key to this, moving to shorter work hours so he could spend a day every week at home looking after Alyssa and her baby brother. Not only did this mean he had evolved from a largely absent parent and partner into a more emotionally supportive role, but it also liberated Grace, allowing her to take on part-time work in a charity shop. For the first time in years, this gave her an identity and purpose beyond that of mother and patient. She was able to feel needed and important without reverting to the panacea of medical attention. Being center stage in her therapy with me also gave Grace an important experience of being heard and seen, outside of a self-created medical drama. I thought that her second child being a boy also helped. Less obviously a narcissistic extension of herself than Alyssa had been, the new baby was an entity she could more easily separate herself from, not simply a familiar vessel through which to reenact the experiences of her own childhood.

In our sessions we talked about how Jason's arrival was changing the family: what it meant for Alyssa to have a sibling to play with, and Marcus to become father to a son. Grace, who had for so long tended to see and describe people as the sum of their medical conditions, was increasingly able and willing to talk in emotional terms about herself and her family. While she still did not accept that she had induced illness to attract care and attention, she agreed that she had interfered in an attempt to treat Alyssa, following her own "medical guidelines" taken from internet and television research, and that this had been wrong. Her conception of love and care, for so long relentlessly focused on the imagining and resolution of medical problems, was transformed into the need to be a consistent provider of emotional support. She began to see Alyssa, once a body to be agonized over, as a mind and a person who could be loved without first being pathologized. The fruits of this attitude and approach became clear in Alyssa's school reports and case notes from the social worker: free from the wheelchair that her mother had once tried to impose on her, better able to socialize among her peers, and no longer suffering the physical intrusion and psychological torture of a constant round of hospital visits and medical examinations. In other words, she became the ordinary, happy, and healthy child that only her mother's misplaced sense of care had prevented her from being.

Like many of the women I have worked with in different contexts and with contrasting problems, Grace was experiencing, and in many ways re-creating, the troubling legacy of her own childhood. Yet her troubles, and the abuse of her own daughter in the name of love, were also the reflection of a simpler and equally prevalent reality: an absence of support and a retreat into her own fantasy world. When meeting women like Grace, professionals often focus on what is wrong with them, some distinctive fragment of their personality or artifact of their life experience that can explain actions that seem inexplicable. By contrast, not enough attention is always given to what the women lack, in her case a support system and a life beyond motherhood that might have mitigated her impulse to seek attention and care through fabricating illness.

Hand in hand with that realization is the reality that it is possible for women like Grace to change the course of their lives and move from a desperate situation to one that offers both security and comfort. For Grace, this was about improving the circumstances she already had—an absent partner and lonely existence that, in its isolation, intensified every echo of her childhood need for love and attention.

What helped her to become a safe and caring parent was not a fundamental character transformation but change within her relationship and in her own sense of herself. The arrival at a crisis point, where she risked losing everything, had finally brought the dangerous charade to an end. Therapy allowed her to give up the pretense of perfection and the obsessive relationship with her daughter's health that was in fact causing the little girl grave harm. Though she never fully acknowledged the extent to which she had harmed Alyssa, Grace agreed to abide by the strict regulations child protective services had set. As these required, she would rely on Marcus to seek medical help and never administer medication to either child herself. She gave up the role of nurse, reluctantly but reliably. Over time, as the couple showed that they would comply with the terms that had been set, social services began to withdraw and give them more autonomy. The threat of the children's removal was taken away.

By separating herself from her children's medical care, Grace became able to access and articulate her own needs for love, care, and attention, no longer projecting them onto her daughter. Her life now afforded her both the reality of support and a feeling of status, a recognition that she existed and was valued in a world outside home and hospital. By leaving behind the urge to fabricate or induce illness, she was finally free to enjoy her own health and her daughter's. Her marriage, once founded on idealized notions that Grace was the perfect caring mother and Marcus the strong provider, with no emotional needs of his own, was now stronger, based in reality. Therapy offered Marcus and Grace a chance to see each other and themselves. Marcus was now an active and involved father, a friend and partner to his wife, able to reflect on how his own childhood had shaped and hurt him.

I always remember Grace, who taught me one of the most enduring lessons of my career: that harm can be disguised as care. Her case highlighted the importance of close relationships outside the consulting room. A patient must also be seen in her social context, with an understanding of who, other than the therapist, is important to them. We are the sum not just of our personalities and life experiences but of our surroundings, relationships, and circumstances. In her treatment, bringing Marcus into the consulting room had been the turning point for Grace, and for the children. And in her life, helping her to build a more intimate relationship with him, in which they understood each other and shared the duties of care more equally, was the essential step in ensuring she felt loved, respected, and secure: no longer in need of extreme measures to find the care she craved.

*

Grace was not just another patient who shattered the taboo of maternal violence. She was also the woman who showed me how effective the cloak of femininity can be, concealing acts of violence so shocking that to many they are simply unthinkable. It is a realization I have often returned to, meeting women I can—to begin with—hardly imagine being responsible for the crimes I know they have committed. The incongruity between someone's appearance and their offense, even though it is a superficial form of bias, is nevertheless one I find myself having to overcome again and again. It would rarely be felt more acutely than with Dolores, a mother whose almost impossibly calm visage masked one of the most distressing crimes I have encountered.

6

DOLORES

Loved to Death

When I first met Dolores, she was still suffering from psychosis, whose paranoid delusions had led her to an almost unimaginable act: an attack on her two daughters that left one dead and saw the other only narrowly escape. So strong were Dolores's delusions that she believed she was saving the girls from a worse fate—a kidnapping by pedophiles that she had convinced herself was going to take place that day. Working with Dolores both in the grip of her psychosis—a paranoid delusion that she and her children were being hunted down—and as it began to subside, was an insight into the devastating effect of severe mental illness and the equally shocking effect of what can happen in recovery as delusion gradually gives way to recognition and realization. The fears underlying such false beliefs, and the absolute conviction that they are real, can lead to terrible acts including murder, inflicted in the hope of rescue. Like the cases of Andrea Yates and Dimone Fleming, who drowned her two young sons in the bath in New York City in November 2022, the awful crimes were driven by severe mental illness. Fleming apparently believed her eleven-month-old and three-year-old sons were devils and asked for mercy only hours before killing them. Only through understanding what can make an apparently ordinary mother turn to such unimaginable acts does it become possible to prevent them. Yet to do so means to enter a world of horror and pain. Our instinctive response is to turn away, to distance ourselves from these mothers, and their terrifying thoughts and actions. Yet intrusive thoughts of harming children are far more common and ordinary than many suppose, and the line between fantasy and action may be more finely drawn than we dare to imagine.

*

When you first sit down with a patient, you are meeting them for the second time. You have already read their file, absorbed their story, and considered how you will approach a consultation. You have developed a mental picture of their appearance, how they might respond to you, what their defense mechanisms will be. Will they be sullen, aggressive, or impervious? Will they see you as a threat to be repelled or a potential ally to be co-opted? You have rehearsed for the initial hour you will spend with the murderer, child abuser, or terrorist who is now your patient: someone whose trust you need to earn and whose problems are now your problems.

My mental picture of Dolores was badly awry. The frightening, hard face of my imagination vanished as I encountered the reality: a calm, composed woman, blond hair perfectly styled around her pale face. She was graceful, girlish, almost doll-like in her carefully prepared appearance and delicate gestures—resembling a child's life-size toy, hair waiting to be endlessly combed through and cared for. I thought about the dolls I had once owned and loved as I sat across from a woman who had killed her own daughter.

As I introduced myself, Dolores smiled. She kept smiling, her eyes trained on me as I described how we would be spending our time together, in this session and the many that would follow over the next four years. As I explained, a psychologist sees people for all kinds of reasons, to deal with behavior that might feel problematic or uncontrollable and for feelings that are hard to bear—such as depression, anxiety, jealousy, or fear. Together, we would look at the events in her past that might have led to these problems starting and explain why they continued to persist.

Dolores nodded encouragingly and said that she understood. The smile remained fixed, but the doll-like body had stiffened, holding itself in place. My words seemed to tumble over her in a soothing, half-heard cascade. Physically present, she appeared frozen in her own private reality.

The eerie neutrality of this one-way dialogue was broken when she asked her first question.

"Is this a factory?"

We were sitting in a small office off the communal space of a secure hospital ward, where Dolores had been moved after just a few days in prison after pleading guilty to manslaughter on grounds of diminished responsibility. The visiting psychiatrist had determined that she was suffering from a psychotic disorder and sectioned her under the Mental Health Act. As her therapist, I first needed to conduct a detailed assessment of her state of mind and identify issues we could address through therapy.

The act of asking a question had unfrozen Dolores. Words and fears poured out, giving the first insight into her private reality: she believed we were in a factory for experimentation, used by the government to test secret drugs on terrorist patients with links to al-Qaeda, including Osama bin Laden, in a program linked to the CIA.

The slew of confessions had broken Dolores's self-containment, and she was almost breathless. From the jagged edges of this shattered calm, her awful story began to emerge. The delusions she had about the hospital unit mirrored those that had led to the death of her daughter Nicole and the narrow escape of an older sibling, Sophia. Dolores harbored a psychotic delusion that she and her daughters had become the target of a pedophile gang, one that wanted to kidnap, rape, and murder them. She believed that she had to save herself and her children from this imagined fate, to her a terrifying reality.

When people are experiencing psychotic delusions, they will often attach huge significance to minor, objectively irrelevant observations that reinforce their fantasies. They will read implications and personal messages into throwaway comments and draw dramatic conclusions from tiny details. On the day of her daughter's death, Dolores dropped her two girls at school as normal. But on her way home, she noticed a man fiddling with his wedding ring. Near her flat she saw more men, also wearing rings, talking on their mobiles. To her, these observations were definitive evidence that the pedophile ring she feared was closing in on her family. The gang was increasing its surveillance on them and getting ready to move in. Dolores believed she had to act.

At the school gate nobody noticed anything untoward about the pretty young mother collecting her children, as she did every day. Dolores had told nobody about her plans, nor shared her overwhelming fears. To teachers and fellow parents she appeared a mother like any other. Her outward togetherness and neat appearance gave no indication of the terrifying delusions churning within, or the appalling conclusion to which they were about to lead her. No one who encountered Dolores that day would have believed a warning that she may pose a danger to two daughters she loved fiercely.

Back at home, she tried to make the girls eat cereal spiked with barbiturates, but they were not hungry and repeatedly refused. The derailment of her plan, to give the children an overdose before killing herself, increased Dolores's already heightened anxiety. She remembered checking the windows to see if the men she had spotted earlier were approaching. As more minutes passed, she became hysterical, eventually grabbing an ice pick from the kitchen drawer and stabbing both girls with it. Sophia, her seven-year-old, was injured but escaped and ran screaming from the house for help. Nicole, aged five, was bleeding from her wounds but did not die. Terrified by noises that she imagined to be the gang approaching, Dolores ran a bath and held her child's small head under the water.

When the police arrived, they found Nicole's body in the bathtub, three empty nooses hanging, and two uneaten bowls of cereal on the kitchen table. Dolores was in a frenzy, searching for Sophia, shouting that she still needed to save her.

As she described the day she had killed her daughter, Dolores started crying. She told me how guilty she felt. I made sympathetic noises as she sobbed. It was a terrifying, overwhelming event to recall. Guilt, shame, and confusion were natural feelings as she began to come to terms with what she had done and the mental illness that had driven her to this unthinkable act. But I was stopped cold when she contradicted me. She felt remorse, but not about Nicole's fate. "I feel guilty that Sophia is still at risk," she told me, eyes shining with tears.

Of all the shocking things I had heard so far, this perhaps affected me most deeply. I realized how ill Dolores was, how comprehensively she remained in the grip of her psychotic delusions, and how long a process of therapy we would now be embarking upon. In that moment, being with her was like meeting a shadow, a frightened, confused creature who lived in an underworld where only ghosts were real.

*

Over the next few years I saw Dolores weekly, to explore the events that had led up to this terrible day and understand how her loss of contact with reality had come about. Even in her ongoing state of fear and paranoia, Dolores trusted and was willing to talk to me. We were about the same age, and I found myself warming to her, though the horror of her crime was sometimes too much to think about.

Like that of many mothers who harm their children, Dolores's own childhood had been one defined by abuse, neglect, and rejection from those who were supposed to be her guardians. She had been sexually abused by her mother's boyfriend and suffered as a teenager from anorexia and bulimia. She told me how she felt her mother had always hated her, resenting the close relationship she had with her father and revealing in anger when Dolores was just five that she had been adopted at birth. This injury was compounded when, aged twenty-one, she traveled to America to meet her biological mother for the first time—eager to find the loving family she had been searching for her whole life. Her dream had been to move there, to start a new life with this family, in a fantasy world where she would be reborn. But her birth mother rebuffed her too, not able to offer her a home. Perhaps she did not want the reminder of her past that Dolores represented as the product of a short-lived affair, or the responsibility in addition to her three younger daughters.

This second maternal rejection was perhaps the defining moment of Dolores's life. It prefaced not only her descent into addiction, as she became dependent on alcohol and cocaine to cope with intense feelings of unhappiness and self-loathing, but her embrace of alternative realities. Poor, struggling, and alone in the UK, she continued to fantasize about the idealized American family of her birth mother, her place in it, and the possibility of gaining the love and care that had so devastatingly been denied her on two occasions.

It was in this period of her life that Dolores had an unplanned pregnancy with her partner, an older man who was sometimes violent toward her. She prepared to become a parent with her examples being the adoptive mother she thought despised her, the man who had sexually abused her, and the biological mother who had turned away from her. Like many abused children, Dolores was searching for a love she had never felt or experienced, and struggled to reconcile her own experiences of childhood with the emotional rigors of parenting. She represented a tendency in those with shattered childhoods not to avoid becoming a parent themselves but to actively seek it as a second chance. By doing so, some invest unrealistic hopes in their children, become frustrated when they do not provide the easy source of love and affection they had expected, and experience the self-loathing of seeing their behavior reflect that of their own abusive parents. They create a tragic inversion of the bond between parent and child, in which an innocent baby is expected to be the giver of love and affection and is resented when its natural demands destroy this fantasy.

Mothers like Dolores can become caught in a vicious tangle, in which they identify simultaneously with their child and with the mother who neglected, abused, or enabled others to abuse them—a figure of loathing they have revived in their own body. As the forensic psychotherapist Estela Welldon has shown, women who cause harm to their children are often treating their offspring narcissistically, as an extension of themselves—revisiting and reenacting the same cruelties they once suffered. By becoming parents, they give new life to the worst memories and experiences of their own upbringing, making their children the victims of violent, vengeful urges aimed at distant shadows.

The testimony of family members revealed that Dolores had at times been cruel to the daughters she repeatedly told me that she loved. For Nicole's fourth birthday she held a party but invited none of her friends, putting the child through the cruel ordeal of a party at which a table set for six lay empty—a lonely ritual that relived the sadness of her own childhood. It scared me that she recalled this episode with laughter and not an inkling of empathy, again reinforcing my suspicion that she was unable to see Nicole as more than an extension of herself, and her daughter's childhood as a macabre replay of her own.

In this graphic reliving of her own troubled childhood, and the association of a child with some of her strongest and most painful feelings, alongside her terror of imagined persecutors, Dolores was typical of the women I have worked with who have reached the unimaginable point where they found it possible or necessary to kill their own child. Like her, most have had upbringings defined by mistreatment and abuse and the absence of any reliable caring figure who can help them to understand and regulate their own feelings. They have not had someone on whom to depend and base their own behavior. For children who have never had such a role model, the consequences can be disastrous: as parents they may be as incapable of assimilating and attending to the uncontrolled vulnerability of an infant as they are their own life experiences. The absence of emotional grounding, the legacy of their own trauma, and the intense identification with the child as a part of that can prove a tragic combination. New mothers who have lacked a caring center to their own life often describe the act and aftermath of birth as an emptiness that mirrors the deprivation and neglect they experienced in their early lives. The reality of a baby for whom they now have to care, with little of the practical or psychological wherewithal to do so, is first a disappointment and can then become a source of intolerable pain. As the psychoanalyst Dinora Pines has suggested, "Mature object love, in which the needs of self and object are mutually understood and fulfilled, cannot be achieved, and the birth of a real baby might be a calamity."

Working with women where birth has led to the ultimate calamity of infanticide or child killing, I have both witnessed these tragic dynamics in action and observed the disturbing detachment with which some of these mothers talk about their dead children—often deeming them almost incidental to the narrative of revenge, anger, or unhappiness that animates them. Diana, a twenty-four-year-old who had killed her son, Otto, at eleven months, consistently delayed talking to me in any detail about the day of his death. She referred to it only as "the incident," giving little sense that she appreciated the emotional gravity of what she had done, or even recognized her child as a human being in his own right. By contrast, she talked readily about her own feelings of rage and desperation in response to her husband's petition for divorce, an act that had triggered overwhelming associations with the many abandonments of her childhood. So angry was she at Otto's father, and so closely did she identify the two together, that she became convinced the boy could not be allowed to live. Unlike Dolores, she was not acting under the influence of psychotic delusions.

For women like Diana, murderous violence is an act of communication and an expression of overwhelming pain, their damaged ego and psyche obscuring even the most fundamental of human instincts. As a psychotherapist, I find it both striking and bewildering how the heat of that anger and trauma often gives way to an ethereal detachment in sessions, with the patient in front of me hard to credit as the person who has committed such an unthinkable crime and equally unwilling to engage with the reality of it.

As much as mothers who kill can be in denial about their actions, the medical and criminal justice systems can also be slow to recognize the real meaning and motivation of their actions and the extent to which they can reasonably be held responsible for them.

This is an especially acute issue in the United States, where there is no Infanticide Act, as there is in the United Kingdom, offering a partial defense for a woman who kills her child within its first year of life, and therefore a woman who kills her baby while experiencing severe mental illness may be found guilty of murder and handed the death penalty. The miscarriages of justice that can result from a failure to understand the depths and danger of postpartum psychosis and depression are illustrated by the tragic case of Andrea Yates, a Houston mother who drowned her five young children in the bathtub in 2001. Suffering severe depression and psychosis, she experienced satanic visualizations and believed her children were going to hell and that cartoon characters were condemning her as an unfit mother. Yet she was nevertheless found guilty of capital murder in 2002 and sentenced to life in prison; only after erroneous testimony from an expert witness was uncovered was the sentence struck down, and in her retrial the jury found her not guilty by reason of insanity. She remains in a secure mental health facility today.

As I found with Dolores, circumventing barriers of denial and self-protection is a gradual process. It requires a constant balancing act of following the patient down paths of their choosing while picking moments to confront them with reality and gradually seeking to disabuse them of their delusions. As our sessions unfolded and we carefully worked through Dolores's distressing life history, I was repeatedly drawn to what I had first noticed in her: the calm self-possession and immaculate appearance, a distinct contrast to most of her fellow patients on the secure ward. She had previously worked as a beautician, a job to which she often spoke of wanting to return, and would usually begin our sessions by talking about her wardrobe or makeup. Her new fantasy was of being reunited with Sophia, her hair groomed and glossy, restored to her former glamour and coveted role as a mother. This shield of self-conscious femininity was not just surface protection. It also characterized her tendency for avoidance and distant communication, as if all the trauma of her life could be powdered away, or the hands that had drowned her daughter could be made innocent again with fake nails and bright colors.

But no amount of fantasy or facade could ultimately shield Dolores from the magnitude of what had happened. As both therapy and the psychotropic medication prescribed for her psychosis began to reduce her delusions, the realization that Nicole's death had not in fact been necessary came with vivid anguish. In the shower she would feel the water falling on her head like a volley of tiny daggers, with sensations of sharp physical pain as she relived the ice pick wounds she had inflicted to her daughter's scalp. These visceral acts of physical recollection were the first language of memory for Dolores. They allowed her to do what she had always done, locating pain and emotion in the body, seeing no distinction between her daughters and herself. For her, physical violence, pain, and disfigurement were possible to assimilate, whereas the pain of the loss and the horror of her responsibility for it were not, at least initially. These were some of the most difficult sessions I have ever conducted, making me want to flee the room and leaving me sick and shaky in the aftermath.

In any long-term therapy, a strong bond will form between clinician and patient. Important as it is to maintain a distance, you also need to become close to the person whose life and trauma you are striving to understand. You are trying to make the patient feel comfortable, encouraging them to disclose painful memories and explore distressing thoughts. Many will be suspicious of the kind of authority figure you implicitly represent, based on their previous experiences with health care, social care, and justice systems. The counterbalance to this need to build bridges with a skeptical patient is the imperative to avoid becoming an active character in their story: someone who inadvertently feeds their delusions, triggers harmful behavior, or becomes an object of obsessive fixation. Any therapist is constantly aware of this balance between the professional and the personal: showing enough of yourself to form a human relationship with someone whose trust you need to earn, without letting yourself become a cipher for the patient to repeat the damaging patterns of previous relationships. Judicious use of transference allows the therapist to notice repeating patterns and bring them to the patient's attention without the burden of reenactment.

For Dolores, I represented multiple characters she wanted in her life. Similar in age, she seemed to treat me like a friend to trade tips with about fashion, makeup, or weight loss. Sometimes drawn in, I found myself wanting to share trivial details about my own life, as though we were meeting for a drink in a bar, not a therapy session in a pale-walled room. I resisted this urge, but it was strong. In parallel she saw me as a kind of mother, and our therapy as almost a surrogate experience of the maternal care and attention that she had been missing her entire life. Dolores was not actually abandoned by the two mothers in her life—both her adopted and her biological mothers made multiple trips to see her in the hospital, including from abroad—but she clung to the pain of their earlier rejections, welcoming their visits without ever softening into forgiveness. She never stopped seeing herself as the little girl who had wanted a home where she could feel safe and loved, or her two mothers as the symbols and agents of its denial to her. Instead she focused on me and our therapy sessions as the latest proxy for the mother-daughter relationship whose absence had been at the center of her life's troubles.

If Dolores saw me in part as a mother figure, I would sometimes feel the same, both acutely responsible and occasionally despairing at my inability to help and protect her. This countertransference was one of the most complex and troubling examples I have known in my clinical career. Dolores's disorienting mixture of sweetness and cruelty, the contrast of her outward femininity and inner brutality, meant I could not stop my own emotions from fluctuating. In one session I could go from feeling like the dutiful mother to feeling suddenly like the scared child, horrified by my patient, left momentarily helpless and uncertain about what to do.

These feelings were compounded by the fact that I was also a young mother at the time, bathing my own daughter in the evening shortly after a session with Dolores in the afternoon. Hours of discussing her homicide in graphic detail meant it was impossible to banish the images of the act from my mind, or to prevent them from tainting the everyday rituals of motherhood with my own child. After the most intense sessions I would sometimes find myself keeping a distance from my daughter, the only barrier I could muster to stop the horrifying visual descriptions of how Dolores had killed Nicole from seeping further into my domestic life. My own daughter was only two at the time and being apart from her felt unbearable at times. I didn't know how I could continue to live if she died, let alone at my own hands. Most disturbing, on the rare occasions when my infant daughter was most demanding or inconsolable, I realized that I could actually imagine hurting her. I was terrified by these fleeting recognitions of my own primitive feelings of rage, by the realization that my own mind could begin to walk the same path that had led Dolores to the unimaginable end of killing the child she gave life to.

This uneasy link between Dolores's motherhood and my own twisted further when I became pregnant with my second child during the course of our therapy. This was after Dolores and I had been working together for several years and Dolores was now living in the community, returning to the hospital to see me on a weekly basis. I waited until four months into the pregnancy, when I was beginning to show, to tell her. As I had expected, this marked a decisive shift in our relationship. By choosing to have another baby, I was turning my maternal attentions elsewhere, becoming the third mother she would feel rejected and abandoned by.

Dolores's response to my pregnancy carried her hallmark, gentleness spiked with cruelty. She would stare constantly at my belly and softly, as if a joke, urge me to lose the weight I was gaining. She seemed to enjoy that I was becoming ungainly and heavy, a contrast with her own thin figure that she could revel in. In turn I felt the guilt of knowing that I was so visibly experiencing the one thing in life she most wanted: to be a mother again. These conflicting emotions—the bond of an experience that instinctively united and painfully divided us—put our clinical relationship under added stress. Most disturbing was a session in which I was overcome with the feeling that my baby had died. Every expectant mother has known this fear, but in two pregnancies I had never felt anything close to this horror, a total conviction that the child in my womb was no longer living. I had not felt him move for some time, and with Dolores's unerring gaze on me it seemed as if she had somehow transferred her fury at being displaced, and her toxic emotions about motherhood, onto my pregnant body. Only hours after the session had ended did I finally feel my baby stir again, allowing the panic and confusion to subside.

The following week Dolores asked that we end our sessions together. I had changed from a source of care and support to a painful reminder of past rejections and a symbol of the motherhood she could never now regain. But I also believe she was thinking of me and my unborn baby. She seemed to intuit both the physical and the psychological effects that our sessions together could have and the harm she was capable of inflicting. Years later, I remain convinced that some part of her wanted to preserve me for my own children as the safe, loving maternal presence that I had temporarily been for her. Like a lone flower among weeds, glimpses of her instinct for love and care continued to poke through the layers of trauma, anger, and self-loathing that had irreparably scarred her life.

Although I was no longer her therapist, I continued to follow Dolores's life from a distance. She lived under the care of her adoptive parents, with medication and regular assessments helping her to lead what outwardly appeared a stable and repentant life focused on volunteer work. But although she had escaped the darkest depths of her psychosis, Dolores did not overcome the patterns of behavior that defined her adult life. When she became pregnant again, by a violent man she had met in the hospital, she opted to go through the pain of birth and surrendering for adoption a baby she could never have been allowed to keep. She said she felt she had taken a life and needed to replace it, but this pregnancy and the inevitable separation from her baby, a son, also reawakened her grief for both Nicole and Sophia. Still, she pinned her hopes on a reconciliation with Sophia, now aged thirteen, even though the girl's father was never going to let this happen, for reasons that I both understood and regretted. As her depression and isolation grew, she continued to pine for the same things that had caused her and those around her so much pain and misery. Having chosen not to continue therapy, she remained under the care of a mental health team as an outpatient until she was deemed fit by a mental health review tribunal to be fully discharged from our clinic.

Twelve years to the day after Nicole's death, Dolores took her own life. On a busy highway she steered her car into oncoming traffic, driving herself headlong into a barrier and causing a near-fatal collision for the passengers of another vehicle. It was a shocking, public suicide, one that contrasted horribly with the calm preceding hours she had spent with her parents, kissing them goodbye before she left them for the last time. It was the anniversary not just of Nicole's death but of Dolores's first attempted suicide. On that day, in the grip of psychosis, she had seen no difference between her own body and those of the two girls. As her health recovered, the intolerable realization dawned that she had not needed to kill her daughters in order to save them. Although she said she had come to terms with her crime, giving this as the reason not to continue treatment with a new therapist, I believe this never happened. Her recovery from the psychosis that had led her to kill opened up new wounds of guilt, grief, and shame that she never overcame. With no place to express her fears and feelings, she felt compelled to release them through one final act of extreme, compensatory violence. That she chose to do so in public, in a way that could easily have killed others, underlined the fact that she remained both victim and perpetrator to the end.

I mourned Dolores for months after learning of her death and still think of her often, even many years later. Therapists are not saviors and must avoid the narcissism of considering themselves in that light, but it is human nature to wonder what more you could have done for a patient whose life ends in this way. I felt my own sense of guilt—for having failed to take the therapy to its full conclusion, to help Dolores deal with the full spectrum of emotions we had released, and for having led her to feel abandoned by me, even though she had been the one to bring the treatment to an end. Inevitably, I could not avoid the thought that she might have lived if we had continued to work together.

Most of all, I was and am haunted by the tragedy of a woman who remained trapped by her unrequited desire to be loved and cared for, whose own abusive childhood and resulting mental illness led her to inflict an appalling, uncontrollable revenge on innocent children. The day before she died, along with a suicide note, Dolores left carefully wrapped gifts for her surviving children, presents she must have known might never reach them. She enclosed small cards with each, simply saying, "Remember, I love you, Mummy." Even as the shame and guilt overwhelmed her to the point of no return, she continued to reach for the idea of love: one final, gentle expression of a desire whose ideal she could never fulfill and whose consequences she could never escape.

*

The tragedies of Dolores's life and death have remained with me, not just because of the nightmarish memories they contain, but also because of their relation to many of the most important themes of my work: the generational legacy of child abuse, the cost of mental illness when kept hidden from view, and the awful power of shame. Social idealizations of motherhood can add to the secrecy and shame of mothers struggling with depression or psychotic illness. For Dolores it was the shame over her actions, once she had become conscious of them, that finally prevented her from healing and recovery.

Shame is an emotion I often encounter as a psychotherapist. It is shame at the abuse they have suffered that leads many of the women I work with to avoid seeking help and instead into using different forms of violence as a coping mechanism. And it is shame about their desires and actions that makes some unresponsive or even hostile patients, reluctant in different ways to engage with the reality of what they have done or with the possibilities of treatment. Sometimes shame is such a powerful barrier that therapy itself becomes impossible: so it was with Amber.

AMBER

Power and Perversion

A serial perpetrator of sexual offenses against children, Amber committed such crimes as distribution of pornographic material, indecent exposure, and sexual assault of minors who included her own daughter. She contradicted the widespread belief that women are not capable of sexually abusing children. In doing so, she also demonstrated the long-term legacy of being a victim of childhood sexual abuse, as she had been at the hands of a relative who would become her co-perpetrator. Amber's tragedy was that she proved unable to escape the clutches of an abusive relationship that had corrupted her childhood and ultimately condemned her own daughter to the same fate.

*

Today the files are sent electronically, but Amber's case was at a time when lever arch binders would arrive at my office, daunting inches of paperwork neatly cataloged within. These anonymous containers chronicled horrors: jigsaw pieces of school reports, police statements, medical histories, social workers' reports, case conference notes, and psychiatric assessments that together told the story of how children had been abused by those responsible for their care.

My job was to provide a psychological report to the court to say whether Amber—who had been charged with multiple counts of child sexual abuse—could be considered a suitable guardian for her children, either now or in the future following psychological treatment. Such reports contain a risk assessment about the parent based on the available evidence, recommendations on possible treatment, and whether this can be delivered in a time frame relevant to the needs of the child.

In some ways it was a typical assignment of the kind I have done numerous times. But I knew from the beginning that this would be an unusual case with acute difficulties. Mothers whose custody has been brought into question are often charged with "failure to protect" their children from physical or sexual abuse. In this case, however, the mother was also one of the suspected perpetrators. As usual, I forced myself to read every page of the file, trying to separate my feelings about shocking details of the case from my responsibility to understand who this parent was, what she had done, and why she had come to be in a situation where she faced my worst nightmare as a mother—having her children removed from her care.

Cases involving children place the heaviest burden on a psychologist's professional objectivity. It is impossible not to pass judgment on what you are reading and the parent whose actions you have been asked to consider, impossible to prevent images of the worst, most pitiless abuse becoming lodged in your mind. I have never been able to forget the five-year-old girl who was so hungry she ate dog food from a bowl on the ground, or the little boy who was punished by being made to stand naked for hours next to an open freezer; he told the social worker that it was his fault for "being bad" and that he "deserved it." I still think about one of the most horrifying cases in which I have been involved, when two boys under the age of five burned to death in their bedroom, after their parents had tied their door shut with string to stop them being "disruptive" and left them alone in the house, with matches in their room.

I still recall with shock how I first encountered child abuse and the instinctive wish to deny it, when working as a tutor in adult literacy as part of a community program between Wesleyan University and Middletown, Connecticut. One of my students was a young woman, with a baby of her own, an alcoholic partner, and two young stepchildren. She worked part-time in a fast-food restaurant and one day had a shift offered to her but no child care for her youngest stepdaughter. Knowing that money was tight, I offered to sit for her. When I took the little girl to the bathroom and helped her onto the toilet, I saw what looked like cigarette burns on her upper thigh and several scabs near her vagina. A teenager myself, I was horrified, ignorant, and scared for her safety. In desperation I consulted my professor, also a reverend, about what to do. He reassured me, advising me to take no action. More than forty years later, I still regret following his negligent guidance, seemingly born of denial and a wish not to see what was in front of his eyes.

These cases inevitably stir personal feelings and memories about both childhood and parenthood. I had been a longed-for child, arriving relatively late in my parents' life. But her strong desire to become a parent did not always make my mother a careful or attentive one. More than once, I have wondered how my beloved mother could have been allowed to keep me had her many instances of neglect been tallied up. As a toddler I would be left by her unattended by the riverbank while she swam some distance away; she often let me wander off while we were out together, which in some cases led to my being returned to her by the police; and she allowed me out in clothes unsuitable for the harsh New York winter. Most concerningly, she would leave me in the company or care of people whom most parents would deem inappropriate, including troubled children she was trying to help, one of whom abused me, as well as an adult who also attempted to do so when I was just nine.

My mother, Lotte, had tremendous trust in the world, despite having survived life in Vienna under Nazi rule for three years. With her mother and two brothers she had escaped via Lisbon to New York in 1941. For them as Jews, life in Vienna after the Anschluss was heavily restricted, and many Jewish men were already being taken to death camps. My grandfather, known as "Papa," would almost certainly have been among them, but he had already died several years earlier of natural causes. "Papa died so that we could live," my grandmother used to say: she meant that, had he lived to be taken to a camp, like so many Austrian Jews the family would most likely never have left, instead remaining in vain hope of his return. A family tragedy ultimately became the reason for our family's survival. Not all of us were so fortunate. My great-grandmother perished in Auschwitz, along with her best friend, and as I grew up, my mother was living with survivor's guilt, the psychological struggle with having been allowed to survive when so many people she knew had not. This made her careless about her own well-being, and not infrequently mine.

Reading files like Amber's, I have often wondered whether my mother's behavior would have been interpreted differently if, rather than being a middle-class academic, she had been a young, working-class woman who had grown up in foster care, already on the radar of child protective services.

Amber's files told a story that was disturbing, even by the standards of such cases. They cataloged allegations that she had sexually abused multiple children, including her own daughter when she was just seven. Doctors' records noted that the girl, Summer, had repeatedly been brought in with symptoms including bruises, thrush, urinary infections, and abrasions that were suggestive of sexual assault. Her school had raised concerns that she was arriving hungry and in unwashed clothes and that she tried to play with the other children in ways that seemed sexual. Case notes from social workers painted a picture of Amber as a mother who showed hostility toward them, resisting any involvement from child-care professionals.

My job was to provide an assessment of Amber, but my attention was constantly drawn back to her daughter, a little girl whose behavior articulated the trauma she had suffered more clearly than any professional analysis could. Her teachers observed a child who seemed neglected, lacking in self-confidence, and desperate to make friends—whom she then alienated through play that they found confusing and disturbing. When a teacher took her aside to talk about this, she first became hysterical, shaking and howling, before moving into a mute, almost frozen state. The file also recorded an incident that I read about with horror, when Summer had walked into the middle of the road and lifted up her skirt, pulling her underpants down. She later said that she was waiting for cars to come and run her over. I was haunted by the image of her suicidal gesture, with its implication of sexualization and its desperation.

As I read through these pages of incident after disturbing incident, it was hard not to agonize over what felt like missed opportunities for intervention, though part of me recognized the difficult situation that authorities are in—charged to safeguard children but unable to intervene or remove them before there is sufficient proof of harm. In cases where the child later dies and the full extent of the abuse is finally known, it is all too easy to see how tragic mistakes were made and how parents misled the professionals involved. In the event, Summer's school contacted child protective services, which placed her on the at-risk register for neglect and abuse. At this point she was still allowed to remain in Amber's care but was monitored through social workers' visits to home and school, though her mother did not allow her to be seen alone at home and Summer was reluctant to say much at school. Like so many abused and neglected children, she was threatened that if she broke silence she would be punished and sent away.

This only changed after the crime that led to Amber's conviction brought distressing evidence to light. With a younger friend, she had enticed to her apartment three children—a girl aged twelve and two boys aged fourteen and sixteen—all of whom she had got to know through her part-time work in a local shop. Having invited them to smoke cannabis and drink alcohol, Amber then encouraged them into a game of strip poker and after that to perform sex acts on each other. She was also alleged to have performed oral sex on the older boy. This episode of prolonged abuse only ended when Summer's father, Shane, called to say that he was bringing her home early. The children were still in the house when Shane and Summer returned, and the smell of weed and drink was evident.

Shane was immediately suspicious about what was going on and a row ensued, with Amber walking out and going AWOL for the next three days. It was at this point that he started looking through her laptop in an attempt to track her down, and found many images of child pornography that she had downloaded. Only then were the police informed, Amber arrested, and Summer removed from her care. Later it would emerge that Amber was part of a network that traded images of child sex abuse on the dark web and that she not only had accessed pictures of children as young as three but also was believed to have created some of them, although this was not ever proven. There was an ongoing investigation into whether Summer was one of the children in the images. Amber denied all charges. Although the apparent assault on the children was what led to Amber's crimes being discovered and all three of the children involved made statements, no charges were brought because she had not photographed them, nor touched any other than the oldest boy, who retracted his allegations about the oral sex, later telling the social worker he was too ashamed and distressed to proceed with making a statement and going through a trial. Like many male victims of sexual abuse by a female, he feared that he would not be believed or taken seriously if he reported it.

As I pored over the files and began to prepare my assessment, two court cases were under way. The civil case, in which my evidence would be heard, was to determine whether Summer should be taken into the care of child protective services, which would then decide whether she should be placed with either a suitable family member or a foster carer, or put up for adoption. The separate criminal case was to determine Amber's guilt or otherwise for the crimes she had been charged with, namely multiple counts of possession of indecent images and a charge of child cruelty and neglect in relation to Summer. In such situations, the finding of the criminal trial has a bearing on the outcome of the civil case: clearly, a convicted sex offender is highly unlikely to be granted custody of a child, while a parent guilty of any crimes against children could only regain custody in light of robust evidence that their psychological health and circumstances have changed since the crimes took place. Even if the criminal trial collapses, a judge in the civil case can make a "finding of fact" about the acts an individual has committed and the risk they pose as a result.

The parameters of my report were clear. I was asked to determine the risk Amber posed to her own child and whether she was suffering from mental illness or a psychological disorder. Could she care for a child, did she require treatment to be able to do so, or was the evidence of past harm and future risk too great for this to be permitted? If she could be treated, how long would this take? Courts, while sympathetic to the role and efficacy of therapy, often ask for an unrealistic degree of certainty around its duration and likely outcome—as if it were a course of antibiotics being prescribed. The reality is much more complex and conditional.

Some of this assessment could be based on the documentary record, but a psychological interview and evaluation were also essential. This would allow me to probe deeper into the situation, determine Amber's understanding of her actions and their effects, and get a real sense of whether she had the capacity to empathize with her daughter or her other victims. I would explore her personal history to assess what it could reveal about the origins of her distorted thinking, sexual deviance, and criminal behavior and the future role that therapy might play.

The interview with Amber was a prospect I found troubling. More than usual, her case had disturbed me and left me with feelings that I knew risked compromising my professional obligations. I had to manage my horror at the thought of Summer, a young child so badly abused that she had been driven to the brink of suicide. As the child psychoanalyst Donald Winnicott suggested in a famous 1949 paper, I needed first to acknowledge and understand my own feelings of hatred so that I could begin to understand the emotions that motivated my patient. An analyst, he wrote, "must not deny hate that really exists in himself. Hate *that is justified* in the present setting has to be sorted out and kept in storage and available for eventual interpretation." As he suggested, the problem for psychoanalysts is not that they feel powerful and common human emotions toward patients they are assessing or treating but that they fail to manage those feelings. "A main task of the analyst of any patient is to maintain objectivity in regard to all that the patient brings, and a special case of this is the analyst's need to be able to hate the patient objectively."

*

The meeting I had spent days fretting over took place in the most anonymous of settings: a small, shabby back room of her solicitor's office, gray filing cabinets lining the walls. I had arrived early and waited for Amber in the makeshift interview room. Ten minutes later she walked through the door with a demeanor and appearance that did little to calm my nerves. She had a cigarette in her hand and a worn leather jacket over her shoulders, and her dark eyes, magnified by glasses, glared at me. She dragged back the chair I offered and sat down heavily, her expression unchanging and gaze unwavering.

I began by setting out the terms of our interview and asked if Amber understood why we were meeting.

"Yeah, because the social are saying I'm a pedo and I can't look after my own kid, right?"

As I explained my role as an independent expert whose report would be sent to all parties in the case, she sighed. Amber had consistently denied the allegations of sexually abusing Summer but admitted she had neglected her at times and that she had found it "hard to bond" with her. Summer's own account, given when she was finally removed from her mother's care and felt in a safe place to talk about what had happened, was shocking. She stated that over the past two years her mother had touched her sexually, photographed and filmed her in sexual poses, and encouraged her to use a vibrator in front of her. The discrepancy between her disturbing, detailed account and Amber's bland statement awakened anger in me. I had the immediate urge to confront her denial directly, but knew this would be pointless, only serving to alienate her further.

I finished my introduction by explaining that I was already familiar with the documentary evidence of the case and that the purpose of our meeting was to hear from her, in her own words. Because I was preparing a report, nothing she told me could be confidential. We would need to go back into her past and discuss her own childhood, as well as cover the charges against her and the question of her suitability for child care.

As I explained this, I felt glimpses of sympathy start to mix with the anger that I had felt at her dismissive attitude. The allegations against her were abhorrent, and her response to concerns raised—the dismissiveness that I had read about in the case file and was now experiencing firsthand—indicated someone with no sense of remorse or responsibility. Amber needed to be held accountable as a perpetrator. But she was also a young woman facing the shame and humiliation of being charged as a sex offender. The prospect of a prison sentence and the loss of her child hung over her. While one part of me simply wanted to see her punished, another saw a defensive and scared patient who needed to be soothed and cajoled into staying in that gray room.

After the combative start to our meeting, Amber became more open as we discussed her early life, one that brought into focus the roots of her feelings of injustice and victimization. When I asked one of my standard questions, about whom she would turn to for comfort as a child when feeling scared or sad, her response stopped me cold. "No one." With her lovelier, more intelligent little sister being the apple of their parents' eye, Amber, whose birth she had been told was "an accident," had always felt lonely. She would spend long stretches of time in her room playing alone and receiving little sympathy if she tried to get her parents' attention. Indeed, the only attention she regularly received from them was punishment for misbehaving, both parents being more than ready to dole out spanking and to deprive her of privileges, sometimes blaming her for misdemeanors for which her sister had actually been responsible. This combination of isolation and vindictive parenting shaped a girl completely lacking in confidence who tried to hide her mistakes, struggled to make friends, and was bullied at school. Recalling these memories seemed to soften her.

It was Amber's loneliness, the lack of care and nurture or any social structure, that left her vulnerable to the defining event in her life, a relationship that developed between her and an older cousin when she was eight. Corey, four years older, had come to stay with Amber's family while his mother was hospitalized for several months. Disturbed and aggressive, he nevertheless showed an interest in Amber, and the two were often left alone while her parents were out, at work, or taking their favored daughter to dance recitals. Starved of affection and attention, Amber became dependent on Corey as her sole source of both.

Over time he began to include sexual elements in their play. While Amber now described how Corey had "corrupted" her, as a lonely and attention-starved eight-year-old child she had had no way of recognizing that she was being groomed for his sexual gratification. She confused his sexual interest with love and affection, and for an otherwise unhappy little girl their games remained a source of interest and even comfort. Corey became increasingly more invasive, and when he started to hurt her with his intrusive touching, Amber was scared. She tried to tell her mother, who didn't believe her and told her off for "fibbing." On several occasions Amber and Corey also involved her younger sister, using physical force to coerce her into sexual touching. They re-created with her the abuse that Corey had inflicted on Amber.

The confused, abusive relationship with Corey was a formative experience in Amber's life, one that shaped her sense of how to give and receive attention. It created an internal template for relationships whereby care and control were equal partners, and the latter was a source of power and comfort in a life otherwise devoid of both. It created a strong association of sexual feelings with abuse, powerlessness, deceit, and secrecy. Having been denied the sense of safety that most people feel from the love and care of a parent or family member, Amber instead identified this with coercive games and sexual exchanges. She was released from a sense of powerlessness and depression through these games and found them exciting, even intoxicating. The result was that as an adolescent and then adult Amber trusted only those she could control and manipulate, assuming that anyone else would reject her. It was this belief, and her troubling early experience, that increasingly moved her toward acts of sexual abuse against children.

These began as her relationship with Corey continued after he moved out of her family home. During adolescence she would send him nude photographs, initially just of herself, sometimes of her sister, and then, as she eventually confessed, also of other children she had access to as a babysitter. As she wouldn't name these children, and there was no evidence of the actual photographs, there was little possibility that I would report her, leading to further charges. Yet her disclosure was a significant indicator of her long-standing risk to children. Like many child sexual abusers, she was careful in picking victims who seemed vulnerable and isolated. Having been a victim in this mold herself, Amber understood the kind of child who would likely stay quiet, internalizing the guilt and shame, too afraid to admit what had happened or to seek help. She knew the signs of a child who had been deprived of parental attention or affection and who, like her, might confuse sexual interest with genuine care. She identified with these children, seeing herself in them.

After she left school at sixteen, the pair's activities became increasingly coordinated. Amber found work as a part-time helper at a local summer day camp where she was placed in a position of some responsibility and authority over kindergarten-age children. Corey took advantage of this, threatening her that their "relationship" would end or that he would report on her unless she continued to provide him with more and more sexual images of children—coercion that he reinforced by praising Amber for her ability to win the children's trust. She later got a job as a nursery helper, working with children as young as three and four. She sent Corey photographs of two of these children semi-naked.

These were among the pictures Shane had found on her laptop and that led to her eventual conviction for possession of indecent images of children. Throughout, Amber used her role as a trusted maternal proxy to access her victims. Like those of other female sex offenders, her main victims were younger than those usually targeted by men, although her daughter was close to the age she had been when Corey first abused her. Amber felt trapped by a combination of Corey's threats and her own impulses. She enjoyed the sense of power that came from being able to control and abuse vulnerable children, and she clung to her cousin as the one person who had consistently shown her care and affection. She was too scared to back out of the arrangement into which Corey had entrapped her and too enthralled by the rare feeling of power and control to break the pattern of abuse, or even to see that abuse for what it was. Instead, she justified it as harmless play that the children enjoyed, even wanted.

Amber's recounting of these events, over two lengthy interviews, was by turns both clinical and emotional. She demonstrated the cold pragmatism that is the mark of many sexual abusers in her calculating approach to identifying and pursuing victims who were least likely to speak against her and a lack of remorse when describing her actions. For Amber these children hardly registered as real people. They were simply objects to be used for her and Corey's pleasure, to service their shared need for control, power, and sexual gratification. She did not feel remorse, because she did not see the impressionable and defenseless children she had abused as victims. They were simply her chosen participants in the power exchange that was her only idea of human relationships. In this sense, her abuse of others reflected a form of sociopathy. Her experiences had led her down a pathway into narcissism, failure to empathize, and lack of trust in the world, all of which had been the gateway to being a perpetrator as well as a victim of sexual abuse. When I pressed her on this point, she simply replied that her victims had only experienced what she had been through and that it had been "okay" for her. She was saying, as so many traumatized and abusive adults do, that the same abuse had never done her any harm. As was often the case with Amber, this was only a partial truth. Later, when we were undertaking a trial period of therapy, she reflected on the encounters with Corey, the force he had used, and the unpleasant physical sensations, along with the sense that theirs was a dangerous secret. She became uncomfortable, almost but not quite able to access the fear, unhappiness, and confusion she had felt as an eight-year-old girl.

Ultimately, confronting her own victimhood was simply too traumatic for Amber, and her defense against this was to reenact the same experience on victims who were as unprotected and malleable as she had once been. By dismissing and discounting the pain of others, she could protect herself from having to face her own. Abuse was simply something Amber relied upon to feel powerful and to access the care of the one person whose affection she valued. Because she had been shown this through the distorting lens of abuse and sexualization, her only way of trying to hold on to love was to do the same to other children, a group of victims that would eventually include her own daughter. Her need for love overwhelmed any wish to care for her child, who barely existed in her mind as a real person, let alone as a vulnerable child in need of protection. The tragedy was that the abuse which had been inflicted on her had a long and destructive legacy—one that turned many more children into victims and transformed a lonely and scared little girl into a persistent and manipulative sexual abuser. The question of whether her victims might go on to inflict abuse on others was one I couldn't address.

*

Two long sessions with Amber, stretching over eight hours in total, left me in no doubt about the conclusion of my report. This was a woman for whom the sexual abuse of children had been a long-term compulsion in which she had willingly participated and about which she expressed no regret. While I thought it likely that she found the abuse not only emotionally but sexually fulfilling, this was too shameful for her to admit.

My assessment concluded that Amber posed a clear and ongoing risk of abuse to children in her care or with whom she had any contact. Not only was the pattern of her abusive behavior long established and evident in various different situations, but she also refused to acknowledge it, something that would have been an essential first step in any kind of recovery. She did not admit that she was excited and aroused by the sexual power she could wield over minors, or how she associated children and young adolescents with sexual pleasure. Her history of harming children sexually and emotionally was likely to be repeated, and she was dishonest about both the extent of her behavior and its motivations.

That dishonesty emerged in small as well as fundamental ways. Amber would lie about apparently trivial details, like the date of her sister's birthday, her address, or how long she had worked in certain jobs. When confronted about this, she claimed to be "depressed" and "forgetful," but the persistent pattern of deceits felt like a deliberate attempt to keep me at bay; it seemed almost instinctive for a person whose life had been defined by desperate secrets and the false identities that were intrinsic to the child sex abuse networks in which she participated. Through a combination of circumstance and design, Amber had created a world almost entirely of its own: one with its own twisted sense of truth, time, and morality. Dissimulation was a way of life for her. Drawn into this universe, I often found Amber to be as elusive as she intended. Her web of untruths, both trivial and important, often left me on the back foot, sometimes questioning whether it was I who was mistaken.

At the conclusion of the criminal and civil cases against her, Amber was found guilty of distributing indecent images of children and of child cruelty and neglect relating to Summer. She received a two-year probation order with a strong recommendation to attend treatment, but no custodial sentence. She was spared prison primarily because it was deemed that she had been coerced by Corey into distributing the pictures. He received a custodial sentence for possession of these and hundreds of other sexual images of children, found after his computer had been seized by the police.

Summer had not wanted to be interviewed by the police, and it was thought too harmful to try to compel this, so her allegations of sexual abuse were not brought to trial. The evidence of her neglect and harsh treatment by her mother, through medical, school, and social services records, led to Amber's conviction on the charge of cruelty and neglect against her. The judge harshly excoriated Amber for her actions and for having abused her position of trust over the many children she had been responsible for. She was registered as what was then known as a "Schedule One" offender, anyone convicted of an offense against a child listed in Schedule One of the Children and Young Persons Act of 1933, in the United Kingdom (a category that no longer exists). She was banned from working with children or vulnerable people in the future. Were she to have become pregnant again, child protective services would have been alerted immediately.

In most cases, my involvement would have ended at this point and left many unanswered questions. Could Amber's state of denial about her actions survive being brought to justice for them? Would she ever be able to recognize the gravity of the abuses she had committed and the damage inflicted on numerous children? Could treatment ever succeed to the point where she no longer posed a threat to children, where she had found other sources of comfort and control and was no longer moved by the compulsion to reenact her own childhood abuse?

As in any similar case, part of my report was an assessment of whether the risk Amber posed to children could be reduced and what role treatment could play in this. With Amber I felt uncertain that treatment would help, given her repeated resistance to acknowledging any agency or responsibility for her crimes. However, with a mandate to reduce the risk she posed to others, I offered her a trial period of therapy, making clear that this would serve as a prolonged evaluation of her capacity to make effective use of treatment and that no results could be guaranteed. I felt that the relationship I had begun to build with her during the evaluation put me in a reasonable position to act as her therapist, if she was actually willing to engage. I therefore made the recommendation in my report that she receive a trial period of therapy with my service, with the objective of reducing the risk she posed to children while living—as she now would—in the community.

I did not accept Amber as a patient lightly. I continued to feel disturbed at how easily she dismissed her responsibility for serious wrongdoing, and to contrast this cold denial with the terrible images of suffering, Summer's especially. With Amber, it was particularly important that I avoid the hostility that can easily arise between a psychoanalyst and her patient, what Estela Welldon terms a "sado-masochistic relationship" in her work on forensic psychotherapy. All of the abuse Amber had committed was ultimately predicated on the feeling of worthlessness and isolation that led her to seek comfort in the one way she knew how: abusing vulnerable children over whom she could exercise power. By getting into arguments with Amber or becoming another authority figure she regarded as persecutory, I would be doing more to reinforce this negative spiral of shame than to counteract it. The art of therapy is to hold up a mirror for the patient so they can see the problem—in this case highly destructive patterns about how relationships are formed—without falling into the trap of reenacting the issue you are trying to address. The role of the therapist is to act as a witness rather than to judge, allowing the patient to explore the most hidden and shameful parts of them-selves. The temptation is to lapse into becoming either collusive or censorious.

I wanted to let Amber describe and explore her own history, hoping that by doing so she would start to understand how her experience of family relationships had left her vulnerable to being groomed by Corey. By suspending moral judgment and being both sympathetic toward her as a victim and curious about her state of mind, I sought to give Amber a sense of safety that might begin to erode her state of denial. The therapy's most important objective was for Amber to acknowledge her role as a perpetrator of abuse and to connect that with what she had first experienced as its victim. Only then could she gradually come to understand and accept what she had done to others and begin to heal the damage in herself.

During half a dozen weekly trial sessions we made frustratingly little progress, but did form a therapeutic alliance. We were able to lay the foundations of a productive patient-therapist relationship in which Amber seemed to feel heard and understood. The overt aggression with which she had greeted me in our early encounters had softened markedly by the end of the consultation period. In turn, I started to feel more compassionate toward her. But I could not get her to move toward an acceptance of the crimes she had committed, their seriousness, and her accountability for them.

Amber was not unfeeling, but the emotions that held sway over her impeded any acknowledgment of the wider truths I wanted her to confront. Her shame at being convicted as a sex offender—and being shunned by her family, employer, and few remaining friends—prompted not self-reflection but an impulsive retort that Corey was to blame. Such remorse as she felt was not directed toward her young victims but took the form of a self-justifying, self-pitying narrative that served only to further insulate her from accepting responsibility. Alongside this shame was her fear that a breach of the terms of her probation could lead to imprisonment and of the fate that may await her, a convicted child abuser, at the hands of fellow prisoners. I was not sure we were making much progress or where our work would lead if pursued further.

Amber clung to the pariah status that attaches itself indelibly to women who appear to contravene all social assumptions by sexually abusing children. So strong was her self-identification as a victim, both from her childhood and in the present, that she was never willing or able to make the psychological space to consider herself as a perpetrator. So wedded was she to her own victimhood that she could not even recognize that of her own daughter, a little girl who felt so desperate that she had walked into the middle of a busy road and hoped for death. Yet Amber described Summer as a liar. It was hard to hear Amber, a girl who had once felt totally alone in the world herself, offer such blank denials of the neglect and abuse she had inflicted on her young daughter. Her own sense of grievance blinded her to the pain of others, leaving her stuck and beyond the reaches of therapy.

As our trial sessions continued, I sought to understand the period before Summer was born and Amber's experience of pregnancy and early motherhood. That she had become a mother seemed almost accidental. Although she had a few casual relationships with other men, Corey remained her obsessional focus. She thought only about how to please him and flared with jealousy at the thought of the other women she knew were in his life. With her family largely keeping her at a distance, and few friends beyond a handful of drinking companions, Corey remained the light of her life in adulthood as he had been through adolescence. The deep association the pair had formed between power, child abuse, and pleasure meant that she did not particularly enjoy sex with other men, from whom she hid her real desires.

She would never have considered Shane, a friend and source of money for drugs and clothes, as a serious alternative to Corey, but they often had unprotected sex, leading to her pregnancy. Although she considered a termination, unexpectedly she found the experience of carrying her baby an affirmative one, enjoying the feeling of being full with life inside her. That positivity dissolved when she learned that, having hoped desperately for a boy, she would be giving birth to a daughter. The discovery triggered her self-hatred: the prospect of a little girl created an immediate and indelible association with the unwanted, vulnerable, and corrupted child that she had been. Significantly, Summer had not been a planned baby, mirroring the "accident" of Amber's own conception. The thought of creating another girl in her own image became overwhelming. Soon the happiness of carrying a life inside her gave way to the opposite feeling, which she described to me as the sensation of something rotten growing within. After giving birth, Amber suffered from postnatal depression, haunted by this idea of history being repeated and scared by the fragility of her baby, its constant crying and endless demands. When I suggested that Summer's cries must have been like hearing an echo of those from her own childhood, which so often went unheeded, she responded with what felt like a rare moment of honesty and connection with me. It was true, she said, that she hated weakness in herself or anyone else. Sometimes this feeling had been so strong that she stifled the sounds of her daughter's crying to stop herself or others from having to hear them.

The same neglectful behavior, bordering on abuse, continued

as Summer became a toddler. Amber described occasions when her daughter would run up to her, wanting stories, hugs, games, and love, only to be turned away and reprimanded, an echo of the neglect she had known as a child. As she told me this, I could see what looked like the beginnings of guilt or regret, but these would be quickly shaken off as she reverted to the comfort of victim blaming—describing her desperate daughter as "clingy." This desensitization of her maternal status and role, shrugging off the most basic needs of an infant and young child in search of care, had been the gateway to the more serious sexual abuse that Amber would perpetrate against her daughter, though this was not proven in court. After her nascent feelings of motherhood had been extinguished, there was nothing to stop her treating Summer as just another child she could exploit for sexual gratification. She could relate to her only as an object, not as a subjective, sentient creature with her own needs and capacity to feel pain. It seemed that in Amber's mind the more powerful bond between them was not as mother and child but as common victims of the same abusive treatment. It was, she shrugged with the coldness that defined her, just history repeating itself. She did not want to talk or think about it.

*

At the end of the six weeks of meeting, I had to tell Amber that I didn't think she would benefit from continuing with therapy. She was too frightened to open herself up to this process, which was unlikely ever to be a meaningful form of treatment or support for her. Although she had turned up in body to the sessions, her mind and spirit were not engaged in the task. She was both insufficiently introspective and too wrapped up in herself to engage with the honest reflection that psychotherapy requires to succeed. Even though she seemed to warm to me a little and had been able to disclose something of her own unhappiness and shame, the work might have taken years and still not been able to reach or influence her, such were the strength of her defenses and the power of her shame.

Amber seemed relieved when I offered this conclusion to her and was only too keen to say that further therapy would be a waste of time. Perhaps no treatment could have weakened the hold that shame held over Amber, nor chipped away at the walls of denial that she had built around herself. Maybe no other therapist could have elicited her cooperation for such a task, but I was left wondering about what, if anything, could have engaged her in such vital work.

Amber's refusal to come to terms with her crimes left her an ongoing risk to potential victims and a source of pain to Summer, who was deprived not only of a loving mother but of even the smallest shred of acknowledgment or apology. Like those of many men who sexually abuse children, Amber's crimes were motivated by loneliness, problems making relationships with other adults, low self-esteem, and a capacity to distort and rationalize her actions. The thrill of power and control over a helpless child was addictive. Her case showed me some of the complexity of criminal sexual behavior—the confusion of affection and sexual contact, the abuse of power, and the particular level of disturbance for children who are used to gratify their mothers or other women.

I learned, depressingly, that Corey and Amber remained in close contact, though she was not allowed to visit him in prison because she had been his co-defendant for some of the charges. They planned to reunite when he was released. It seemed that the strength of this toxic coupling overwhelmed all other considerations for Amber and that she was irreversibly bound by his influence. She remained, in a sense, the young girl who had first been groomed by him and had matured into his trusted and unbreakably loyal accomplice. This abusive love killed off the possibilities of a healthier alternative ever replacing it. The relationship had left her unreachable, imprisoned inside an exploitative partnership that had become her life.

Amber's was one of the defining cases that brought me to see the reality that women, as well as men, sometimes exploit children for their own sexual gratification and for comfort and control. Based on my experience, I then believed it was rare for a child sex abuser to be a woman, and rarer still that that woman be a mother. I have learned that this is something of a myth, for female sexual abuse is not only a hugely damaging reality but one that appears to be severely under-estimated. In the United States, a study by the Centers for Disease Control and Prevention found that nearly 25 percent of females and 16 percent of males who reported being sexually abused as a child said that at least one of their attackers was female.

Amber's case encapsulated society's tendency—perhaps even desire—to turn a blind eye to the sexual abuse of children by women. The image of the pedophile as seedy, male, and middle-aged, com-bined with the cherished belief that women are not by nature sexu-ally predatory, leaves little space in the collective consciousness to recognize an abuser like Amber. As her case proved, this idealization of mothers carries a social cost, driving female abuse underground and hiding the experiences of both victims and perpetrators. The general refusal to consider women as potential sex offenders can also give them a dangerous degree of access to children, just as Amber was able to secure over a number of years as a teenager and young adult. Her case was in some ways typical of the model whereby a female predator, working with a male co-conspirator, can act as the primary recruiter and groomer for potential victims (although it is far from the case that women only sexually abuse children alongside or under the coercion of a male; they also abuse children alone, for their own gratification). In other contexts female sexual abuse can even be given an acceptable or glamorous face, with the stereotype of the "teacher-lover" and the assumption that adolescent boys who are groomed and sexually abused by young women must have wel-comed this attention—something that makes it doubly shameful and difficult for these victims to seek help. There are also some rarer cases where the women involved in child sexual abuse have not been victims themselves. They may be motivated by financial gain, by the wish to please their partner who is sexually aroused by children, or by their own sexual desires, directed toward children. This "perver-sion" of maternal instinct and femininity is viewed with particu-lar horror by the public at large, threatening as it does deeply held beliefs about womankind. It has been hard for society to bear that women as well as men can be aroused by the physical appeal and vulnerability of children, and thrilled by the ease with which they can be manipulated for their sexual gratification.

Amber's story reinforced how, even when cases of child sexual abuse by women come to light, a second layer of mitigation will often be applied: the idea that the woman is acting primarily under the coercion of a male partner. For a public imagination that struggles with the fact that women can sexually abuse children, it is more reassuring to assimilate this trope than to recognize the agency of these women, and the complex interplay by which an individual can be both victim and perpetrator. Amber herself found it much easier to accept that she had been under Corey's coercive control than to admit the excitement and pleasure she had actually derived from abusing children in her care.

Her internalized sense of victimhood underlined the power of the narrative that defines women as passive participants, complicit in acts of sexual abuse rather than direct and active perpetrators. This notion—as well as its counterpart in which female abusers, once discovered, are publicly vilified in a way that permits no understanding—perpetuates a harmful falsehood that helps to drive female sexual abuse underground. Amber had been the victim, first of neglectful and callous parents and then of sexual abuse on the part of her cousin. But she had also been responsible for choosing the path that followed, for blinding herself to the realities of her actions, and for perpetrating unthinkable abuse of multiple children over an extended period and cruelty toward her young daughter. Not all former victims choose this path; those who were able to see their treatment by perpetrators as the sexual abuse it was, and were believed when they disclosed it, are more able to separate themselves from their abuser and at reduced risk of reenacting it. For Amber, this dark secret lived inside her, and she identified with her abuser and accepted the distorted version of "care and control" it offered her. Society's widespread ignorance of sexual abusers in her image meant that her actions went unheeded by others and unreported for more than a decade, coming to light only after her partner's chance discovery.

Amber was a patient whom I found impossible to help because

she could not take the first, hardest step of recognizing that she had, in any way, done wrong. I continue to hold out hope that a time will come when that may change, because my experience shows me some patients do, in the face of advancing age and shifting life circumstances, relinquish beliefs that would once have been unshakable.

*

Working with Amber was, at times, chilling as well as frustrating and forced me to confront the limitations of therapy. Amber's was a story of abuse and shame that found its only outlet in reenactment. It was also an example of the force exerted by toxic partnerships such as her relationship with Corey. It had been in part to please and placate him, as the one person in her life who represented some form of love and care, that she had abused so many children with such coldness.

Amber epitomized the tendency among female child abusers to regard their victims as narcissistic extensions of themselves: deserving of maltreatment and suitable targets to express their anger or gratify their needs. Most are reenacting their own childhood in some form, whether perpetrating the abuse they once suffered, reliving the feeling of cruel neglect as Dolores did by torturing her daughter with the empty birthday party, or seeking to rediscover a past place of safety as Grace did by fabricating and inducing illness in Alyssa. Difficult as it may be to understand or empathize with, these women were dealing with pain through the only outlet they could find. Desperate for some source of power, comfort, and control, they picked on their own vulnerable and needy children, taking advantage of the intimate privacy of motherhood and the assumptions of safety that come with it. That desperate need to feel control and expel feelings of self-loathing twisted their sense of acceptable behavior and blinded them to the pain of their own children.

In all cases, these women's search for control was exacerbated by their relative isolation and lack of status outside the home, driving them inward in the search for relief, rather than reaching out to seek help. Amber's troubling story also underlines how relationships in which a male partner's needs and life are primary can be a catalyst for this kind of abuse: her bond with Corey gave her both the need to abuse children, for fear of losing him, and some kind of rationalization for what she was doing.

While the child abuse cases I have discussed illustrate the different kinds of abuse that women may perpetrate against children—Amber's sadistic sexual abuse being clearly distinct from Saffire's angry outbursts or Grace's calculated acts of deceit—they also reveal common threads. Perhaps most telling and affecting is that, in all these cases, the child became lost as a human being.

When I first began doing assessments in child-care proceedings, I started from the premise that mothers love their children and their children should almost always remain with them. At twenty-two, Bryony was the first woman I met for an evaluation of her fitness to care for her child. She had grown up as one of seven, in a poor white family, who had moved around frequently and had no schooling. Bryony was in prison for a violent assault on a woman in her eighties whom she had tricked into allowing her into the house and then stolen from. Because Bryony was pregnant, the old woman had felt sorry for her, falling for Bryony's request for a glass of water as she was so thirsty on this hot day. Bryony was charged with a felony of grievous bodily harm and theft and was now serving a three-year sentence. Seven months pregnant when first incarcerated, she was offered a place in a mother and baby unit within the prison after her son was born. There she was deemed a perfect mother by the staff.

When I met with Bryony, visiting the strangely soft and nurturing unit in the otherwise shabby northern prison, she was desperate to prove to me that she would do anything to protect her son and raise him with the love of which she had been deprived. She explained the influence of her father, a racist man who had threatened to put her first baby, Kinsley, whose father was black, into a trash can, saying she was garbage. She cried as she told me that the father of her daughter had been violent and she had no one to turn to other than her family. She seemed broken as she reported how the baby had to be taken into care and how she had not been allowed further contact with her. Kinsley was now three, and Bryony had recently signed adoption papers, having little choice in the matter. She told me she still dreamed about her.

In prison, Bryony had learned to read and said her wild youth, running crimes with her younger brother, was behind her and she had been "taught her lesson" through this sentence, swearing she would put her son's welfare above all other concerns. Her son, Elias, was a beautiful eight-month-old boy who was reportedly thriving in her care. Like Kinsley, he was dual heritage, with a different father from her, who Bryony said had been "a one-night thing." In my own twenties, not much older than Bryony, I was impressed by her description of her changes and her apparent and reported sensitivity to Elias. I spent hours with her and with the prison staff who worked with her, all of whom had nothing but praise for her mothering and dedication. She followed all the rules and showed willingness to learn. Agonizing over the more gruesome details of her crime, and the violence and deceit she had shown to gain entry to the old woman's house, I focused my report on whether she posed a risk of violence to her child, rating it low, and highlighting her positive mothering. I felt the main risk was of the pain of separation and the trauma that both she and Elias would experience as a result. The risk of re-offending was a separate matter. Going to court for the first time, I was measured but clear: her mothering was not to be faulted, within the prison. My colleague, an older male, gave a noncommittal report too, hastily written on a train, and clearly outlined the risks versus benefits of baby staying with his mother. The prison governor gave a passionate account of Bryony's mothering. The magistrates' court was swayed, and Elias remained with his mother.

All went well during the prison sentence, for Bryony and Elias, until the termination of the mother and baby unit when Elias turned two. A possibility of a longer-stay unit arose, but it was in a prison farther from the family home and Bryony refused it. Elias went into short-term care while she finished her sentence in the prison where he had been with her. She was reunited with him on release, and there were difficulties immediately. She left him with her younger sister, going for a night out. This contravened the agreement made with social services that strictly limited family contact with Elias, as many members of Bryony's family had criminal offenses and were deemed a risk to children. Only her mother and eldest sister were considered safe to care for Elias. Worst of all, her father, with known racist views, a previous attack on Kinsley, and a long history of alcohol abuse, was found in the home alone with Elias. When child protective services made an unscheduled visit to the house, they found Bryony out. On her eventual return she seemed high and had difficulties focusing on Elias, who seemed disturbed, clingy, and inconsolable. Elias was taken into care briefly, until a mother and baby unit in the community could be found, giving Bryony another chance to prove herself. Sadly, this placement broke down quickly because she would not stick to the rules and regulations of the unit, finding it impossible to resist the invitations of friends and family to come and meet them in another city, returning late, breaking curfew, and starting to feud with other residents. Elias was taken into short-term foster care, by now a deeply troubled little boy, while social services began the painful process of returning the case to court and identifying suitable long-term carers, should he not be placed again with his mother.

Back to court I went, having reinterviewed Bryony in the new unit. Far from the persuasively dedicated and devoted mother she had seemed in the prison, she was now angry, fiery, challenging decisions made, and complaining that she was being harshly restricted and punished and had done nothing wrong. She hated being in the mother and baby unit in the new city, pining for her family and unable to see why she was not allowed to take Elias there, to see his relatives. It was as though history were erased, and her longing to return to her old life had obliterated concern about forging a new one, where Elias came first. I had to report this and sadly recognize my own part in the chaos that the pair had experienced. While Bryony could be "the best mother we have ever seen" in the highly controlled environment of the prison, her new "family" and far removed from her actual one, once set free, she was desperate to return to her previous life, with no restrictions, rules, or sense of responsibility. I was shocked by her transformation and the flares of anger and wildness I now beheld. Gone was my naive belief about the sanctity of the mother-baby bond. Even worse, Elias was to spend eighteen months in various short-term placements until a suitable family, matched for his cultural and ethnic background, could be found. Eventually placed at five, he was no longer the calm and contented boy I had met in prison, playing happily at his mother's feet, but now an anxious boy with sudden fits of aggression, insecure, unsurprisingly, and desperate for a reliable home. Having no internal sense of mothering and containment herself, Bryony was unable to take on this role with her own needy and vulnerable child, outside a highly regimented structure, over which she had no choice or control. Not seeing what was actually inside her, the wildness and rage that still burned, but seeing only the image of an idyllic mother-child bond, convincingly presented within the prison, had left me blind to danger. This, of all the cases I have worked, was a turning point, having revealed the force of my unconscious and conscious wishes to have a mother and her baby stay together, no matter what. I learned that such sentimentality is dangerous.

Whether choosing to put their relationship first, as Jackie and Amber did, or like Grace being so overwhelmed by their own needs that they became blind to the harm they were doing to a child, all these women ultimately lost sight of their children as vulnerable human beings. Perhaps no woman ever sets out to harm a child, but there are so many ways that they may become desensitized to the horror of doing so: the child can be an unbearable reminder of their own experiences, or a dependent whose needs can overwhelm them, spurring extreme feelings of inadequacy and self-loathing. Or the child can effectively disappear as a human being altogether: simply a faceless vessel through which to relive past trauma or meet present needs, including the wish to inflict pain on another being. Maternal child abuse can occur because the hugely significant events of becoming pregnant, giving birth, and bonding with a newborn can create emotional turmoil as well as reward. But it may also occur simply because the child is there, in the home with the desperate mother who feels trapped and has no one or nothing else as a container for overwhelming feelings.

The tragedy of maternal child abuse is dual: that it happens at all, and that social attitudes toward motherhood impede greater prevention of it. The trust and belief that are placed in the idea of a mother, combined with the lack of support that vulnerable women are offered to deal with the challenges that motherhood may present to them, allow problems to go undetected and put children into harm's way. The traumas that women have experienced in their lives too frequently go ignored and untreated, while their potential as perpetrators of violence is denied. The two together can lead to disastrous outcomes.

When women do come out of the shadows as violent, or struggling with dangerous fantasies and impulses, they are often vilified, reflecting the bias in society that still pervades, and one in which the voices of women and girls who are victims of sexual abuse, violence, and degradation are silenced.

Baroness Helena Kennedy, an eminent barrister in the UK, has been at the forefront of cases where women have been on trial, successfully pleading for rulings of self-defense where abused women have finally retaliated against their violent partners. She has championed the fair treatment of women on trial and been instrumental in changing laws. Her research has pointed to the particular vilification of women who commit crime and their unjust treatment by the courts. She has been one of the most important feminist voices in justice in the UK and continues to fight for justice, as shown in her recent report into the Scottish criminal justice system, where she poignantly describes institutional biases in the courts:

> I have been a legal practitioner for five decades, and during that time have seen the rising tide of anger over the inability of the criminal justice system to address the violence, abuse and degradation that is so much part of women's and

girls' daily lives. Debates about the failure of the system to deliver justice for women have now moved to centre stage, in a climate of increasing polarisation and divisiveness where vicious conduct seems to have exploded, turbo-charged by online disinhibition and social media invasiveness.

Increasingly in recent years, women have broken their enforced silence over the extent to which domestic abuse and sexual violence have blighted their lives and have complained about the inadequacy of the law's response. As a result, these issues moved up the political agenda. New laws were passed.

Understanding women's violence in the context of the most important relationships of their lives—with those who raised them, with intimate partners, and with children—is fundamental to recognizing its nature and motivations. It also leads us to the final aspect of female violence—that perpetrated either with or against romantic partners. Love, sex, attraction, and obsession are some of the most important forces in all our lives and can all be catalysts for violence in their own right. Women may act violently for fear of losing a partner or because a relationship unearths past trauma. They may lash out against the partner who has been abusing them, in some cases over the course of many years. Or they may be driven to violence by a relationship that exists partly or entirely within their own head, when what started as a pleasant fantasy threatens to turn into a harmful reality. Women's violence can rarely be understood in isolation. It is almost always a reflection of the relationships they have or do not have with other people, with the partners they choose or the family they cannot. It is only by probing the dynamics, the legacies, and often the trauma of such relationships that patients like those I will discuss next can first be understood and ultimately treated.

TANIA

Trauma and Revenge

Aged twenty-four, Tania had known only instability in her life: often forced to fend for herself as a young child, removed from the care of her mother, a sex worker, and never finding a foster family with whom to settle. Her short life had been defined by two shocking events: a sexual assault she had been subjected to as a preteen, and a prolonged torture that she later inflicted on a man, with her partner as co-perpetrator. Hers was a deeply troubled story that brought the nature of trauma to the fore, revealing the complex legacy of childhood abuse and raising the question of how a cycle of violence that begins so early in life can be averted.

*

What made her do it? When I met Tania for the first time, a slight figure wearing jeans and a pink Juicy Couture sweatshirt, an image of my teenage daughter flashed through my mind. I struggled to see how this tiny and delicate woman—vulnerability peering through carefully applied makeup—could have been the perpetrator of such a cruel crime. I wondered what combination of trauma, provocation, and fear had been needed to turn this scared girl into a sadistic torturer.

It would take many months of meetings to get even close to

the truth, gently unpeeling the layers of physical and psychological defenses that guarded the terrified child that Tania still was,
underneath the veneer. And it took months more to untangle the
past from the present, detach the traumatized girl she was from the
woman she had become, and persuade her that childhood history
did not have to be a lifelong destiny.

Appearance and demeanor give the therapist some of their first
clues about a new patient. Tania's told me that she was someone in
conflict about whether to unburden herself or to lock her trauma
away, to hide the shame of her guilt or feel the liberation of being
caught and held accountable for the wrong she knew she had done.
Her long, false eyelashes and talon-like fingernails were emblems of
glamour that spoke of defensiveness, but hers was an armor with
chinks, perhaps conscious ones. Her high-heeled sandals, a size too
big, revealed naked feet bearing an ankle bracelet and a delicate tattoo. The bold, almost combative ensemble belied her inability to
look directly at me and meet my gaze.

She came to me having just been released after a jail sentence for
false imprisonment, grievous bodily harm, and robbery of Alan, a
man twenty years her senior—in a crime committed with her partner, Lee. They had tortured and humiliated their victim for four
hours: tying him up, burning him with a cigarette lighter, kicking
him, and pouring urine over his head. Some of the ordeal was filmed
and shared with friends over social media, with both Tania and Lee
laughing and inviting suggestions for what they should do next.

I knew from the witness statements that this prolonged assault
had only stopped when a downstairs neighbor had knocked on the
door, alarmed by the noises he was hearing late into the night. Lee
and Tania had been scared he would call the police, so they left Alan,
bleeding and doused in urine. He was lying on the floor barely conscious as they ran out to the local park, drinking and watching the
films they had made, still "high" from the night's events. The neighbor had telephoned the police, who arrived to find Alan, groaning
and injured, lying in wreckage. When he regained full consciousness in the hospital, he named his assailants, and the pair were both
arrested.

The relationship between the three lay at the root of this complex and distressing story. To Tania, Alan was something between a friend and an admirer. He was vulnerable, had learning disabilities, and, like her, abused both drugs and alcohol. His interest in her appeared mostly platonic, and they had often spent time together previously without incident. Lee, the third corner of this fateful triangle, had been Tania's partner for six months. Tania, a victim of multiple abusive relationships during childhood, saw in Lee someone more confident and assertive than her, a source both of sexual attraction and of protection. Lee was a trans man whom Tania referred to interchangeably as her "man" and "partner." He provided a comforting, protective masculinity without evoking the men Tania had known only as abusers throughout her short life. It would later emerge that Tania, not Lee, had been the main instigator of the violent and prolonged assault.

As our sessions began, Tania's life, which had never enjoyed stability, was at a particularly fragile moment. She was living in a halfway house where she would be able to stay for twelve months following her release from prison on license, under threat of being reincarcerated if she committed further crimes, broke the rules of the hostel, or failed to attend her probation appointments. This situation was especially precarious for a woman terrified by her own impulses to anger, worried that her relative freedom would lead her back into a world of alcohol, drugs, and violent sexual partners, and afraid that every misstep would take her further away from being able to regain custody of her son, Luke, now aged seven and still in the care of his paternal grandmother.

One phrase she used in our early meetings lodged in my mind. As I explained how our sessions would work, and acknowledged the difficulty for her of having to go back over familiar ground with someone new, she smiled, saying, "Same trailer, different park."

Even as a young woman, Tania's life had been one in which people had been coming and going—social workers, psychologists, police, and probation officers. She trusted none of them; she thought they existed only to judge and blame her after her anger, self-loathing, and fear had boiled over into a criminal act. As far as

Tania was concerned, no one who was meant to be on her side had ever really helped her. They had just stood by and ignored signs that she was being abused or neglected, observed the damage she was doing to herself and others, and intervened only when it was too late. Why, she quite reasonably thought, would this be any different?

*

Tania's abiding sense of distrust was the product of a childhood in which she had been failed by almost every adult who should have cared for her. The eldest of five children, she was exposed to alcoholism, domestic violence, and the realities of her mother's sex work from a young age; she felt responsible as a young girl for trying to protect her siblings and her mother, May, from abuses she could not possibly have prevented.

When she was ten, her mother's violent partner, also her pimp, moved into their flat. He brought drugs into the home and was violently abusive toward May, Tania, and one of her younger brothers. Often banished from the house while her mother saw customers, she would roam the streets looking for something to do, someone to take her in, and somewhere safe for her three brothers and sister to stay. When she found one, she would leave them and return to the house, fearing for May's safety. Witnessing her being beaten up on more than one occasion led to nightmares: faceless bodies that would emerge in the darkness and strangle her mother while she was powerless to move.

Such traumatic circumstances indelibly shaped the contours of Tania's personality. Her mother's neglect—a form of abuse that leaves no bruises but can cause lasting damage—left her with an abiding feeling of being alone in the universe, an emptiness and isolation that would make her vulnerable to the violent relationships that lay in her future. She both loved and feared being alone, craving the independence that would free her from the horrors she had known, but also wanting someone to protect her and care for her. This search for safe harbor would lead her to multiple relationships that proved as damaging as the life she so desperately wished to escape.

For Tania, no relationship was straightforward. The mother she loved and sought helplessly to protect was also an alcoholic who tried (mercifully without success) to coerce her daughter into prostitution at the age of ten. May also prevented Tania from calling the police to report assaults in which she had been hurt. May worried that she would be arrested for solicitation and repeatedly talked her way out of difficult questions from social services when neighbors called them out of concern. Tania grew up feeling helpless, confused, and scared.

Tania's first boyfriend, Darren, in his thirties while she was a teenager, introduced her to cocaine, ketamine, and the synthetic drug known as spice and inveigled her into having sex with some of his friends. Only when a mutual friend bragged to Tania that she was also one of "Darren's babes" did she realize that she had been mistaking the abuse and exploitation of a pimp for the love and attention of a partner. She later came to see the initial *D* he had tattooed on her lower back not as proof of his devotion, but as the form of branding and marker of possession that it was.

Even Nan, Tania's grandmother and the closest thing to a mother she knew, was, like May, an alcoholic. Tania remembered how they would dance together in her grandmother's kitchen, listening to American country music and dreaming of another world, another life. But even these memories were not uncorrupted. Alongside the dancing, hugs, and feeling of safety Nan offered, Tania recalled the smell of booze and sweat and the sense of preoccupation that emanated from her grandmother when she had been drinking. It was a vivid, piercingly sad memory, one that encapsulated how no adult in Tania's life had been an uncomplicated, pure source of love and protection.

The neglect of her home life spread across Tania's entire childhood. Hungry and forgotten, Tania would often find that school lunch was the only meal she would eat all day. Pride and self-denial became part of her makeup. She learned to associate being hungry with being in control and being fed with being pitied, or singled out as different in a way that shamed her. Her ability not to give in to hunger pangs or ask for food was a tiny island of authority she could own amid the chaos and brutality that surrounded her. At other times she would binge on junk food. This toxic relationship with food and hunger evolved into bulimia: when we started working together, Tania was having bulimic episodes every day and night, making herself sick as a habit, seeking not just to stay slim but also to purge herself of the anger, shame, and guilt that stalked her. She took pride in her slender, tiny body—one that, in common with many anorexia and bulimia sufferers, also represented a symbolic protest against the aging process and the arrival of adulthood that in Tania's experience heralded yet further abuse, pain, and suffering.

When Tania was eleven, child protective services finally acted and removed the children from May's custody. But it was impossible to house them together, and multiple placements with foster families broke down as Tania repeatedly ran away, often returning to her mother's house. Eventually, she was sent to a "secure children's home," a forbidding institution filled with other children deemed unsafe to remain in foster homes, liable to seek a return to the familial home they had been removed from, or convicted of crimes but too young for prison. For Tania, this was just another version of the unsuitable, unstable homes that were all she had ever known. It was a volatile environment in which the staff often resorted to physically restraining children when they felt they had no other means of imposing boundaries. There she met Brandon, who would become her boyfriend. When they both left the home at the age of sixteen, she discovered she was pregnant. She had neither taken precautions nor wanted a baby, but she found that the idea appealed to her. Like so many unparented girls, part of her longed for a baby to provide the pure source of love that nothing and no one ever had. They had a boy, Luke, who was in her care for the first six months of his life and then looked after by Brandon's mother because Tania was using drugs and seemed indifferent to the baby, who was not thriving. A year later, staying in a homeless hostel, she met Lee.

Out of this history of trauma, exposure to sexual violence, and deprivation, Tania developed a wild fantasy world, filled with dreams of revenge. She had often imagined tracking down the men who had hurt her mother and subjecting them to the same abuse they had meted out. She could visualize holding a knife to their throats, stripping them naked, and humiliating them. It was shocking to her how vivid and enlivening these images were to her, and how they offered her a welcome release from the pervasive anxiety she suffered. Therapy with Tania was a slow process in which a history of desperate violence and abuse had to be approached with care, even gentleness. So powerful were the memories of what she had seen and suffered that the constant risk was of reviving trauma, making Tania experience again the most acute pain of her childhood as we sought to understand its lasting effect on her.

But no amount of careful support could shield Tania from the legacies of these events and the physical form they took. As with so many women who have experienced significant trauma, her memories were encoded in the body, stored physically so that she would feel as if she were not just remembering events but actively reliving them. As the psychiatrist Bessel van der Kolk writes, "the body keeps the score," with an alertness to danger that can mean the smallest of triggers sends a trauma victim back into the time and place where they experienced the worst moment of their life. The sound of a light being switched off, of footsteps on the floorboards, of a bottle being opened, can be sufficient to re-traumatize someone for whom the sound was once the harbinger of brutal abuse and suffering.

For Tania this risk was ever present. She would describe to me in great detail the feelings she was having, of being hurt, touched against her will, smelling the stale scent of body odor and sex, seeing her mother's twisted face, hearing her baby sister cry. Such recollections go beyond memory. Trauma victims like Tania are not simply recalling what happened to them but reexperiencing it through an act of bodily memory. They are back in the room where an alcoholic caregiver abused them, where their mother was beaten, or where the sexual assault first took place. They can see the stains on the walls, smell the alcohol on the abuser's breath, hear the music that was playing in the background.

One of Tania's most viscerally traumatic memories was of an event that had taken place after she was removed from her mother's care. Living with her first foster family at age twelve, she had run into some older boys she knew and accompanied them to what she thought was a party. Instead, they took her to an empty house and sexually abused her, holding her hostage for several hours during which she was forced to give them oral sex, an assault that was filmed and posted on social media. When she was finally released, she returned to her foster mother, too ashamed to tell her what had happened, meaning the police were never notified. Tania would recall this episode in almost physical shock, becoming shaky and flushed, even putting her hands to her throat as she reexperienced the sense of gagging. It was her first experience of sexual contact and implanted associations of guilt, shame, and self-loathing that remained with her.

For patients such as Tania the process of reliving and remembering can be horrifying, but it serves an important purpose. As our sessions progressed, she was able to link some of the abuses she had suffered with the damaging feelings and patterns of behavior she continued to exhibit. She increasingly recognized that her bulimia was best understood as a response to trauma and an extreme form of exerting control over a body that had been so brutally violated, making herself sick to expel from her body what did not belong there, regaining the agency that had been stolen from her. Bulimia was also a twisted form of purification, the fulfillment of her belief that she was somehow guilty for every bad thing that had happened to her. Her frequent purges were a way of voiding every vivid memory, every intrusive thought, every painful feeling, that amounted to the grim legacy of her childhood. For this frightened child in a woman's body, they were a manifestation of the punishment she felt she deserved and the control over her life that had always, agonizingly, felt out of reach.

It was not difficult to understand why Tania felt the urge to harm herself, a damaging train of thought that we gradually addressed through therapy—helping her to understand where these feelings came from, what triggered her most visceral moments of recall, and how she could find healthier ways of managing them. More complex was the question of why, on that one afternoon when she was seventeen, Tania had decided to cause harm so destructively to someone whom she had trusted and thought a friend. Getting to the point where she felt able to talk about this, and safe enough not to fear becoming totally overwhelmed by its horror, was in itself significant, and I was aware of how carefully I would need to tread.

Eventually Tania felt she had the courage to go through the events of that day. It had begun as time spent with Alan normally did, drinking and smoking weed, with no indication of what was to come. Then Lee left the flat to buy booze, leaving Tania alone with Alan. At this point, she said, Alan started to come on to her, trying to hug her and touching her breasts. It was a shock, because she thought he was her friend, not "a typical guy." When Lee returned, he found them lying on the couch together.

It was the confluence of two emotional responses—two spikes of fear—that turned a humdrum afternoon into a day that would define the next seven years of Tania's life. The moment Alan started looking at her, a look that at seventeen she had seen on the faces of too many men who wanted only to take something from her, she began to shake, transported to another room where she had been held hostage and assaulted. This terror was compounded when she saw the hurt and angry look on Lee's face, returning to find them entangled on the sofa. Lee's expression heightened her fear of abandonment: that she might lose the one person in her life who represented love and protection.

Seven years on, as we worked week by week to understand the events that had followed, some things became clear while others remained clouded in ambiguity. Tania readily admitted and accepted that she had done to Alan what had been done to her five years earlier: denying someone their freedom, assaulting them physically, and later humiliating them on social media, making this attack public. She recognized that a reenactment of one of the worst days of her life, with roles reversed, had offered a tremendous sense of power and feeling of release. She also recalled how often she had seen her mother hurt by men who used her sexually and how outraged and helpless she felt as a little girl exposed to such horrors. Alongside the boys who had abused her, these faceless shadows also lurked in her memories as the attack on Alan intensified.

The impunity with which others had once abused her was now Tania's to wield. She did so, in a vicious and prolonged assault whose intensity was frightening for her to recall. This mirror image of victim turned perpetrator was one she struggled to face. It took months of sessions in which we covered the events of her childhood before it was even possible to broach what had happened between her, Lee, and Alan.

Other aspects of that day were more elusive. While the triggers of past trauma might have suggested an instinctive recoil, the assault on Alan went far beyond a firework of fear and anger. As a series of events over several hours, it took on a calculated, unemotional character that was harder to reconcile with the idea of Tania reveling in a transient and retributory moment of emotional release. Her own recall of events was inconsistent. At times she suggested that she was too drunk and high to have understood what was going on. In some sessions she blamed Lee's influence and said she had been acting out of a desire to earn his approval. In others she told me how she saw Alan's face take on the form of the boys who had assaulted her, becoming confused about who he was, where she was, and the danger she might be in. The past intruded on the present.

One aspect that haunted Tania was their filming of the attack, a recording she had been forced to watch in court during her trial. The experience of seeing the attack again had proved so painful that Tania had attempted suicide in the aftermath, cutting deep into her wrists. We spent several difficult sessions exploring the question of why she and Lee had chosen to film their crime, before concluding that there was no reason beyond an impulse, an instinctive need that added to the exhilaration of an event whose power had become addictive. Like soldiers who have committed war crimes after losing their moral and ethical moorings, Tania and Lee had lost touch with their humanity. In those hours, Alan had become nothing more than an object to them, something to be beaten, tormented, and humiliated for their gratification. Unconsciously, the choice to film completed the process of objectification—one in which assault became almost impersonal: mere entertainment for others to share and participate in virtually, enhancing and glorifying their assault.

This physical and emotional frenzy, one fueled by its own sense of intoxication, collided in retrospect with the cold reality of the film they had created. The indelible record meant there was no ambiguity about what Tania had done: no tricks of memory that could deflect from the cruelty and viciousness or soften the emotional blow of realizing how far she had slipped beyond humanity and morality. Tania had to live not just with her own memory of that day but with the camera's objective record of it. It was irrefutable evidence of something that terrified her, an inner wildness with the power to obliterate her compassion and capacity for reason. That in turn spurred another question that loomed large in our sessions: Was Tania's disastrous loss of inhibition and self-control a one-off, or was there an active danger that it might happen again? Had she expelled her need for retaliatory violence against the ghosts of her former abusers, or did that wildness still live in her? In the wrong circumstances, might it yet be reanimated?

*

The appalling abuses Tania had suffered, and finally perpetrated, in her life meant that our therapy sessions were an exercise in tiptoeing through the minefield of old traumas and potential triggers. The constant battle was to help Tania establish a sense of self in the present, as an adult whose existence was both separate and safe from that of her childhood. Becoming lost in the past represented a danger both to Tania and to those around her. The shame, guilt, and self-loathing that were the legacy of those years amounted to emotional kindling. As the assault on Alan had shown, only the barest of sparks was needed to light it into a blaze with an all-consuming power.

What Tania had so lacked throughout her life, and what we sought to equip her with through therapy, was a sense of control and containment. Her entire life had been a series of shocking events in which she had little to no agency. She had felt unable to protect her mother or siblings from the abusers who surrounded them; power-less to prevent the boys who had sexually assaulted her; vulnerable to the behavior of predators like Darren. And, ultimately, she was either unable or unwilling to stop herself from an act of sustained violence that had left her victim traumatized and cost her seven years of freedom. The presence of another person with similar depths of unspent rage had endorsed her cruelty, fueling the assault. Her only means of exercising control were forms of self-harm: abusing drugs, drinking until she blacked out, eating until she was sick, and then trying to void her body of every physical and emotional thing she could not bear to hold. Breaking this cycle required two things of the therapy: that it help Tania to distinguish effectively between her past and her present selves, and that she develop safe mechanisms for discharging the emotional burden that she would always carry, traumas and memories she referred to as demons.

Her inability to self-soothe was a legacy of the fractured rela-tionship with her mother and the absence from her childhood of any reliable source of love and care. She had never experienced what the psychoanalyst Wilfred Bion defined as the relationship between container and contained—in which an infant projects feelings they cannot comprehend or process onto their mother, who acts as the container for them, modifying and reflecting these emotions back in a way that soothes a crying baby, and ultimately helps a develop-ing child to identify, understand, and manage their own feelings. The mother detoxifies the infant's early experiences of terror, rage, hunger, and fear and feeds them back to her baby in a manageable, digestible form.

No one in Tania's life had provided this for her, the sense of complete safety that is such an essential part of emotional develop-ment. Where protectors should have been, she encountered only predators and abusers. Even her own mother, herself an abused and terrorized woman, had tried to prostitute her. No one had effectively cared for Tania, which left her uncontained, without any ability to handle the overwhelming emotions that were the imprint of her young life's experience.

The process of therapy was initially about providing Tania with a container and ultimately helping her learn how to become her own: processing her own fears and feelings to the point where they no longer threatened to overwhelm her or leave her trapped in a purgatory between past events and the present day.

In this work we were helped by a setting for therapy that would normally have seemed uncongenial. Our sessions took place in a small room in the basement of Tania's probation hostel, an anonymous space that felt like its own private world, cut off not only from the outside but from the buzz and murmur of people going about their daily lives in the hostel.

Like many of therapy's significant but unspoken details, the setting matters. With patients who are often hypervigilant and accustomed to assessing their surroundings for signs of danger, it is essential to have a reliable space that feels both safe and neutral: a blank canvas rather than one whose details might send unwanted signals. Our basement room inadvertently proved perfect for the purpose of helping Tania to feel grounded and protected. As a dark, remote, almost womb-like enclosure, it represented a place of safety and a physical manifestation of the emotional containment that we were working together to achieve. We had to meet at the same time, in the same room, on the same day of the week to ensure that Tania had a sense of therapy, and me, as being reliable and safe.

An equally important container was the relationship between us as therapist and patient. In our initial sessions, Tania's appearance made clear that her guard was up. It took time to even begin broaching the issues at the root of her troubles, because she quite reasonably feared what confronting her demons might unleash. Tania also felt self-conscious about being the one to receive treatment when she was painfully aware of the physical and psychological scars she had left on her victim. At this early stage, she was largely focused on external changes—wanting to alter how she looked, return to work, and see her son—without any apparent recognition of the internal ones she so desperately needed to make.

Slowly, as our weekly meetings went by, Tania started to soften.

No longer dressed defensively for our meetings, she would appear in comfortable slippers and tracksuit bottoms. Gradually, we started to piece together a puzzle of many parts: the abuse she had suffered, the legacy of trauma that had imprinted itself on her, and the violent manifestations that had resulted, both in the form of harm caused to her own body and in the assault on Alan. Tentative progress, my nonjudgmental and reliable presence, and the consistent use of grounding techniques helped Tania to relate differently to her past, no longer being transported back into it, but able to observe, reflect, and rationalize from a point of emotional distance. My maternal countertransference to her was helpful, in that I felt and conveyed understanding of her distress and uncontainment, allowing her to feel "held" in the sessions rather than cast out and rejected as monstrous and bad. She could, in turn, both trust me and, at other times, berate me for "not caring enough" as she projected onto me the feelings of abandonment she had toward her actual mother. Her transference to me was powerful: in her mind I was variously the neglectful mother she had known, the caring mother she had wanted, and, like her grandmother, a loving but unreliable presence. Unlike her mother, I could bear her anger without feeling the impulse to retaliate or walk away. This allowed Tania to process her anger, integrating and assimilating aggressive feelings that she would once have tried to bury, with the inevitable result that they would later reemerge, twice as destructive as before.

Over the course of the therapy I helped Tania to deconstruct her life experiences, to name her feelings, and to untangle the complex emotional relationship with her mother, one that encompassed blame for being unable to protect her children, hatred for her attempts to coerce Tania into prostitution, and sympathy as a persistent victim of abuse whose suffering it had deeply pained her to witness. We had to confront Tania's anger and soothe her guilt, allowing her to realize that hating her mother for some of the things she had done did not invalidate the love she still felt for her.

Months of this work helped her to see how the abuses of her childhood, alongside neglect, had left her with feelings of guilt, self-loathing, and a desire for punishment that were the roots of her self-harming behavior. It also enabled her to recognize that her attack on Alan had been akin to an attempt to undo what had been done to her, inflicting equivalent and compensatory suffering on another.

Throughout this cautious, dangerous journey into Tania's past, I acted as her container and archivist. My role was to help her talk about what had happened to her, to recall events that she had never previously spoken about, and to share feelings that terrified her, notably the interplay between her sense of being worthless and her desire for revenge, to inflict the humiliation that lived in her on others. When we first met, I had been far from certain that we would ever reach this point of reflection and self-knowledge. Tania's body language revealed that she was barely keeping the lid down on a lifetime of secrets, but she openly expressed her fear of delving into them and her thought that it may be better to take them to the grave. She was an uncontained soul who had in parallel repressed and internalized her short lifetime of horrendous suffering. This unsustainable conflict of the psyche had burst open, with disastrous results, seven years earlier. Across many sessions in our basement cocoon, we worked to unpack it, allowing Tania to develop a durable sense of self that could live in the present, which in turn helped her to see the past as a place of discrete memories rather than nightmares that retained the power to consume her. Through this process, Tania gained control over the most untamed parts of herself: memories that had existed only as feelings became thoughts that could be interrogated, digested, and rationalized; the triggers that had been such a danger to her and others became recognizable, in a way that allowed her to anticipate and prepare. She could distinguish the past from the present, fact from fantasy, and herself from her own mother. She no longer felt that she was doomed either to avenge her mother's pain or to suffer as May had done. This emergence of an identity that was truly her own—independent from generational trauma and existing in the present—marked the beginning of Tania's recovery.

After Tania's term in the probation hostel came to an end, she moved into a studio apartment and continued to see me as an outpatient. These meetings, in a more ordinary room at the probation office, lacked the intimacy and intensity of our earlier sessions, but also reflected the progress Tania had made. She was increasingly capable of being her own container, no longer in need of physical props or my presence to provide a feeling of security.

She had also become involved with a local church, and it intrigued me to see how this tight-knit community provided a parallel source of containment, its combination of faith, structure, and social support enhancing Tania's growing sense of stability and morality. For perhaps the first time in Tania's life, she had been welcomed by people who had neither a malign motive nor a professional obligation toward her. The church connection appealed to the emphasis on sin and punishment that remained central to Tania's psychology. Being more aware and in control of her emotions did not mean she was liberated from the strength of them. At one of our final meetings, she told me that she knew she would never forgive herself for what she had done, but she hoped that, eventually, God might. Although offering no comment on a subject outside my remit, I silently took comfort in the thought that Tania had found an outlet, one that offered her the prospect of release from the tormenting guilt that had accompanied almost her entire life. Although not religious myself, I understood the sense of belonging and safety that this community offered her.

Six months after our last regular session, I saw Tania again for a follow-up appointment. I was almost taken aback by the confident young woman who walked into my office and looked me straight in the eye. The frightened child that had been barely under the surface when we first met was no longer to be seen. This part of Tania would never be gone entirely, but she had found ways to soothe and separate it from her life and identity in the present. She was working daily in the church's café, enjoying weekly visits with her son, and dating a woman in the congregation who bore little resemblance to the violent partners who haunted her past. That past, she said, was something she could feel herself leaving behind. Tania smiled a very different smile as she referred back to one of the first thoughts she had ever expressed to me. Finally, it was a different trailer, a different park.

As that session, our last meeting, came to a close, she surprised me by asking if she could give me something as a gesture of thanks.

Although accepting gifts from patients crosses a boundary and is not strictly speaking permitted in psychoanalytic psychotherapy, the therapist must weigh up what it means to be offered such a gift and whether accepting it will distort the course of therapy or create a conflict of interest (in this, the financial value of the gift is also an important consideration). While I could have rejected Tania's request and reassured her that her progress was gift enough, this did not feel right. Looking at Tania's earnest face, and catching the sight of leaves, I decided in that split second to accept the small rose plant, saying it would remain in the hostel for all to enjoy. She wanted me to have it, she said, so I might look at it and think of her, continuing to thrive and grow as the flowers did.

Tania had experienced an extraordinary life cycle, one that began with betrayal and abuse, twisted into a horrific orgy of revenge, and had somehow, like the rose, flowered again into a fragile emergence of calm, a degree of self-knowledge, and the prospect of stability. Her rose remains in the hostel's garden today: a reminder of the possibility of renewal.

*

Tania's story exemplified the strength of memory and the power of reenactment: how trauma that lives below consciousness can suddenly intrude on present moments with devastating consequences. It underlined the injustice of revenge, Tania's victim having been as vulnerable as she had been when so terribly abused as a child. Above all, it emphasized how even this suffering does not dilute the need for love and care, or distract people in their search for it. Tania's discovery of care and nurture in the form of community was a reminder of how healing and fulfillment are possible.

Yet that quest for love, one of our fundamental drives as human beings, can also be the root of problems and a spur to violence in the wrong circumstances. What begins as a timeless story of falling in love can, sometimes, end in obsession, hatred, and violence. With Maja I was to see how the universal need to find love and be loved can turn dangerous.

MAJA

Objects of Obsession

Maja, a twenty-one-year-old university student, had fallen in love with a man who rejected her. In her delusional conviction that he still loved her, she stalked him and threatened to kill his new girl-friend. She was charged with stalking, harassment, and threats to kill and given a restraining order to prevent contact with him. She avoided a prison sentence but was given a probation order and was referred for therapy to help her relinquish her erotic fixation on her victim and to restore her grip on reality. In her case, love itself was dangerous, and the obsession bordering on madness.

*

With each new patient, a forensic psychotherapist has to decide one thing early. How much of the truth can the patient handle? Is she yet ready to confront reality, or is it too difficult and potentially too damaging to try to detach her from the belief or delusion that led her to commit extreme acts?

Maja was a clear case of the second category: people who can only be untangled from the barbed wire of their own impossible logic with great care, patience, and caution. So extreme were her fantasies that they had turned what began as a straightforward relationship between young students into an obsessive spiral that culminated in her criminal conviction.

The fantasy life Maja had created was a kaleidoscopic marvel of reality contorted, its pieces broken apart and rearranged into a pattern whose beauty only she could see. Even after her conviction for stalking a former boyfriend, Theo, and threatening to kill his new girlfriend, she was convinced that he still loved her. She believed that it was Theo, not she, who was obsessed and that all the evidence to the contrary could be explained because he had fallen under the coercive control of his new partner. The denial was not with her but with him, refusing to recognize the truth of their love. All the rejections and legal consequences she had faced were simply steps along the road to that truth being revealed and fulfilled.

The fire of these beliefs contrasted with Maja's soft, even gentle appearance in our first session, held in the outpatient department of a forensic psychiatry service. We met in a bright room with posters on the walls and big windows, a setting that was designed to put people at ease. She spoke softly, so much so that I found myself leaning forward over the table to hear her. But the actions that had brought her into that room with me were far from meek. After Theo had ended their relationship, she stalked him for a year, bombarding his phone with calls and messages and following him around campus. She then turned her attention to his new girlfriend, contacting her three times in the same day with messages whose escalating menace culminated in a threat to put a knife through her throat. After this was reported to the police and the couple both gave statements, Maja was charged with and convicted of stalking, harassment, and making threats to kill. Her eighteen-month community order included a requirement for psychological treatment, and she was referred to my clinic by her probation officer.

All of this had done nothing to dent her intense certainty that Theo still loved her and that they would one day be reconciled. For her, the hard currency of witness statements, a conviction, and a court order faded into irrelevance compared with the hidden messages she had read into the choice of songs on Theo's Spotify playlist.

Maja's continuing obsession was clear as she described the early days of their relationship to me, a detailed and often sexually explicit portrait that she demanded I pay attention to, even as I tried to steer the conversation elsewhere. She was at her most alive talking about the sexual tension that had grown silently between them sitting in lectures at the university where they met, the touch of his fingers on her skin, and the intense pleasure of their lovemaking. She described his body in the kind of detail that would have been awkward even among very close friends.

These early interactions were troubling, not just for what they revealed about the depth of Maja's infatuation, but because they brought me directly into the teeth of a classic therapeutic dilemma. As with any patient, I needed to gain her trust and for her to see that I was sympathetic to her, not someone else who thought her mad for believing what seemed to her undeniable truths. Yet to encourage her version of the story too enthusiastically, in effect colluding with her delusions, would lay the foundations for an even worse outcome. It would position me as an ally who was ultimately destined to betray Maja as our relationship evolved and I sought to help her detach reality from beloved fantasy.

This dance between patient and therapist, treading the agonizingly thin line that separates listening to someone's problems from inadvertently reinforcing them, is a staple of any psychologist's work. I have to understand a patient's delusions, and encourage them to elaborate on them with me, but at some point I also need to confront them with reality, shattering those same illusions. With Maja, as I was to discover, it would be an especially acute problem, closely linked to her own distorted template for forming relationships and the dangerous unraveling of her romance with Theo.

That had begun at college, where she was studying for a psychology degree. She met Theo through one of her friends, a mostly female group whose privileged backgrounds and private school education contrasted with her own. During their second term she was introduced to him and immediately attracted by his good looks, easy confidence, and attentive manner. She quickly found herself "totally besotted" with him, so much so that she decided to ignore the few things that concerned her—the way he used cocaine as a mood enhancer before sex, and how he encouraged her to be more sexually adventurous, acts that he sometimes filmed. She rationalized these doubts: proof, she made herself believe, of how much he wanted her.

Her growing sense of attachment to him deepened when she was invited to stay the weekend with his parents. For Maja this was a defining moment in their relationship. The home she was visiting quietly radiated wealth, a world away from the cramped council flat in which she had grown up with three siblings. The invitation itself was something that she believed to be deeply significant: not simply a token of hospitality and a signal of support for a nascent relationship, but a formal welcome by Theo into his world and a statement of meaningful commitment. It was during that weekend, Maja remembered, that she began to dream of marrying him and raising a family in a home much like this one. Alongside these reveries, intruding bitterly into her daydreams, were pangs of doubt and fear, the belief that she must be unworthy of his love, and the certainty that one day he would abandon her. This sense of paranoia would prove as significant to her condition and subsequent actions as her passion.

It was at this point that I believe Maja began to experience symptoms of De Clérambault syndrome, named after the French psychologist who described it as psychose passionnelle, a condition more popularly known as "erotomania." This is characterized by obsessional feelings, typically from a young woman about a man she believes to be in love with her. The perception that the person is from a higher class than she is is also significant. Often it arises in cases where two individuals never actually meet and the person suffering will become fixated with a public figure into whose actions they interpret hidden meanings. In his 1885 paper that first defined the syndrome, de Clérambault cited the example of a patient who believed that King George V was in love with her. This was apparently confirmed when she visited Buckingham Palace and observed a curtain moving, which she read as a secret signal to her. In his 1997 novel, *Enduring Love,* Ian McEwan beautifully describes the resistance of erotomania to reason, contrary evidence, and the passage of time.

Maja's growing obsession with Theo reflected many traits characteristic of erotomania. She had the tendency, both during the relationship and in its aftermath, to overinterpret signals or dream up those that never existed. The invitation to meet Theo's family, for him a small step, to her represented a prelude to marriage. Moreover, by fixating on someone from a very different background from hers, she had entered an unfamiliar world, giving physical manifestation to the fantasy life she had mentally begun to construct. The further down this path she walked, the more she risked losing touch with her real self, and in turn with reality. At the same time, her prevailing sense of insecurity and controlling personality ensured that her love for Theo was a deeply suspicious one, in which affection and attachment lived alongside the constant, obsessive fear of abandonment.

Romantic obsession may begin with attraction, but it hardens with fear and becomes absolute when passion fuses with the anticipation of betrayal. Although only a tiny minority (around 5 percent) of people with erotomania become violent, a study by the psychologist Park Dietz in the 1980s found that rare incidences of violence tend to be directed not at the object of obsession but at people whom the obsessed individual deems to be standing in their way, or trying to take that object away from them. Maja's case reflected this. She threatened but did not carry out violence, and her ultimate target was not Theo but the girlfriend who had taken her place, under whose tight control she believed he had fallen.

Maja was experiencing the devastating grip on the mind that can come from the romantic idealization of another person. Most people know what this feels like in the form of sexual infatuation. But obsession does not wane, soften, and evolve in the same way as lust. It feeds off itself, requiring no reciprocation and eventually making its object almost incidental. Then, if that object fails to respond or moves away, the obsessed lover becomes frantic, increasing their efforts to retrieve what they are at risk of losing. It is at this point that a state of mind to which anyone can relate becomes a dangerous fixation bordering on psychological breakdown.

This was exactly what Maja began to experience as the relationship entered its second year. She could feel Theo distancing himself from her, committing to see her less, and no longer responding to messages with the same frequency. They were having sex less often, and he seemed to be more dependent on drugs when they did. As the relationship dwindled, her fear and mistrust grew. She began to question him about where he had been, with whom, and why. She was spending more and more time thinking about Theo and trying to build up a picture of his movements when they were not together. Both her work and her mental state suffered accordingly. She began to feel shaky and fragile, ate and slept far less than was healthy, and found it impossible to concentrate on her coursework. Her friends noticed that she was becoming withdrawn and seemed to talk or care about little other than Theo.

Their observations were an accurate impression of Maja's deteriorating mental state. Her obsession with Theo meant that in his increasing absence she felt both herself and her world falling apart. Her self-identification as his lifelong partner had become so overwhelming that she was struggling to see who she was and what purpose her life had without him. As she declined both physically and mentally, suffering from depression and the effects of undereating and lack of sleep, her obsessive desire to be reconciled with him only grew stronger. Their time together was becoming less frequent and less meaningful, and she tried to compensate by sending a constant stream of messages and nude photos, interspersed with more requests to know where he was and with whom. Several weeks of this behavior brought matters to a head and Theo broke up with her, saying that he had only ever wanted a casual relationship and that her intensity was too much for him. He held firm even as she threatened to kill herself if he walked away.

The end of the relationship accelerated Maja's decline. Her fixation on Theo developed still further as she committed entire days to tracking his movements through social media, zooming into pictures to work out exactly where he was and imagine what he might be doing. She tortured herself with thoughts of Theo and a new partner together, taking long walks in the park, watching movies on his laptop, and making love. Once it became clear that Theo had indeed started a new relationship, with a girl named Saskia who was physically different from her in almost every way, Maja's anger and paranoia fused. She obsessively revisited the cherished memory of her weekend with his family, imagining that he would soon be repeating it with Saskia and tormented by the belief that they would prefer her.

As Maja's depression worsened, she began to stalk Theo in person. She cornered him and begged to reconcile, saying that she would do whatever it took to please him and on another occasion becoming angry and again threatening suicide when he told her to leave him alone and that he had never wanted a serious relationship with her. These desperate, failed bids to win him back only deepened her paranoia. She became convinced that he had kept the recordings of them having sex and was showing them to his friends, laughing at her. Then, when she was following Theo on a night out, she saw him kissing Saskia, something that sent her into a frenzy of rage and anxiety and turned her obsession in a new direction. A new idea formed in her mind: if she were to kill Saskia, a grief-stricken Theo would be sure to turn to her for comfort. She would be doing him a favor and setting him free. She began contacting her, culminating in the threat of murder that would lead to her arrest and conviction. Counterintuitively, it was not the despair at losing Theo that finally pushed Maja to acts that could no longer be ignored but the hope that she could recapture him and her plans to do so.

*

By the time I became involved in Maja's case, the criminal case had already been decided. She had been convicted of stalking and making threats to kill and sentenced to a community order, one of whose conditions was the therapy I would provide. The only question was how to devise a course of treatment to help a young woman who had been a high-achieving, well-liked student before erotomania led her into paranoia, depression, disordered eating, and ultimately harassment and threats to kill. My aim was to help Maja understand her crimes, their meaning, and the underlying motivations and experiences that had brought her to that point. Hers was simpler, but also opposing. She wished to be reconciled with Theo and believed that it was he who needed to change for the situation to be resolved. She said, in a quiet voice I had to strain to hear, how important it was that I understood *she* was the victim.

Maja craved my attention as a willing audience, but she evidently also feared I might at any moment choose to leave my seat. Even though I felt almost a hostage to her version of events, more cautious than usual of challenging a patient for fear of losing her trust altogether, it was Maja who radiated insecurity. Some patients actively relish sessions, while others hardly engage and are tangibly desperate to leave as soon as possible. But, unlike anyone else I have worked with, Maja seemed almost to be clinging to me. There was a desperation to her body language, which prompted me to offer a rare observation: she seemed to be anticipating and dreading the end of each session almost as soon as it had started. She nodded, saying that it felt as if things were falling apart when we were not meeting, that she had no one else and nothing other than the time we spent together.

Maja's neediness, and her transference of the demands she had once made of Theo onto me, began to illuminate for me her relationship template and the problems that had brought us to this point. It was increasingly evident that what she sought was not a specific individual but simply another person, a being with whom she could achieve some kind of fusion, to calm the agony of her insecurity, her terror of being left alone, and her overwhelming fear of abandonment. Hers was a narcissistic universe in which she was at the center and other people existed to provide affirmation, to meet her desperate need for love and admiration. She did not feel real without this reflected sense of herself.

In this way Theo, the object of her obsession, had been not so much a real person as a symbol: an idea of the perfect boyfriend come to life. I too existed not as a distinct individual but as a generic one: a faceless receptacle into whom she could pour her stories, allowing her to feel heard and accepted. The irony was that she sought physical presence and human connection without being willing to accept the reality of what another person is: an individual with a mind, a life, and a being of their own. She demanded intimacy with another person's body and presence without being willing or able to tolerate contact with their mind. She wanted love, but without any of the complexity, the tolerance, and the compromise that love requires. Hers was a brittle conception of human connection that left her perpetually feeling on the verge of being broken.

Searching for the roots of this deeply flawed relationship template, I began to steer our conversations toward her childhood. It became clear that in different ways both her parents had caused her lasting psychological harm. Her father had left the family home when Maja was only six, planting the seeds that would grow into the fear of abandonment that had become such a defining part of her life. Her contact with him in the years since had become sporadic as he remarried and had children with his new wife, leaving Maja feeling locked out of his life. Her memories of time with her father were physical and even had a faintly erotic dimension. She recalled sitting in his lap, being held in the crooks of his strong arms, with him singing to her. Ever since, she said, she had been seeking a man who would provide that same sense of comfort and safety. She agreed with my suggestion that as she went through adolescence and early adulthood, she had often confused sexual attention with loving affection, conflating the two and assuming that the physical connection of the first would naturally yield the stable bond of the second.

Maja's mother, Jade, was a carer who worked long hours and had little family support in raising her four children, of whom Maja was the eldest. As a single mother struggling to look after her family alone, and having to deal daily with the distress and aggression of her elderly patients, she often took out her frustration and anxiety on Maja. She expected her oldest child to take on responsibility for looking after the other three, but rarely offered her kindness or understanding in return. Instead, Maja found herself constantly facing new demands, subjected to cruel punishments, and criticized for fashion choices that her mother deemed unsuitable.

Having undergone puberty early and been expected to be responsible for her siblings from a young age, Maja hardly had a proper childhood in which she knew love, nurture, or stability.

Because I had also had an early puberty, her story struck home, and I remembered vividly how uncomfortable unwanted male attention was and how hard to reconcile with a wish for some kind of affirmation. Unlike Maja, I was lucky enough to feel loved at home, but still had a troubled relationship with my out-of-control body and its unexpected power to attract attention. This was a key moment of identification with a patient, when their struggles and one's own are writ large and feelings of real understanding and connection are easy to access. I found it easy to empathize as Maja described how her fast-developing body had attracted attention for which she was not emotionally ready, and how at fourteen she began truanting from school and going out with older boys, the first sign of her need for male care and protection to fill the gap her father had left. This premature sexualization had left Maja with overwhelming and conflicting emotions. Part of her was ashamed by how she believed others at school saw her, and how readily boys seemed to approach her with unambiguous intentions. Another part took comfort in the rare boost to self-esteem that their attention represented.

At fifteen she had her first sexual relationship, with Max, a seventeen-year-old who lived in foster care. He introduced her to drugs and the intoxicating sense of relief they could offer, an escape from the drudgery of her home life and the anxiety of school. But he was troubled, desperate to escape the care system, and terrified of becoming entangled in a serious relationship. Maja was heartbroken when he ended the relationship and moved away. In response she cut her arms, took an overdose of paracetamol with vodka, and threatened for the first time to kill herself.

Such an extreme event was a terrifying reflection of the pain she had experienced in her short life, but it did change the balance of the relationship with her mother, who belatedly recognized how much her daughter was suffering and then became closely involved in nursing her back to health. Her support, along with that of a school counselor, helped Maja to thrive for perhaps the first time in her life. Still distraught at how Max had abandoned her, she sought distraction in her schoolwork. The controlling instincts that were to become so destructive during the decline of her relationship with Theo served her well during this final period at school. With a ruthless focus on work, she outperformed all expectations to earn strong A-Level examination results and her university place. It was here that she hoped to reinvent herself: to reset the course of a troubled life in which she had so rarely wielded the control she craved.

*

The meetings in which we discussed Maja's childhood began to break through the facade that had initially caused me so much concern. After our first four sessions I worried that, such was her unstinting obsession with Theo, we might never get past the familiar script of his continuing love for her and the inevitability of their future reconciliation. Her dreamworld seemed so certain, and the beliefs it rested upon so unbreaking, that I seriously wondered if progress was possible and whether Maja could ever be helped to discern fantasy from reality. For her the fusion of the two had become so complete that I was now unsure if a decoupling could be achieved.

But in therapy, as in life, sometimes it is a chance event that tilts the scales and shifts the odds in your favor. Bus timetables do not feature on the list of clinically tested psychological treatments, but in this case they provided a catalyst, when a last-minute change meant Maja arrived late for our fifth session. She was angry, distraught, and loudly insistent that we should continue the session beyond its planned duration to give her the usual amount of time. When I said this wasn't possible because I had another appointment afterward, she became enraged, shouting that I obviously didn't care and was putting other people before her. How, she demanded, could I not see how important the therapy was to her? Why wasn't I willing to make someone else wait so that she could have her full session?

As she accused me of being callous and indifferent, I had the rare experience of feeling physically afraid during a session. Her fury was so hot and sustained that I thought there was a chance she might attack me, this young woman who had started our sessions speaking so quietly that I could barely hear her.

Eventually, I took advantage of a gap in her ranting to make an observation. She was upset not that our session would be cut short but at the unwanted realization that I had patients other than her to see. For her this was akin to a betrayal. If I wasn't only for her, then I couldn't be for her at all. This very obvious interpretation seemed to stop Maja in her tracks. She looked startled, rudely displaced from a mental groove that was so comforting and familiar. The events of the day had inadvertently contributed to her first recognition of me as someone who existed outside these sessions and with responsibilities to people other than her. This was a jolting dose of what Freud once called the "reality principle" after she had initially succeeded in co-opting our sessions into the strictures of her fantasy life. Her anger drained and was replaced by tears as the quiet voice returned to tell me how the thought of other patients had sparked her self-loathing and the immediate conclusion that I must like these people better and have an easier time treating them.

The boundary I had set initially felt cruel and unjust to her, apparent proof of my lack of care, but confronting her with it proved important. She had run into one of the essential parameters of therapy—that it must be reliable, at the same place and same time, providing a safe and dependable environment in which to explore destabilizing thoughts and feelings. Testing this boundary and seeing it upheld despite her protests was a sobering and important moment for Maja. Tears rolled down her cheeks as she admitted how frightened it made her when she was out of control, and how scared she was of being punished by me the way her mother had used to. She shared for the first time how she had been abused physically as a child, told that she was bad and evil for any behavior that Jade deemed an infraction. During the remainder of the short session we were able to begin exploring her childhood in detail for the first time, touching on the legacy of her father's abandonment, her mother's brutality and indifference, and the scars of her early relationship experiences.

This marked a turning point in several ways. My failure to respond as Maja had expected, by accepting and interpreting her rage rather than seeking to punish her for it, was another blow to the certainties of her worldview. So convinced had she been that I would abandon her that she could not hide her surprise, not prevent herself from a rare and precious moment of introspection. She was forced to acknowledge that her preconceptions were personal expectations, born of experience, and not immutable realities. Our confrontation had become an unplanned showdown with some of her deepest fears: the belief that she was worthless, that others were ridiculing her, and that every person to whom she so desperately clung in life was destined to abandon her. The wave of these feelings, simultaneously crashing over her in an already emotionally fraught situation, had a profound effect on her. It felt as if we had finally exposed a tiny chink in the armor of a fantasy that had previously seemed impregnable.

Moments of surprise such as this can be crucial breakthroughs in therapy. The difference between my actual behavior and Maja's transference of feelings about her mother onto me shocked her into a moment of recognition about her personality and the powers that had shaped it. She was forced to confront a boundary and to realize that while help within limits was possible, her hope of blissful fusion with another, therapy without end, and infinite love was an impossible one. It was another significant moment, another knot untied in the rope that bound Maja's reality to her fantasies.

As we discussed her childhood, a change was also evident in her demeanor. No longer was she the star of her own show, preening herself with a familiar narrative and closely watching how her audience responded. All the dramatic intensity fell away as the helpless, scared little girl began to reveal herself. This fragility, although alarming to her, was something that needed to be endured for her to connect with the moments in her life that had conspired to cause her so much pain. By stripping away the grandeur of her delusions, we brought her closer into contact with reality, with the shame and shabbiness that she needed to confront before she could overcome its legacies.

The scales were also falling from my eyes as these sessions proceeded. Having initially been incredulous about Maja's wild, ungrounded fantasies, I was starting to understand the purpose they served: protection from the grim realities of a childhood that needed to be escaped, not just physically, but in the mind. The pain, poverty, and abuse of her young world had been too great for her to confront, so she had learned to conceal them, first from other people and eventually, unconsciously, from herself.

The progress in the sessions following her lateness and outburst of rage had been significant, but our work together was far from complete. Maja had achieved the first degree of separation between fantasy and reality, but was not yet ready to relinquish her obsession with Theo, nor the transference of her need for attachment onto me. At the end of each session, after our conversation was over, she would linger while slowly gathering her things and then hover in the door, looking intently at me as though trying to memorize my face. Then, at the beginning of the next session, she would be cautious and cagey, as if we were meeting for the first time and something might have changed in the intervening week to threaten our equilibrium.

The abandonments of Maja's early life had left her without a sense of constancy, and ever suspicious that the people she relied upon would not be waiting for her when she needed them. Her desperate struggle to avoid the demise of her relationship with Theo reflected this. Unable to reconcile herself to letting their story end with the grim familiarity of separation, she clung to the idea of Theo as a savior, one who would ride to her rescue, slay the dragons of her deepest fears, and provide the fairy-tale ending in which she would be cherished and not abandoned, never again left alone and unloved.

Building on the faint inklings of self-recognition that Maja had begun to discern, our subsequent sessions focused on two themes. The first was that there was no external savior and never would be. Only Maja could rescue herself from her worst fears by recognizing that abandonment is not inevitable, relationships do not follow a script, and intimacy requires an acceptance of people as they actually are, not as we wish or believe them to be.

The second was mourning, a central task of our therapy. Maja's troubled relationship with Theo was directly connected to the fact that she had never come to terms with her father's leaving, nor mourned his departure from large parts of her life. Their sporadic contact in the years that followed compounded the problem, reawakening her longing to connect and providing straws of hope at which to grasp. In later years she had also continued to see him in defiance of her mother's wishes, because Jade's means of coping with his abandonment had simply been to pretend he did not exist. This was a dangerous example that imprinted itself on Maja, teaching her that bitter reality could be undone through the power of will and the force of the imagination.

Mourning the loss of her father helped Maja to reconcile the pain it had caused her and to identify the tentacles that had stretched through her life as a result. Gradually, she began to see that she had transferred her need for a strong male protector first onto Max and later onto Theo. She recognized that her intense hatred for Saskia was a transference of her feelings toward her father's second wife and younger children: the people who had taken away the object of her desire. She also began to accept that by outsourcing her deepest emotional needs onto other people and expecting them to make her feel whole, she had let her own sense of identity erode to the point where it had almost disappeared altogether. Maja had allowed falling in love to become synonymous with falling apart. She had surrendered to fantasies that were an unconscious means of protecting her from pain but that ultimately dragged her into a deep pit of depression and self-harm.

It was only by escaping the dreamworld, freeing herself from the endless loop of cherished memories and disappointed dreams, that Maja was able to climb out. By coming to terms with the most painful events in her life, she regained her sense of self and control of her story. Most important, she began to recognize that she would never be able to have healthy love for another person until she rebuilt a relationship with herself: accepting strengths as well as faults, owning her past without being controlled by it, and abandoning the idea that she was a lost soul needing to be saved by another. Our relationship as patient and therapist, one that confounded her template for attachments and denied her the certainty of abandonment, provided a life raft during this process—helping her to navigate through mists separating fantasy from reality, and offering solid ground on which to experiment with healthier thoughts and feelings.

This was a slow, unsteady process that occupied two years of weekly therapy sessions. It took months of work to finally escape the maze of Maja's residual obsessions and lingering faith in her relationship with Theo. The script to which she had so closely clung in our initial meetings was not easily relinquished, even after she had started to doubt its veracity.

But her recovery, though gradual, was persistent. One milestone was restoring contact with her father, which led to regular visits with him and his family. The patient love he showed her allayed her fears about how he would treat the news of her conviction and helped to bolster her sense of identity as a person worth caring for. Another was her decision to return to college and begin a business studies degree. Here she began a new relationship with another student, Oscar, whom she told early about her history of stalking. Although we were both aware of the risks this posed, I encouraged the relationship, believing that Maja needed to prove to herself that she was capable of forming healthy bonds of attachment we had spent so much time exploring together. As their relationship developed, our sessions acted as a pressure valve when she was occasionally overwhelmed by the old feelings of insecurity and paranoia and the need to track Oscar's movements bubbled up. These intense fears and needs never left Maja, but she had learned to talk about them in preference to acting on them.

For Maja, as with so many patients I have worked with, recovery meant not elimination of the pain, trauma, and emotions that occupied her but control over them: an ability to recognize overwhelming feelings, work through them, and form them into a manageable shape. She was not free from her demons, but nor was she hostage to them any longer. It was her childhood experience that had left her vulnerable to pursuing the search for love in an extreme, almost desperate way. But this alone might not have led her to the point of stalking one victim and threatening deadly violence against another. That had come when her innate vulnerabilities fused with circumstances that detached Maja from her sense of self, the life with which she was familiar, and any kind of meaningful support system. Being away from home, in an unfamiliar social setting, and without friends or family to rely on had all contributed to Maja's separation from reality, allowing her to become subsumed by her fantasies. Reestablishing some of those familiar bonds was, therefore, an essential part of the recovery.

As the time came for our sessions to end, we both knew that there was one final hurdle to overcome. The conclusion of our work meant that, unavoidably, we would be confronting one of its abiding themes, that of abandonment. This was challenging for both of us. Maja was understandably wary of how she would cope without sessions that had become part of her routine.

Our final sessions were emotional. Maja told me about dreams in which she had been drowning at sea and watched me walking past, indifferent or oblivious. This left me concerned about how much she might struggle to recognize danger signs and self-soothe without my help. Yet I knew, difficult as it was, that this was the natural next step in Maja's recovery. A therapist can be a guide and guardian to help someone explore their past and steer their psyche toward safer ground. But there always comes a time when that individual has to be left to take the next steps independently, when further growth is not possible without first relinquishing contact with the therapist. I knew that I had to let her go out into the world without my watchful eye. I shared with Maja a thought that my own therapist had given me when our sessions were ending. In the year that follows the ending of the relationship, the patient can internalize their therapist, providing for themselves the voice of reason, patience, and challenge, as if they still had them to talk to. The therapist may be gone in reality, but a former patient can still benefit from their influence and imagined voice.

For someone who had once nurtured such an all-encompassing fantasy life, this idea of the imagined, internalized therapist was an intriguing one. Maja left me for the last time after commenting on how much she had learned about herself and how she had finally discovered that she did not need to be with a person all the time to trust them. I comforted myself with the implications of this parting gift. This woman whose life had been dominated and nearly destroyed by the fear of abandonment was at last able to bear the thought of being alone.

*

Women's violence toward their partners can arise, as it threatened to with Maja, from attachment that has turned into obsession. More common and often more serious is the violence that occurs within an abusive relationship, when a woman who has suffered years of relentless abuse from her partner reaches the point where she responds in kind. As the cases of Rachel Bellesen and more recently Penelope Jackson have shown, these are circumstances that can lead to extreme violence and even murder.

The questions of aggression and culpability within intimate partner relationships can be difficult to answer in the absence of medical evidence, police callouts, witness statements, or admissions of guilt by perpetrators. The recent verdict in the case of Amber Heard, who, without naming her ex-partner Johnny Depp, declared herself a victim of domestic abuse, was found in his favor, despite her allegations. He had sued her for defamation and won the case. In her statement, Heard attributed Depp's win squarely to that profile. "I'm heartbroken that the mountain of evidence still was not enough to stand up to the disproportionate power, influence, and sway of my ex-husband," she said. "I'm even more disappointed with what this verdict means for other women. It is a setback. It sets back the clock to a time when a woman who spoke up and spoke out could be publicly shamed and humiliated. It sets back the idea that violence against women is to be taken seriously."

I have worked with numerous women who would never have come into contact with me if they had not become entwined and trapped in a relationship with a man who was controlling and violent in a way that made their lives unlivable. These are stories that, in extreme cases, become tabloid fodder. Yet they are routinely told in a way that obscures the most important truth: how an abusive relationship that unfolds over a long period of time can become a trap in which a woman, fearing for her life, sees no outlet or escape except violence.

LILLIAN

Breaking Point

After suffering more than two decades of abuse from her aggressive and frequently violent husband, Lillian had stabbed him to death. She was sent to a psychiatric hospital for evaluation of her mental state and was eventually found guilty of manslaughter by virtue of diminished responsibility. Her story illustrated the complex dynamics of intimate partner violence: how abusers groom and entrap their victims through a combination of seduction, aggression, threats, controlling behavior, and the pretense of care. It also reveals how the victim of such abuse can become a killer. And it articulated a crucial question in such cases: How much responsibility should its victims bear for the violence that they have apparently been driven to by years of relentless abuse?

*

I knew from the start that Lillian would be different. That much was clear before a word had even passed between us, because she entered the room for our first session in a patterned dress and pearl necklace, a contrast to the slippers and sweatpants that were standard issue for patients in the secure unit where she was being held on remand. Over the top of the dress was a lavender cardigan, whose sleeves she picked at throughout our conversation. Completing this carefully considered appearance was her graying hair, held together in a neat bun. The first impression was of someone who was most likely to be here working with the unit's younger women, perhaps providing pastoral support. In fact Lillian had killed her husband of more than thirty years, stabbing him repeatedly while he slept. With a murder trial pending, multiple psychiatrists and psychologists were undertaking clinical assessments of her mental state to appear as expert witnesses. My job was not to support the legal process but to help Lillian, offering psychological treatment both while she awaited trial and, ultimately, in its aftermath.

As I concluded my opening explanation of how our work together would explore the factors that had led her to commit the offense, and that it would be treatment through talking rather than medication or occupation, that first impression solidified. This was not a patient like most I had worked with in the hospital setting. As her response made clear, she knew exactly why we were sitting together. I ended by asking if she had any questions. "No, dear. I know perfectly well what psychology is, the understanding of human behavior. You need to work with me to see if what I did was justifiable and rational, in the context of the abuse I suffered, or if I just went mad, for no reason. If I was a 'battered wife' who snapped. You are going to write reports about me and determine the rest of my life. I understand all too well. We had best get started, then. Fire away."

It is not unusual for forensic patients to present a challenging, even confrontational face. Some will try to gain control of the interaction as they see it and to probe for what feel like potential weak spots. But I had encountered few women who did so with such cool and clinical efficiency, prompting the rare feeling that a patient had seen right through me. It was not just Lillian's appearance that set her apart. In her tone, manner, and world-weary confidence she immediately established that she would be leading me through these sessions as much as I did her.

This self-possession was markedly at odds with the nature of her offense, a frenzied knife attack that had left a temporarily defense-less man dead, undertaken with the kind of brutality that does not normally come wrapped in pastel cardigans. It was that offense we now needed to unravel and explore, though not through the lens of guilt, innocence, and culpability. That much was in the hands of her clinical assessors and defense lawyers. My job was simply to develop an understanding of the patient and to establish whether she would benefit from treatment, and in what form. I had dozens of questions for and about Lillian, but the issue of her criminal responsibility was—on this occasion—not one of them.

*

The nature of Lillian's offense meant it was hard to begin our work with an entirely open mind, untouched by the questions and assumptions that such cases present. The tabloid binaries of a wife murdering her husband are hard to fully dispel. Did he deserve it? Was it cold-blooded revenge or an almost unconscious response to years of suffering? I also found myself torn between personal beliefs and professional experience. As a feminist, I was naturally disposed to see first the horror of domestic violence and to think primarily of the countless, often voiceless victims of toxic masculinity—abused or killed in a society that has consistently normalized the dehuman-ization of women and girls. Yet as a forensic psychotherapist I also knew that sometimes it is the woman who is the intimate partner terrorist, using tyranny to protect herself from the shame and terror she herself feels. I was disinclined to consider the possibility that Lillian's killing of her husband, Ray, was a calculated act of revenge for infidelity rather than a helpless, defensive act of violence against an abusive partner, but I knew that it was nevertheless possible. I recalled the much-reported case of Jean Harris, the killer of "the Scarsdale Diet doctor," Herman Tarnower. She had shot him four times, after their relationship had cooled and he had taken up with a younger woman, a secretary from his office. Though Harris claimed she had gone to his house armed with a gun in order to shoot herself in front of him, she was ultimately found guilty of murder, admitting in court that she was "certainly guilty of something." While the defense attorneys maintained that jealousy was not a factor during cross-examination, the prosecutor introduced a letter written just prior to the shooting in which Harris referred to her rival as an "ignorant slut" and "a vicious, adulterous psychotic."

Yet in Lillian I did not sense a vengeful nature, instead a calm, regretful world-weariness—a disbelief not only that she had committed an act of such uncharacteristic violence but that her life had ever turned out this way, so far from what she must have imagined when she met and married Ray. I thought I saw tears in her eyes as I asked her to tell me about her children and the family home. Both were now grown up—Jimmy, in his thirties and with children of his own, and Alice, a "career girl" who worked in marketing. There was pride but also bitterness in Lillian's voice as she described them to me: a happiness that they had built lives of their own beyond the abusive home in which they had grown up, but also a sense of shame at what they had seen and experienced, and perhaps a note of jealousy, alongside pride, toward the daughter who was now pursuing the kind of career that a controlling, domineering husband had consistently denied her.

Ray's violence, a consistent feature of their decades-long marriage, had started when Lillian was pregnant with Jimmy, hitting and bruising her in places that clothing would naturally cover up. He was a binge drinker who brooded over problems at work, both of which could be the precursor to violent outbursts. She recounted how this had led to a consistent pattern of verbal attacks at least twice a week and physical violence maybe twice in a typical month. The threats of such violence were enough to keep her on constant alert. As well as being a manifestation of his own fluctuating mental state, Ray's assaults were a means of controlling his wife. They had subsided while she took her first maternity leave after Jimmy was born and restarted when she expressed the wish to go back to work, resuming her career as a medical secretary.

As Lillian narrated the story of her early life with Ray, I was struck that she seemed to be reminiscing over it with a degree of affection as well as recalling events with fear and anxiety. Theirs was a marriage that had been scarred by abuse and ended in death, but those truths, while defining, were not the totality. It had also begun as a romantic pursuit like so many others and produced two children to whom Lillian continued to be devoted. That is not to imply a balance sheet of good and bad, but simply to recognize that even relationships that produce trauma and tragedy have much in common with those that would be considered normal. Women in Lillian's position are better served when their whole stories are heard, not apportioned into a grim highlights reel of the worst moments and most piercing traumas. Although I am probing for insight into the moments of greatest significance and meaning, I also need to let a patient tell me about their life in their own way and through their eyes. In this way I can understand how those moments arose and what they signify to the patient. It is a constant tussle between following and leading, prompting the patient and sometimes pressing them for extra details while trying to avoid imposing my own preconceptions.

Equally important is to remember the mental toll for a person of immersing themself once again in past trauma. Even for a woman as evidently self-possessed as Lillian, this was something that had to be managed carefully, the work done in small doses to avoid her feeling overwhelmed, as though she were back in the rooms of her home where the abuse had happened rather than in the hospital with me. I had initially suggested that we could begin at the end, focusing on the killing itself, but she demurred, making clear that she would rather work toward this and preferred to begin on the safer ground of their early relationship history and the lives of her children. Of course, I said, and reminded her that she was in charge of setting the pace of what we discussed: I was there to support, not interrogate. Even this was clearly fatiguing her, and after half an hour she asked if we could end the discussion early, a suggestion to which I quickly agreed. Lillian looked both relieved at having begun to unburden herself and exhausted by the effort it had taken.

As I wrote up my notes after she left, I was full of more questions, including about what had drawn this apparently unlikely couple together. While he was from a rough background, with little experience of care or nurture, Lillian's own history spoke of someone who took an instinctive interest in the needs and struggles of others. As the youngest child of well-off parents, she not only received good schooling and developed a lively interest in tennis and netball but spent time volunteering with the Samaritans, a telephone charity for people in states of distress. By the end of the meeting I was satisfied that an introduction that had begun in a struggle for control had ended in what felt like productive cooperation. Right at the end of the session, as Lillian's eyes lingered on me, it felt as if we had now met and the therapy itself could properly begin.

*

My work with Lillian was potentially a traumatizing undertaking for her, done at a time when she was already under significant strain, awaiting a trial that seemed likely to end in either a long prison sentence or a stay in a psychiatric hospital, regardless of whether the conviction was to be for murder or manslaughter on psychiatric grounds. Lillian's violent escape from decades of domestic violence had brought her to a point where she was on the verge of losing her liberty and access to the most precious things in her life: her children, her pets, and her home.

Initially she had been sent to prison to await trial, but her obvious state of distress and dissociation in the aftermath of Ray's killing meant that she was swiftly remanded to the hospital to be assessed under the Mental Health Act. This meant living under the microscope of the secure unit, moving at the age of fifty-five from a suburban home to a psychiatric clinic where all the doors were locked, patients had to be escorted everywhere by a nurse, and many of her fellow inhabitants were overtly mentally ill—whether displaying out-of-control behavior, acting violently toward each other or the staff, or self-harming in extreme and alarming ways. The deliberately soothing decor of the unit—potted plants, comfy furniture, and floor-to-ceiling windows—ultimately did little to dispel the threatening ambience that permeated the hallways, a barely repressed sense that violence was always about to explode into the piercing alarm that would send nurses running to find out who had "kicked off" now.

Alongside these sober realities was the psychological burden of knowing that she had killed another person, someone she had once loved. Whatever the circumstances, to take the life of another person is an action that carries an incalculable weight, one that is likely to make the perpetrator question their sanity. Individuals who have crossed this line will never be able to entirely trust themselves again, never be absolutely sure of the level of their self-control, or capable of dispelling the thought that it could somehow happen again. The line between the imaginary and the real has been irrevocably crossed, meaning they no longer feel safe in their fantasy worlds. Paranoia, PTSD, and depression are serious risk factors, and I had to consider the possibility that Lillian might become suicidal. It was for this reason that my work with her had to happen when it did, even though it meant asking her to confront her traumatic past with yet another psychologist, at a time of intense vulnerability and turmoil.

Unlike most of her fellow patients, Lillian did not decorate her room with posters, pictures of family, or stuffed toys. She had none of the comfort objects that were standard issue on the secure unit, nor did she allow herself to be seen as most did in dressing gown, pajamas, and slippers. She continued to be the neat, put-together woman I had first encountered, as ordered in her appearance as she appeared to be in her mind. When we convened for our second session, she met me in the ward's dayroom and sat waiting with a notebook. It contained notes she had been making from an old diary, which detailed the abuses and cruelties that she had consistently suffered at Ray's hands. Revisiting these entries from a former life, which revived events she had instinctively sought to repress, had helped her to remember more and made her eager to resume our conversation. The words seemed to tumble out of her as she recalled events from the past and the effect these memories continued to have on her. Even in death, Ray still haunted and scared her, now visiting her in a recurring dream in which he would hold out his hand and beckon her toward a door, a red rose in his hand, only to slam and lock it shut behind them as Lillian realized she had been lured into a narrow passageway with no escape. Beyond the locked door she could see Jimmy and Alice, appearing in the dream as children. Her body began to shake as she relayed this dream, one that appeared to be rooted in the recent experience of being locked away in prison, something that had caused her panic attacks during her first nights of incarceration. Other than seeking to reassure Lillian, reminding her that she was no longer in prison but in the hospital, that her children were grown up and Ray could no longer hurt her, I did little to disrupt a flow of confession that was picking up speed. Even as her hands shook, it was clear that she wanted to carry on and to continue her story.

Doing so seemed to bring her alive, as if a return to the certainties of the past were a balm against the anxiety and torment of the present. She lost herself in the story; having been so weighed down by the thought of blood on her hands, she temporarily shifted the burden, forgetting for a moment the prospect of the trial and incarceration that lay ahead. Lillian wanted to begin at the beginning, not hers or theirs, but his, a "feral" childhood on the streets of a city in the North of England, with a mentally ill mother who was in and out of psychiatric hospitals, a father who was rarely present, and siblings it was left to Ray to provide for. He became a familiar face in the area, first to family and neighbors as "a charity case" and later to the police as a teenager who was drifting into a life of petty crime and street fighting.

Even now, after years and years of abuse from Ray, she seemed to be interested in the reasons why he had done these things to her; what had compelled him to become such a brutalizing force in the life of another person. Remarkably, some part of her still seemed to care for him, to want to understand his struggles and empathize with them. There was bitterness and shame in her voice as she recounted the often grim details of his domestic violence, but it was impossible to ignore that the same voice sometimes conveyed interest, compassion, and even the faint shadow of affection.

This unlikely couple from opposite backgrounds had met at the GP's surgery where she worked as a medical secretary and he was a patient. She was charmed by his accent, his humor, and his unsubtly determined pursuit of a date with her. At thirty-one to her twenty-five he was unlike any of her previous boyfriends, or indeed any of her friends. She quickly found herself swept up by the wave of attention he showered on her, his athletic good looks, and the bond she felt between them as he shared traumatic details of his early life and how his childhood had left him feeling unlovable. She set aside her natural caution about letting a relationship move forward too quickly, instead allowing Ray to drive the intense pace of their dating life, enjoying how much he obviously wanted her and the compliments that made her feel like the most desirable woman in the world. Within a year they were married, despite the quiet warnings of friends who suggested that Lillian was acting out of character. She thought them snobbish, looking down on a man who worked in a factory while they held comfortable white-collar jobs. As they entered married life, she said, Ray became her whole world. It was only now, with more than thirty years of perspective, that she could see this was exactly what he had intended.

Having already overcome creeping doubts to come this far, Lillian continued to dispel them into the first year of their marriage. The characteristics that had so drawn her to Ray began to reveal themselves as problems. His vulnerability was beginning to manifest itself as insecurity; his intense affection for her as possessiveness. She was making adjustments to her life to accommodate and placate him, without fully recognizing the trap into which she was falling. She stopped wearing makeup because Ray preferred her "fresh-faced," and she began to withdraw from nights out with her girl-friends in order to avoid the conversations when she returned home to find him waiting up, pelting her with questions about whom she had been with and what they had been doing. His behavior was becoming overtly controlling: even if he knew she was out with friends, he would insist on Lillian calling him before midnight with an estimated time for her return home. He bought her blouses he described as "feminine," to be worn in preference to the low-cut tops she favored. And when she went out with a male friend, Sam, his questioning of her became so intense and bad-tempered that she started seeing him in secret and eventually stopped altogether, even though these were nothing more than platonic social occasions between childhood friends.

Ray's control and possessiveness only intensified after Lillian became pregnant with Jimmy, emotional abuse that was presented as loving concern. This reflected a common pattern in domestic violence cases where abuse may first be seen during a pregnancy, often a warning sign of future escalation. He would talk to her daily about the possibility that she might harm the baby or miscarry, using this as a pretext to insist that she not meet friends at night. When she did so during the day, he would insist on coming to collect her, bringing the car over at a time of his and not her choosing. He was also beginning to drink more, going on heavier binges that would usually culminate in his breaking down in tears, shouting at Lillian, and accusing her of cheating on him. When she was six months pregnant, he went out to a bar after being passed over for a promotion at work, returning drunk and demanding that she hand over her phone. Having interrogated her about every innocent message on it, he then found one from Sam, an exchange from a week earlier when she had been venting about a recent argument, after Ray had stopped her from going to a close friend's bridal shower. Discovering the conversation with another man and seeing that he had been disparaged sent Ray into a frenzy. Without warning he grabbed her by the throat and shouted that he would kill her if she didn't confess to the affair with Sam. Just to make it stop, Lillian heard herself begging him for forgiveness and crying that she had not betrayed him.

It was at this point that Lillian stepped back from the flow of a story that seemed to be gripping her, as if she were encountering it for the first time. This was perhaps the pivotal moment in their entire marriage, she thought, one where it became unambiguously clear that Ray posed a danger to her. It was the first time in Lillian's life that she had ever faced physical violence or intimidation. She woke the next morning shaking and ashamed, going through in her head a plan to leave Ray, return to her parents, and call the police. It was, she now believed, the closest she ever came to getting herself out of the relationship, escaping its shadow before the worst of the abuse had begun. She now blamed herself for having stayed, even as she recognized that it was impossible to know then how perilous her situation would later become. Instead, she had allowed herself to be swayed by a desperate and penitent Ray, who was on his knees apologizing and beseeching her to forgive him. He said he felt suicidal that he had hurt her and vowed that it would never happen again.

He had taken the day off work and proceeded to shower her with attention reminiscent of their early dating days, taking her out to lunch and for a walk in the park, bringing her cups of tea and ice packs for the bruising that was visible around her neck. In retrospect, Lillian could see a malign intent she had not recognized at the time. By staying at home and attaching himself to her for the day, Ray was effectively closing off her escape route, ensuring that she could not flee to the safety of her parents' home, call her close friends, or contact the police. Like many abusers, he purported to be caring when he was actually controlling. He was also gaslighting his victim, claiming that it was he who was vulnerable, at risk of harming or even killing himself if she chose to leave him. His insistence on her power and his relative weakness confused her, seeming wrong and illogical. He told her she was crazy not to see he was right. The strangulation itself—a symbolic form of intimidation that has now been written into legislation as a specific criminal offense that can carry a prison sentence—was matched by Ray's desire to restrict his wife's options in its aftermath. He left nothing to chance, ensuring that she had little choice but to accept his apologies and turn further inward. His ploy succeeded, because she cut off all contact with Sam and began to be more selective about relationships with her female friends, avoiding those for whom Ray had expressed his dislike.

The harder Lillian tried to placate her abusive and controlling husband, the worse his abuse became. With the help of her diary,

Lillian recalled that he had been violent to her for a second time late in her pregnancy. Ray had been checking and cross-referencing dates and had convinced himself that Jimmy's conception matched one of the occasions when she had met Sam. He became certain that the baby was not his and, after another binge-drinking session, lost control, pushing Lillian against the frame of an open door and threatening to punch her in the stomach, over which she had protectively wrapped her arms. He ended up kicking her in the leg and spitting in her face, before storming out and spending the night sleeping in his car, returning with a note that again threatened suicide if she refused to take him back and promise that the baby was his.

The abuse, intimidation, and coercion continued throughout what became a long marriage, at a constant low pitch that would sometimes explode without warning. Although Ray was only infrequently physically violent toward Lillian, the memory of when he had been, and the threat of it, were enough to ensure that she effectively remained his hostage throughout their children's early lives and for years after they had left home. More persistent was the controlling behavior. Ray would monitor her phone relentlessly and act toward her houseguests in such a way that discouraged further visits. As well as seeking to limit her social life, he chipped away at her confidence, berating her especially harshly if she ever tried to assert herself and calling her an unfit mother. His abuse led to Lillian's becoming depressed and more reliant on alcohol, which precipitated further verbal attacks as he played on her fears that she was an alcoholic and could lose the children into foster care if he notified them of her "unfitness"—another threat that he consistently held over her head as leverage.

He was also a hypocrite, engaging in the kinds of extramarital affairs that he had frequently and falsely accused his wife of, projecting onto her the reality of his own infidelity. Ray made little attempt to cover his tracks, but when Lillian questioned him about seeing other women, he simply told her that it was her fault and that she was incapable of satisfying his high sex drive. On other occasions he simply denied it and called her crazy and paranoid. By this point his psychological hold over her had become so strong that she did indeed sometimes doubt her own suspicions. While Ray was increasingly flagrant in pursuing affairs, he continued to use the false accusation that Lillian had been unfaithful to abuse her. On one occasion he put the family's dog collar around her neck and threatened to walk her down the street naked wearing it, before finally taking it off and beating her with it, shouting to the children, who had been woken by their mother's screaming, to stay in their rooms.

Ray's treatment of Lillian fitted a characteristic pattern of domestic violence in which the abuser subjects their partner to a level of intimidation, coercion, and aggression that affords them control over almost all aspects of their life. The abusive partner exercises psychological control to the point where physical violence is no longer necessary. The victim can often be so accustomed to suffering abuse that they become numb to it, accepting their fate and making no effort to escape it, believing that any attempt to do so would either fail or lead to worse consequences.

The law around domestic violence in the UK has evolved significantly in recent years. The introduction of the principle of coercive control into legislation has given a criminal definition to a reality that clinicians have long recognized: an abuser does not actually have to physically hurt their victim in order to harm them. I have worked on countless such cases over my career, but rarely had I heard anyone articulate as fully as Lillian did the torture of an abuse that pulls its victim in deeper with every angry word or violent outburst. She read an entry to me from her diary, written after the second time Ray had assaulted her while pregnant with their son: "I hated him so much for what he had done, but loved him too. His pain was unbearable to see and I knew he hadn't meant to harm me, but what will he do next time? What do I do if I leave him? I know if I leave, he will kill himself, and I can't bear to bring my son into this world without a father. I have no one I can tell this to. Never felt so alone. I just hope if I can bring him joy with this son, and he loves him too, he will finally feel reassured, and stop this craziness. I can't quite believe this charming man I fell in love with has become a monster."

*

While the shocking details of Lillian's story were sadly familiar to me from similar cases, the ending to it was not. Over sessions spanning several weeks, Lillian had talked me through her relationship with Ray, tracing its many humiliations, the constant low hum of undermining or controlling behavior, and the occasional peaks of shocking violence. Yet she had consistently deferred the moment at which we would address the event that had brought her here in the first place. Only as the trial approached did she finally feel ready to talk to me about the day she had killed her husband.

The killing was the culmination not just of three decades of abuse but of a more recent escalation in their relationship and his behavior. With the children having now left the family home, Ray had progressively been losing control, hitting Lillian in places that could not be covered up. On one occasion he had left her with cuts under a black eye, which had led to her canceling a visit to her now elderly parents. On another he had strangled her for the first time since she was pregnant with Jimmy. Lillian felt that she was increasingly in danger from a man whose abuse was becoming even more consistent and who was no longer making any attempt to conceal his extramarital activities, which included openly using telephone sex lines within her earshot. His potency waning, he needed ever more extreme sexual fantasies to arouse him, and this seemed to feed into his careless use of chat lines. If he was aware that Lillian could hear him, he didn't care or, worse, enjoyed the pain and humiliation it caused her. Had he been my patient, I could have confronted him with the sadistic way he treated Lillian and how his rage at all womankind was being enacted against her. I would have tried to move away from his aggression, to treat the depression that underlay and fueled it, and taken practical steps to safeguard his family—asking him if he had weapons in the home and what he could do to ensure he didn't lose control entirely. But he was not my patient and I had no controls over his aggression, either internally or externally imposed; nor, it seemed, had he.

As well as being more fearful about what Ray might do next, Lillian was beginning to see the possibilities of a different life for the first time in decades. When the children had been at home and Ray had successively threatened that he would either call in child protective services to have them taken away or turn the force of his abuse toward them, she had simply hunkered down and determined that accepting her fate was the best way to protect the people she loved most. Now the focus of her fears had switched. She worried that, trapped in Ray's dark universe and with her own life at risk, she might miss out on her children's adult lives and lose the chance to play a full role in those of her grandchildren. She started to consider telling her parents, who had never liked Ray but knew only a fraction of the abuse to which he had subjected their daughter, the truth of her marriage. And, as her fifty-fourth birthday approached, she recognized that not much time remained in which to salvage anything from the career she had once dreamed of having. This spurred her into applying for jobs, something she had been too afraid for years to attempt but that now quickly led to a job offer in her old role as a medical secretary.

It was this return to work that caused an already volatile situation to escalate to an unbearable peak. Due to attend an induction at work on the Monday morning, Lillian was faced with a drunk and angry Ray returning home from the bar on Sunday night. He was immediately in her face, threatening to prevent her from leaving the house the next day and accusing her of trying to start a new life without him. Lillian had experienced so many of these verbal assaults over the years that she was accustomed to keeping herself calm and limiting the damage. But, faced with a threat to the independence she had again begun to dream of, on this occasion she snapped and returned like with like. Yes, she screamed at him, she did want a new life. She was going to leave him. She would rather die than remain a hostage in her own home. There was nothing left to keep her here. Ray flew into an even greater rage. He put his arms around her throat, pushed her to the floor, and retained his stranglehold for what felt like forever, threatening to stop her breathing. He spat on her and kept her on the floor with his hands, at which point she thought she was about to die. He finally released her but kicked her while she lay and then punched her in the face so forcefully that she almost passed out. He staggered away and kicked one of their dogs, hard, as he walked toward the living room.

In sickening pain, Lillian realized that a bruise was already beginning to form around her eye. Almost as quickly, she concluded that she would have to call in sick for the induction. She was horrified to see the dog whimpering in pain in the corner of the room, a vulnerable creature who had done no harm to anyone. She felt like that dog, helpless and injured—a creature that Ray would say he loved and cared for, denying his cruelty toward it. Animal abuse is not uncommon in situations of intimate partner terrorism and is a form of intimidation and cruelty—the perpetrator effectively conducting a rehearsal of future violence, giving a demonstration of what he is capable of, and revealing his absolute willingness to attack something beloved.

In the most brutal manner, Ray had destroyed the dream of freedom that Lillian had begun to nurture in the preceding weeks and months. As the argument raged, he had taunted her for being a washed-up old bag, saying that he was seeing a younger woman who was much better in bed than she had ever been. He then wielded one of his perennial threats. If Lillian tried to leave him, he would punish Alice—hurting her, her children, and their dogs. She was used to his macho posturing and threats, but this one she believed. He had often boasted of having been involved with organized crime, being able to get hold of guns, and she had no doubt that he was capable of almost anything, including harming his own daughter just to punish her.

Amid this gruesome assault, Lillian remembered a moment of almost calm clarity settling over her as she caught sight of her reflection in the mirror and took in the horror of her bloodied nose and bruised face. This was the moment she realized her life had been destroyed and her dream of freedom was never going to be fulfilled. Hot terror and pain had given way to cold rage and resolve. Walking into the living room, she found that Ray had fallen into a drunken sleep, a half-finished drink spilled in his lap and the glass on the floor by his feet. She remembered a feeling of elation that in this state he was temporarily incapable of harming her. She said that she had felt calm, determined, and composed—as if all the adrenaline had suddenly drained from her body. She walked into the kitchen and took the sharpest knife from the drawer. After she had punctured his chest multiple times with it, he was dead.

*

When we sat in the small consulting room on the secure ward, it was eighteen months since the day she had killed Ray, but Lillian was speaking as if it had just happened. After stabbing him, she had called the police, who arrived to find her shaking, repeating words over and over to herself. Arrest and incarceration followed, but mentally she kept finding herself back in the living room of her house, revisiting the final argument of her marriage, the feeling of his hands strangling her and that of the knife entering his chest. These recollections, she said, would often prompt panic attacks that left her shaking, sweating, and forced to take short, shallow breaths.

At the time we began working together, Lillian was approaching trial and considering how she intended to plead. She had two serious options: to plead not guilty and argue that she had acted in self-defense, or to plead guilty to manslaughter on grounds of diminished responsibility, positing that she had been of "unsound mind" when she stabbed Ray. When she chose the latter path, I was both relieved that she was spared a prison sentence—instead being committed to the psychiatric hospital until she was deemed fit to reenter the community—and frustrated that she had found herself in a position where she effectively had to plead insanity to avoid the consequences of an action that had become inescapable to her. The legal record would always show not that a serially abusive husband had forced her into a trap from which she felt that the only escape was to kill but that Lillian had been suffering from what the Mental

Health Act defines as "an abnormality of mental functioning," in her case a depressive disorder with features of "learned helplessness" or "battered woman syndrome." Although I understood the logic of her legal team—that a plea of self-defense would incur the unreasonable risk of relying on a jury to agree that she had faced a legitimate threat to life—I found the decision hard to take. It felt, at least in technical terms, as if the wrong victim were being blamed. The killing was a rational one, if unpalatable. I understood Lillian's appraisal that her life would be at risk if she were to make an attempt to escape Ray, and could see how her crime might be considered one of self-defense. Charles Ewing describes the term "psychic extinction" as an aspect of years of intimate partner terrorism, adding further weight to the notion of killing an abusive, controlling partner as an act of rational self-defense in an intolerable situation. The eminent lawyer Baroness Helena Kennedy outlines the historical difficulty of securing justice for women who have killed violent partners after suffering years of abuse. Baroness Kennedy has been influential in creating welcome changes in judicial outcomes for women similar to Lillian and greater acceptance of the pleas of self-defense on the basis of provocation.

For years Lillian had discounted the possibility that she could leave the marriage that had scarred her adult life. She had entered a state of learned hopelessness, resigned to her fate. Yet her situation was not a static one. From the moment she had expressed the desire to return to work and regain a little of the personal freedom her younger self had taken for granted, Ray had increased his controlling behavior. His appalling attack on her that Sunday evening was a marked escalation that left Lillian believing that he really meant it when he said he would kill her and harm their daughter if she tried to leave him. I felt there was no question that she had taken Ray's life out of fear for her own and her daughter's, killing him because the levels of control, violence, and abuse had become such that she simply saw no other way of escaping her predicament.

Her plea of manslaughter on grounds of diminished responsibility was accepted. I was pleased to resume my work with Lillian when she returned to the hospital after her trial. Following this we had two years of weekly sessions, focused on further unpacking the legacies of her abusive marriage and supporting her recovery from depression and PTSD. The sessions then continued for another year on a fortnightly basis while Lillian was living in the predischarge unit on the grounds, preparing for her return to a home that would now finally be safe to live in.

Our work together illustrated the disturbing realities of domestic violence and coercive control, a form of abuse that by its very nature helps to guarantee its own continued existence. It is parasitical, feeding off the love and affection that brought two people together in the first place and the equally vivid emotions it then supplants them with. Lillian described the many ways in which she had felt trapped, unable to escape a relationship and a home that placed her at constant risk of harm. Partly this was the shame that so many domestic violence victims experience: the feeling that the only thing worse than what they are experiencing would be for anyone to find out about it. Partly it was guilt, an inescapable sense that she must be somehow to blame, one fed by Ray's constant gaslighting. And most of all it was pure fear, a fear that the consequences of leaving would exceed even those she faced on a daily basis. Fear not for herself but for her children and of what would happen if she left and Ray gained full custody of them. And she still feared that Ray would kill himself if she left.

The question "why didn't she just leave?" is often asked of women in Lillian's situation. To those without direct experience it seems so easy. Lillian's case was one of many in my career that have underlined how simplistic and misguided a view this is. Alongside the emotional snares of the abuse are its practical implications: a woman trying to leave a violent relationship faces the reality of also cutting herself off from many shared friends and family. Shelters do exist, but their reach is limited and some women are put off by the perceived stigma or very real insecurity associated with them. Often there are children to take into account, with a mother valuing the stability of their lives within current arrangements above their own safety (it is also true that the need to protect children can be a factor that finally compels some women to leave). Even going to social workers, child protective services, or the police to report domestic violence carries the risk that the household will be declared unsafe and the mother unable to protect the children from harm; that they will be taken into state care. When combined, these practical and psychological forces amount to a forbiddingly high wall to climb. And, almost always, there is not just a voice in someone's head telling them it's better to stay but a real one, a voice they once loved and have come to fear and despise. There are threats of suicide or, worse, homicide followed by suicide. As with Ray, the jolting episodes of violence are so often followed by pleas for forgiveness and vows to change—yet another hurdle separating the idea of leaving from the reality.

Dealing with the psychological legacies of this act was a core part of our work over several years, helping Lillian to understand that she was in effect an abuse and trauma victim, not a murderer or monster. Even though she knew she had acted out of fear and necessity, the weight of having killed the man she once loved still had a profound effect on her. The guilt that she had unreasonably felt as Ray's victim had now taken on a new form as she absorbed the gravity of her actions, necessary as they might have appeared to her. His last, perhaps even cruelest, legacy to Lillian was that he had driven her to commit an act of such extreme consequences that they would always remain with her. She felt, in a sense, that she had become him.

Alongside this guilt was Lillian's growing feeling of anger as she was able to look back on the years of her marriage from our shared vantage point. Even though she had gone to great lengths to conceal the truth of Ray's abuse from others in her life, she felt certain that her friends and family must have had some inkling of what was going on, enough instinct and intuition to read between the lines and see that all was far from well. Reliving her marriage in the cold light of day forced Lillian to confront not just her own actions but the silence that had surrounded decades of domestic abuse and the belief that others could have done more to help her—that perhaps some part of her long ordeal could in fact have been averted.

Therapy could not help Lillian fully relinquish these thoughts and feelings. The emotional landscape of an abusive marriage had become an inseparable part of her, too entwined with her sense of self ever to be left behind. But that did not mean she was doomed to remain fully at the behest of her past. By understanding her actions through the lens of trauma and being treated for her PTSD, by learning to identify the triggers to her panic and using techniques to reduce the effect of traumatic memories, she began to gain control over emotions that had once overwhelmed her. Through painstaking psychotherapeutic work she began to explore conscious and unconscious forces within her and to see the toxic dynamics of her marriage that had bound her so tightly. She learned that the anger was a part of her, one that needed to be understood and ultimately deserved to be forgiven.

In parallel, we focused on rebuilding the corners of her psyche that had once been equally intrinsic to her sense of self but that the long years of abuse had persistently worn away. We found opportunities for her to be an educator, as well as carer and nurturer: she became an increasingly central figure in the life of the secure unit, a maternal influence to those around her who took a leading role in many activities and helped patients with little or no literacy to write letters home. This, more than anything, helped provide Lillian with a viable path back from the secure unit to her life in the outside world. It gave her a sense of purpose and identity, helping her to feel like a person again, not the monster she had believed herself to be during the eighteen months she had spent constantly reliving the moment of Ray's killing. She continued to find outlets for that purpose once she had left the ward, spending much of her time advocating for women's rights, alongside a fulfilling life with family and friends.

Lillian continued to battle with her feelings of guilt and shame even after some degree of normality had returned to her life. She was able to resume life in the community, but carried the notoriety of her crime with her, along with a sense of fear that would overwhelm her at times, waking in a panic after the nightmare of being trapped by Ray returned. She found herself ruminating about whether and how she could have found a different way to escape from Ray and to keep her mind from fragmenting to the point where she felt killing was the only solution. To this day she still writes me occasional letters that detail these inner struggles. As was the case during our years of therapy, the question of forgiveness is a running theme, something she was never fully prepared to accept. Lillian was and is a complex, highly intelligent woman, reluctant to accept simple explanations or embrace the comfort of broad brushstrokes. She resisted some of the conclusions toward which I was trying to draw her even as she acknowledged their truth. But she learned to live with herself, to carry the burden that years of trauma had left her with, while also enjoying a life with the people she cared about most, free at least in body from the man who had terrorized her. She came to understand that she had exchanged his life for hers.

*

Lillian's case showed how years of enduring private, hidden violence can finally break a woman, until the moment when she swaps roles with her abusive partner and takes on his rage in a desperate act of self-preservation. At last the body speaks, and years of pain and violence break through. Violence for Lillian felt like her only way of surviving and might actually have been so.

Her experience is common to so many women who entered relationships with men who appeared to be caring and considerate but over time revealed themselves to be abusers. Some are able to escape these relationships at the early signs of trouble or after an initial incident, but many are not. Toxic relationships can drag women into committing acts of violence that otherwise appear entirely out of character and that they would never have believed themselves capable of. The tabloid sensationalism that surrounds the most high-profile of these cases means they are presented as salacious soap

operas, rather than the grim stories of domestic abuse and men's violence against women that they really are. The apparently inconceiv-
able act of a woman committing serious violence becomes the focus
of attention, while the man's violence against her that precipitated it
is viewed as unremarkable.

My work with Lillian showed how violence can stem from
abusive relationships and the desperation that they create. While
the case of Maja demonstrated that it is not just the experience of
romantic partnership that may take a dangerous turn but the search
for it. Almost everyone has romantic and sexual fantasies of some
description, but for women like Maja these become more than a
pleasant distraction from life or occasional daydream. Over time
they overwhelm reality itself, detaching those who experience erotomania from normality in a way that can be dangerous to them and
others.

Every human life is defined by relationships, romantic or otherwise, and the experience of them, both good and bad. A relationship of some description has been essential to understanding every
violent woman I have worked with. These women are motivated by
the deep human need to form attachments, but are often led toward
violence by relationship templates that substitute abusive behavior
for love. Their search for love, which they might never have experienced or known only at a particular point in time, becomes an
experience of violence, whether as victim, perpetrator, or both. The
act of violence, especially if a singular one like Lillian's, becomes
defining, erasing everything that has come before. I believe we owe
these women understanding: not to think of them solely in the context of their crime, but to give credence to the years or even decades
of abuse that put them into a position where it felt unavoidable and
inescapable. Only then can we understand how frequently the pursuit of love and the committing of violence prove to be two sides of
the same coin.

Conclusion

The hundreds of women I have worked with during my career encompass the full spectrum of female violence: women who have harmed themselves, their children, or their partners, and a few who, while experiencing delusions, have attacked total strangers. My patients have variously been trapped in repeating cycles of trauma, been compelled to re-create the twisted bonds of attachment imprinted in early life, and acted out of fear or desperation, or in the grip of severe mental illness that takes them outside the realm of reality. Their stories have moved and shaken me, prompting feelings of concern and shock about the horrors many have survived and some have perpetrated. A few have left me—even with years of training and decades of therapeutic experience—feeling helpless in my capacity to change the relentless power of delusional conviction or to deter the compulsion to repeat and reenact past trauma. But many more leave me inspired: women who have endured some of the worst things imaginable yet have gradually been able to reclaim and rebuild their lives, turning a legacy of trauma and abuse into a future of tentative hope and possibility. It is these women who live in my mind, giving me hope in the possibility of recovery and redemption.

One reality unifies this work, with women of all ages, backgrounds, and life experiences. Every therapeutic encounter that begins will end, whether at its natural conclusion or foreshortened by circumstance or the patient's choice. Every woman whose life I have temporarily lived alongside—whether for a few hours or a few years—will one day leave my office for the last time, rarely to return. These partings sometimes come amid concern and worry about what awaits that patient. With others, there is hope and optimism about their potential to find a form of safety and stability. Although I cannot know what will happen next to the woman with whom I have become intimately acquainted unless she writes to tell me, I generally feel hopeful. I believe that a good therapeutic relationship endures beyond the limits of the actual sessions: the containment that I offered, the ideas and understanding we shared, and the relationship we established can all remain with and within the patient, anchors and reminders to return to at times of stress. This inner sense of "home" and being kept in mind can endure, sustaining a patient for years to come.

In turn, the memory of my patients also stays with me. I think often about Mary, who was able to live a quiet and fulfilled life again in the community after decades of suffering in near silence; and about Paula, whose fear and anger had cast such a long shadow, but who was finally able to emerge from it and allow herself to love again. Both women, who for so long obscured their pain with violence, were examples of what psychotherapy can achieve: a secure relationship that acts as a springboard back toward others, helping a patient to learn again how to give and receive care. Others whose stories I have told in this book, including Tania and Maja, remind me of how therapy can be an act of acceptance for people who have mostly known rejection in their lives. For both of these young women, a critical step was being understood for their vulnerability rather than decried and exiled for their crimes.

The cases that most frequently haunt my dreams are those of mothers who have killed, often out of love, deluded and tragic. The recent case of a mother shortly before Christmas 2022, who appeared to have major mental illness, killing her two young sons and concealing their bodies, shocked New York City. And yet, like Dolores, this mother, Dimone Fleming, may have been unaware of the irrevocable nature of her actions, taken over by a delusional belief that she had to murder these boys, the very sons she loved. That their father discovered their bodies hidden in the bathtub, a horror beyond his wildest imagination, may be construed by the prosecution as evidence that Fleming's acts were fueled by revenge fantasies, and, if the jury is sympathetic to this notion, will be accepted as such. This could, in certain states, result in her death. If, however, the defense is able to attest to her likely mental illness, potentially a postpartum psychosis, she may be spared life-sentence imprisonment. But this will not free her from a lifelong sentence of grief and self-loathing that may ultimately lead her to suicide.

In March 2023 a fifty-six-year-old Belgian woman, Geneviève Lhermitte, was euthanized at her own request. In 2007 Lhermitte had killed her son and four daughters, aged three to fourteen, while their father was away. Like Dolores, she had tried to end her own life after killing the children, but this failed and she had then called for help, eventually being sentenced first to life imprisonment and later to a psychiatric hospital. With echoes of Dolores's story, she had used a knife to end the short lives of her children, and ultimately found another method to end her own.

How are we to understand the motivations of someone who betrays all of our cherished notions of maternal love? How is a jury? And, finally, how can a woman who enacts such a crime ever feel at peace? The description of Fleming outside a shelter, "ranting" and repeating the harrowing question "What I did?" is both poignant and revealing. While a part of her seemed to have been overtaken by a conviction that she had to kill, this would have been only a portion of her personality, a part of her encapsulated in space and time, disconnected with her "real" self, the mother who loved and nurtured her children. Like Dolores, she is a woman whose violence and illness went underground, until, tragically, it was too late. The devastation of the father finding the bodies of his children, as he did, and of Fleming, when she, as one imagines she will, recovers from what appears a transient state of dangerous delusion, is hard to bear. How can she ever feel at peace? Like Dolores, will she find the only solution to profound guilt and grief to lie in her own death? And most of all, one thinks of the victims, the little boys whose mother was the person they turned to for love, protection, and care, but who dealt them death. The fear and pain they may have felt is perhaps too awful to contemplate, and yet through understanding the complex factors that led to their deaths, and imagining the unimaginable, it might be possible to spare the lives of future victims. With this aim in mind, we, as a society, must attend closely to these kinds of crimes rather than relegate them to acts of individual evil. Through careful analysis of these offenses, despite the pain it may bring, and deconstruction of the mental state and social circumstances of the mothers, we can begin to identify the warning signs of maternal danger more accurately.

Societal and medical neglect of such phenomena as postpartum psychosis and depression-desperate states of mind that can lead to such crimes only take us further from this goal. Tragedies like the deaths of Andrea Yates's children, Lyndsey Clancey's, and those of Dimone Fleming might have been prevented with greater knowledge and awareness of these conditions. As Jessica Winter described in her recent article in *The New Yorker*, " 'Postpartum psychosis has been around for thousands of years, and yet it is not an official disease category in the *DSM-5*,' Veerle Bergink, the director of the Women's Mental Health Program at Mount Sinai, told me. 'There is no money for it, not for research, not for treatment. There are no guidelines. This is one of the most severe conditions in psychiatry, one that has huge impacts on the mother and potentially on the child, and there's nothing.' "

My contact with violent women has taught me not just about trauma and how victims of abuse may become its perpetrators, but also about my own impulses, fears, wishes, and intense feelings. At different times I find myself wanting either to protect or to punish my patients, or to magically transform their lives and undo their pasts.

I have also learned much about the violence and intolerance of a society that cannot bear the truth of women's agency and complexity, choosing instead to idealize and then vilify women, casting out those who are violent as pariahs rather than recognizing the complex reality of their situations and offering support. This attitude will only further perpetuate the cycles of abuse and trauma by continuing to stigmatize some of the most vulnerable women in society, imprisoning them both psychologically and physically.

The forces that lead women to acts of violence are not simply related to their own psychology and trauma histories, but are also responses to societal pressures. In the United States today, there are immediate and pressing concerns that increase the risk to women and whose significance has to be highlighted. Most acts of violence are not cases of individual evil or psychopathy, but the manifestation of complex toxic forces acting together to create a perfect storm. A vulnerable and isolated woman experiencing a traumatic event may find herself taking action that she will regret forever. And yet greater numbers of young females in the United States are being harmed; the recent report on Youth Risk Behavior published in 2021 by the Centers for Disease Control and Prevention's Division of Adolescent and School Health, citing ten years of data collected from high school students, found that the prevalence of experiences of violence, including sexual violence, suicidal thoughts, and mental health difficulties, had dramatically increased, especially in adolescent girls, over the past ten years. Against this bleak picture, there was some reduction in risky sexual behavior and substance misuse.

Key findings related to female students in this population study, representative of students across the United States, included shocking statistics:

> Nearly 20 percent of female students had experienced sexual violence by anyone, and nearly 15 percent had ever been forced to have sex.

> The percentage of female students who experienced sexual violence by anyone increased from 2017 to 2021.

> Young people who feel hopeless about their future are more likely to engage in behaviors that put them at risk for HIV, STDs, and unintended pregnancy.

The escalation of risky behaviors in young women and its link to those who have been subjected to physical and sexual abuse have direct relevance to this book's exploration of female violence. These young women are at risk of turning this violence against themselves in the form of self-harm or harm to others, including their intimate acquaintances or, in teenage mothers, their children.

In conjunction with the findings of the increase of risky behavior and experiences of sexual violence in women, and mental health issues that could lead to increased reliance on substances—also linked to sexual risk-taking, itself leading to sexually transmitted infections and unintended pregnancy—the new abortion laws following the June 2022 case of *Dobbs v. Jackson Women's Health Organization* are highly relevant. In this landmark case the Supreme Court overturned the constitutionally protected right to access abortion, leaving the question of whether and how to regulate abortion to individual states. A recent report on human rights describes this as a human rights crisis and notes that approximately 22 million women and girls of reproductive age in the U.S. now live in states where their access to abortion is severely restricted, and often totally inaccessible.

As described, thousands of women who become pregnant may find themselves with no choice but to go to term, and for some, this may become an impossible situation. Additionally, there are serious implications for those pregnant girls and women who are under correctional services in the U.S., many of whom may not yet have come to trial, or are under parole or probation restrictions, which mean they are not free to travel to those states that would allow them legal abortions. For some women, the fact of their pregnancy is so shameful that they conceal it from friends and family and may even kill their baby within the first twenty-four hours of life—neonaticide—to hide their shame and terror of stigma.

This crime of neonaticide is one whose true prevalence rate is not known but is thought to be significantly higher than those cases that are detected. The phenomenon of women whose pregnancy is so shocking and unwanted that it is not even acknowledged by their conscious minds is known as hysterical denial of pregnancy and can also result in a woman giving birth without full awareness of what has been happening within her body. Various motivations for neonaticide have been described in a recent study in the United Kingdom, highlighting the role of distress and desperation in women who kill their babies in the first twenty-four hours of life.

An analysis of neonaticide in the U.S. revealed the significance of the stressors facing the mothers and some of the characteristics that increase risk of this outcome, outlining some strategies to prevent this. Many of the mothers committing neonaticide are young and unmarried and have concealed their pregnancies. An unwanted pregnancy, sometimes denied by the woman unconsciously, or consciously concealed, could send an already vulnerable and traumatized woman over the edge. Faced with an unplanned pregnancy, one that might even be the product of rape, she may now face great difficulty and even fear criminalization if she seeks a termination or is forced to travel to a state in which it remains legal, at high emotional and financial cost.

Given what we know about the risk of neonaticide in young females with poor social support, the criminalization of abortion is likely to increase the prevalence of baby deaths and concealed pregnancies. Furthermore, according to Planned Parenthood, the group most likely to have terminations in the second trimester are girls under the age of fifteen. Often scared, ashamed, alone, and confused, these girls will now find themselves criminalized if they take a decision to terminate a pregnancy when they are in no position to care for a child. Forced to have a baby they do not want, or to commit what may now be deemed an illegal act, or to travel many miles to another state where abortions after fifteen weeks are still permissible, their risk of psychological or physical harm increases. Unplanned pregnancies are a documented risk factor for later violence in women, and the likelihood of neglect or abuse is a real one, unless this young woman is lucky enough to be surrounded by a community that will offer her baby, and herself, support, acceptance, and care.

*

In general, protective factors, which reduce the risk of young women behaving in dangerous ways, include stable housing, school connectedness, and parental monitoring, highlighting the importance of their immediate social context and community. Women who are socially isolated or removed from their parents' care, or who either have dropped out of school or find it alienating, will be most at risk. Those who lack stable housing are also at risk, and it is evident that in the United States, as in the UK, the female homeless population is especially vulnerable to sexual, financial, and physical abuse.

The women I have described in this book are predominantly those who lacked such protective factors in their youth and sought connection through violent partners, mistaking control for care and coercion for guidance; who were exploited by those they turned to for sanctuary. Tragically, risks build on one another, and those who have experienced the most traumatic experiences early on are most likely to remain at highest risk of future harm. Particularly relevant to women are the experiences of forced sex and sexual violence. These, in turn, are directly related to HIV and STD risk, but also to the experience of psychological trauma, which has also been linked to substance use, mental health problems, and suicide risk.

*

As I have shown throughout these pages, the legacy of trauma can lead to women inflicting such harm on others, perpetuating what can appear to be a relentless cycle. There are ways out of this cycle, and the earlier the intervention, the more effective. Encouraging parental monitoring where possible, increasing the sense of connection at school, and reaching out to those women most at risk through youth workers, dedicated mentors, and accessible mental health services can be significant.

In the United States women who commit violent crimes receive extreme punishments, and women of color are disproportionately sentenced to extreme punishment compared to white women. At the present time, fifty-two women sit on death row. Additionally, the United States has one of the highest rates of incarceration in the world.

According to a 2021 report by the Sentencing Project, "Extreme punishments, including the death penalty and life imprisonment, are a hallmark of the United States' harsh criminal legal system. Nationwide one of every 15 women in prison—over 6,600 women—is serving a sentence of life with parole, life without parole, or a virtual life sentence of 50 years or more. The nearly 2,000 women serving life-without-parole (LWOP) sentences can expect to die in prison. Death sentences are permitted by 27 states and the federal government." A significant proportion of the women serving life sentences without parole who commit serious acts of violence, including homicide, were under eighteen at the time of their offense. Two of these women were awaiting execution, even though, in 2005, the U.S. Supreme Court ruled the death penalty unconstitutional for people who committed their offense under the age of eighteen.

My wish is also to end such draconian measures of treating violent women and to reduce the risk that these crimes happen at all. Almost without exception, the women I work with have experienced trauma, abuse, and pain, and have survived experiences that should be unimaginable. The task I face, not just to evaluate and treat women who have committed terrible acts but to change societal attitudes and understanding of how and why they do so, is huge, and sometimes daunting. The nature of my job has meant that the two halves of my life have often existed in close proximity. The most important events of my adult life have all taken place against the backdrop of my professional work. I became a mother and raised my children as I spent agonizing hours working to help women untangle the truth of how they neglected, harmed, or killed their own. I lost my own beloved mother, grandmother, and uncles as I heard women describe abuse at the hands of those who were meant to love and protect them. And I watched my own children grow up as I listened to the often-unbearable testimonies of women whose childhoods had been dominated by physical and sexual abuse, traumas that set an unavoidable course for their adult lives.

As one body and mind trying to absorb and contain all these stories, I have never been able to keep the personal fully separate from the professional. Instead, I accept that to share so closely in the life of another person means that, in some small way, their story becomes a part of mine, opening my eyes to experiences, thoughts, and traumas that can never fully be forgotten, and which sometimes even appear in my dreams. Living with that reality can be painful, but it is also the privilege of being trusted with another person's worst experience and deepest fears—trust that must be repaid with the patient, professional diligence of helping women understand what has really happened to them, why they may think and behave as they do, and what it will take to eventually break the cycles of trauma that have defined their lives.

I begin every contact with a woman believing that it is possible to break the cycle of abuse and trauma, even if, as the patient histories detailed in this book have shown, sometimes it is not. We are all vulnerable to cruel and unexpected events, but equally, with the right support, many of us have the capacity to recover. Even with the most complex women I encounter, and the women whose histories and actions most unsettle or frighten me, I keep in mind this simple belief. My duty is to try to understand and help, not to judge, and I will honor it until it is clearly no longer possible to do so.

Knowing something about the force of social factors, the deep wish to love and be loved, and the vulnerability that underlies even the most brutal facade helps me to refrain from judgment and work with each woman in her complexity. How I get to this place is not always straightforward to describe, but one of the main anchors for me is focusing on the fact that the women who are perpetrators of violence are almost always victims too, and this dual status is essential to hold in mind. Holding in mind the vulnerability of the women, as well as the fact that their aggression may have grown out of necessity, is essential. Additionally, trying to imagine the child inside the adult, the fear underneath the rage, and the pain that shapes the violence are powerful in transforming confusion and anger into curiosity and empathy.

*

There are no simplistic or straightforwardly happy endings to the complex stories of violent women who abuse and kill. Yes, they are perpetrators and the justice system exists to determine their guilt and appropriate sentence. But if the crime and its punishment become the entire story, we trivialize lives that have much to teach us, even if many would rather not hear those truths. As the stories in this book have shown, a woman's violence is so often the culmination of years of trauma: abuse endured in childhood or within a relationship. Although it is certainly the case that women as well as men can be violent without cause, my career has shown me that female violence is very often the product of suffering that needs to be understood before a criminal act can be explained and any future risk reduced. My patients were almost invariably victims of either child or partner abuse before they themselves became perpetrators. As such, most of the crimes I encounter tell a story about what it means to live as a girl and a woman: in childhood and adolescence, as intimate part- ners, as daughters, and as mothers. As the stories in this book have illustrated, abuse and violence are desperately common occurrences at all these stages of life.

For Lillian, her history of abuse at the hands of a violent partner resulted in her own act of murder, a horrific outcome that she could never before have imagined being driven to. The shame and stigma associated with being a victim of such abuse prevented her from seeking help, making public what was happening behind closed doors, and possibly averting the fatal ending. Amber's experience of incest and grooming distorted and perverted her sexual feelings, leading her to seek comfort and gratification through abusing and photographing children, then offering the results to her partner, whom she was desperate to keep, as a form of gift and tribute. In both cases the women were victim and perpetrator alike.

Focusing only on the disastrous outcomes of female violence

is not just reductive, but a stance that denies the reality of trauma and the prevalence of violence against women and girls. No violent woman I have known came from nowhere: she was the product of a society that fails women too readily, enables their abusers too frequently, and condemns those who violate its stereotype of womanhood too impulsively. Only when we replace the urge to vilify with the instinct to care and protect will we make a fairer and safer society for women, preventing many from becoming first the victims and then the perpetrators of abuse. By contrast, if violent women enter our collective consciousness only as the grisly faces alongside tabloid headlines, then we should not be surprised that their crimes continue to live underground and their future victims remain tragically at risk. Consider how the widespread denial of women as child abusers shielded Dolores, Grace, and Amber—and their victims—from view until the fact of serious harm came to light.

In the United States, as in the United Kingdom, the majority of incarcerated women have serious histories of trauma, contributing to their trajectories into crime. Understanding this is not to exonerate violence, or other crimes, but to understand it, in order to prevent it, to guide women and girls to lives in which they are not at risk, nor do they put others at risk. Despite the important work of psychologists and justice campaigners, including Stephanie Covington, who works on creating trauma-informed and -responsive prisons for women, the situation of most incarcerated women is that their histories are invisible and they are seen solely as perpetrators, not as the victims they also are. The disproportionate incarceration of women of color is of particular concern. Mary Enoch Elizabeth Baxter's 2021 film *Ain't I a Woman* powerfully illustrates this. Here Baxter, aka Isis Tha Saviour, depicts her own experience of giving birth in shackles while imprisoned, highlighting the inherent racism and inhumanity of incarceration. Initiatives within female prisons, in both the United States and the United Kingdom, including the Becoming Trauma Informed (BTI) groups, are attempts to combat this unidimensional treatment of women inside prisons. However worthy and essential this intention is, the goal of creating a trauma-informed criminal justice system for women has not yet been reached in either country. The dual status of violent women as both victims and perpetrators of violence seems almost impossible to reconcile.

The situation in the United States is particularly stark, as the Vera Institute of Justice reports, "although American women comprise just five percent of the total global female population, we represent nearly a third of the world's female prisoners." Furthermore, the population of incarcerated women has grown significantly between 1980 and 2021, increasing by 525 percent, and there are currently two thousand women (one in fifteen of all incarcerated women) serving life-without-parole sentences, some of whom face the death sentence, as described above. Recent reports on female imprisonment shine a light on this urgent issue, and the fact that women and girls in prison have significant vulnerabilities, including histories of trauma, such as sexual and physical victimization, mental illness, and poverty. Their imprisonment does not contribute to public safety and is damaging to the women themselves and to their families.

Never has it been more urgent to address the underlying roots of violence and to understand and treat it, viewing violence not as a manifestation of an individual "evil" but as an expression of societal malaise whose origins and meaning require understanding. This stance is fundamental in forensic psychotherapy and has yet to be embraced in the United States, a country with the highest rates of homicide in the developed world. As illustrated throughout this book, the roots of violence are deep and transgenerational, requiring us to begin at the beginning—to meet and understand the lives of those women at greatest risk of violence, most of whom have already encountered abuse, multiple traumas, and gross neglect over many years.

These stories are difficult and distressing, but also ones we can and must learn from. If we as a society open our eyes to the realities of mental illness, maternal despair, and aggression, and the ways in which women and girls may be groomed and abused before becoming perpetrators themselves, we will better prepare those working in the health-care, education, social services, and justice systems to identify individuals at risk. To do so, we need to give up sentimental and idealized visions of femininity and motherhood. Only by acknowledging that female violence exists, understanding where it comes from, and recognizing that it can be treated can we hope to change social attitudes and support women who otherwise struggle to find help. The need to identify signs of abuse and violence is essential. These can be seen in the behavior of children who come to school with bruises, signs of neglect, or aggressive behavior. Women with dental injuries or who isolate themselves from friends and family, change their appearance and habits dramatically, and stay away from work may be victims of domestic violence or intimate partner terrorism but afraid to disclose it. Instead, like Lillian, they are filled with shame and blame themselves until they can stand it no more.

Supporting and safeguarding women who have suffered abuse before becoming perpetrators of violence has been an important part of my work outside psychotherapy. With colleagues from across the health-care and criminal justice systems, I have engaged in initiatives to improve prison conditions for women—including the provision of therapeutic spaces, mother and baby units, culturally specific practices, and access to the outdoors—and to encourage policies that divert women away from the prison system and help those who have been prisoners to find work and stability when they leave. In both this and my therapeutic work, I have been motivated and inspired by the individual stories of the women I meet, their struggles, and the way many have achieved a form of renewal.

I think often of how Skye learned to contain her wish to harm her body, and found her voice in other ways, through writing and reflecting on our conversations; how Saffire learned to control her anger and focus on the needs of her young sons; and of the painful journey that Grace underwent, acknowledging the harm she had inflicted on her daughter and freeing herself and her daughter from a cycle in which abuse had become synonymous with care. These battles were not easily won. It took profound courage for these women to admit their disturbance and the way they had abused both their own bodies and those of their children. Yet the fact that such remarkable personal journeys were possible gives me hope and reaffirms the purpose of my work.

*

Seeing women evolve from using violence as their only form of communication toward self-knowledge and understanding never stops being both beautiful and remarkable. Like the moment when Skye, who in one of our last meetings before she left the prison, looking at the skin she had so relentlessly mutilated, said: "I think my scars are just the tears I never shed." In one of our last sessions, she was finally able to cry: a sign of change, self-realization, and trust. It was the kind of moment that can be years in the making, and which I sometimes worry will never arrive. Skye's words encapsulated how violence is so often the expression of a pain that has found no other voice. My work with her, and so many other women, is about finding ways first to understand and then express the truth of what was done to them, and what it led them to do. For a violent woman to lay down her weapons, she must be capable of understanding the forces that formed them. Only then can she eventually hope to gain control of them, of herself, and of a future that can at last find meaning beyond the shadow of her past.

Acknowledgments

My thinking and writing have been inspired by the work of many colleagues and friends in forensic psychotherapy, especially Anne Aiyegbusi, Gwen Adshead, James Gilligan, the late Gill McGauley, Jessica Yakeley, and Estela Welldon. Close colleagues and friends have also encouraged me to express my outrage at injustice and to create change for women who are imprisoned, both actually and symbolically, especially Julia Blazdell, Danny Brunt, Joanna Burrell, Jackie Craissati, Maxine Dennis, Eleanor Fellowes, Maggie Fishman, Charlotte Fox Weber, Tony Gammidge, Rebecca Lowe, Christy Pitfield, Charlotte Proudman, Sheila Redfern, Yiftach Resheff, Benjamin Ross, Ana Sauma, Julie Tartakover, Sue Thorp, and Kate Thompson. I am grateful for the work and friendship of Siri Hustvedt and Paul Auster, who have been both supportive and inspirational in the later stages of writing. Other good friends have offered sustenance and encouragement throughout, especially Jean and Laurie Burrell, Ted Colman, Christian David, Sean Hand and Maoliosa Kelly, Melissa Midgen, Paul and Ellie Montgomery, Susan Salvati, and Phyllis and Elyse Weiner. Conversation and debate with my friends about the nature and treatment of violence, especially in criminalized women, has shaped my ideas and strengthened my wish to give voice to the women's experiences, so often silenced.

Colleagues and friends at the Health and Justice Division of Central and North West London NHS Foundation Trust, the Female Offender and Offender Health Team at the Ministry of Justice, the Expert Group for Women in the Criminal Justice System, and Sodexo are too numerous to name in full, but I want to thank them for their dedication, insight, and support for this project. I am especially grateful to Sarah Allen, Emily Bunje, Sam Hunter-Briscoe, Kayleigh Holden, Christine Morrison, Louise Minchin, Michelle O'Sullivan, Vicky Robinson, Yvonne Singh, Katie Trewick, Ian Whiteside, and Kai Wong. The staff at HMP Bronzefield, including the chaplaincy, especially Kate Hartley and Simeon Sturney and the librarian, Francesco Calzolaio, also deserve thanks and recognition for their dedication and support for the women in the prison and for my work there. I also owe thanks to Lucy Baldwin, Laura D'Cruz, Joy Doal, Helena Kennedy, Jude Kelman, Caroline Logan, Kate Paradine, and Laura Seebohm, whose creativity, scholarship, and commitment to making changes for women within the criminal justice service are inspirational.

I am very grateful to the editorial team at Knopf, especially for the wisdom and guidance of Victoria Wilson, whose engagement and close reading has shaped this book throughout. I want to thank Belinda Yong of Knopf for her dedication and support. I also want to thank the editors at Orion, particularly Jenny Lord, Maddy Price, and Clarissa Sutherland, and Adam Gauntlett of Peters Fraser and Dunlop. Their interest, suggestions, and faith in this book have been invaluable.

I owe deep thanks to my loving family, Hannah, Joshua, and Nigel Warburton, who have been patient, kind, and supportive, despite losing me to the book for months on end, and am grateful for their comments and thoughts. Hannah's close editing and suggestions were greatly appreciated at all stages of writing. Joshua has read this edition closely, and helped improve the text significantly. My aunts Trudy and Marian Wassner, and Gael Neeson, have also been interested companions on this journey, and my cousin Susan Edlis has always encouraged me. Although no longer alive when this book was written, the love, humor, and intellectual curiosity of my parents, Lotte and Hans Motz, Uncles Herbert and Stefan, and my courageous grandmother, Gizi, have been guiding forces throughout my life. Their stories of exile and immigration and the unfolding secrets of our family history are still alive in me.

Finally, it is to the women with whom I have worked in therapy over many years, and who allowed me to enter their lives, that I owe the greatest thanks. They have taught me about the possibility of overcoming unimaginable trauma, and finding hope where there appeared to be none.

Notes

INTRODUCTION

xiii While only 5 percent: While roughly 10 percent of the total incarcerated population, women still represent a larger portion of people in prisons and jails than in previous decades. Moreover, in many states, women's incarceration rates are continuing to grow faster than men's. A. Kajstura and W. Sawyer, "Women's Mass Incarceration: The Whole Pie 2023," Prison Policy Initiative, March 1, 2023, www.prisonpolicy.org.

xiv Too often, the women: A. Motz, M. Dennis, and A. Aiyegbusi, *Invisible Trauma: Women, Difference, and the Criminal Justice System* (Hove: Routledge, 2020).

xviii For this reason, the case studies: H. Watson et al., "A Systematic Review of Ethnic Minority Women's Experiences of Perinatal Mental Health Conditions and Services in Europe," *PLoS ONE* 14, no. 1 (2019): e0210587.

xviii They are more than twice: E. Cardale et al., *Counted Out: Black, Asian, and Minority Ethnic Women in the Criminal Justice System* (London: Prison Reform Trust, 2017).

CHAPTER 2 SKYE SPEAKING THROUGH THE SKIN

24 "a brick mother": H. Rey, *Universals of Psychoanalysis in the Treatment of Psychotic and Borderline States: Factors of Space-Time and Language.* (J. Magagna, ed.), Free Association Books, 1994.

26 She showed how the social defenses: I. Menzies, "A Case-Study in the Functioning of Social Systems as a Defence Against Anxiety," *Human Relations* 13 (1959): 95–121.

30 It brought to mind: S. Freud, *The Ego and the Id,* Standard Edition, vol. 19 (London: Hogarth, 1923).

30 In this Skye was typical: Prison Reform Trust, "Majority of Women in Prison Have Been Victims of Domestic Abuse," Dec. 4, 2017.

30 a finding also replicated: Ministry of Justice, "Statistics on Women and the Criminal Justice System 2019," Nov. 26, 2020, 33.

33 The psychoanalyst Betty Joseph: B. Joseph, "Addiction to Near-Death," *International Journal of Psychoanalysis* 63 (1982): 449–56.

CHAPTER 3 PAULA THE VOLCANO AND THE VOID

46 She was an example: K. Slade, "Dual Harm: The Importance of Recognising the Duality of Self-Harm and Violence in Forensic Populations," *Medicine, Science, and the Law* 59, no. 2 (2019): 75–77, doi:10:1177/00258 02419845161.

48 All our attempts to form: C. L. Whitfield et al., "Violent Childhood Experiences and the Risk of Intimate Partner Violence in Adults: Assessment in a Large Health Maintenance Organization," *Journal of Interpersonal Violence* 18, no. 2 (2003): 166–85.

CHAPTER 4 SAFFIRE AND JACKIE MOTHERHOOD ON TRIAL

66 In typical development: M. Klein, "Notes on Some Schizoid Mechanisms," *International Journal of Psycho-analysis* 27 (1946): 99–110.

67 "Love and hate are struggling": M. Klein, *Love, Guilt, and Reparation, and Other Works, 1921–1945,* vol. 1 (New York: Free Press, 1975).

68 Confirming that you are: Sigmund Freud articulated this in his statement that "the doctor should be opaque to his patients, and like a mirror, should show them nothing but what is shown to him." M. F. Gibson, "Opening Up: Therapist Self-Disclosure in Theory, Research, and Practice," *Clinical Social Work Journal* 40, no. 3 (2012): 288, doi:10:1007/s10615-012-0391-4.

69 As I so often did: D. W. Winnicott, *Playing and Reality* (London: Tavistock, 1971).

70 Beyond the physical evidence: M. D. S. Ainsworth et al., *Patterns of Attachment: A Psychological Study of the Strange Situation* (Hillsdale, N.J.: Erlbaum, 1978).

82 According to the National: "Statistics Briefing: Child Deaths due to Abuse or Neglect," NSPCC, Dec. 2021, learning.nspcc.org.uk.

82 In that year, California: Statista Research Department, Jan. 26, 2022.

CHAPTER 5 GRACE UNDER COVER OF CARE

95 As one woman with this diagnosis: S. Crawford, "I Have Munchausen's Syndrome Like Corrie's Curtis and I Hurt Myself to Feel Loved," *Mirror Online*, Dec. 2, 2021.

96 But as the psychoanalyst: D. Pines, *A Woman's Unconscious Use of Her Body: A Psychoanalytical Perspective* (London: Virago Press, 1993).

97 A UK study found: RCPCH, *Fabricated or Induced Illness by Carers*, 2002.

98 Contemporary guidance encourages: RCPCH, *Perplexing Presentations (PP) / Fabricated or Induced Illness (FII) in Children: RCPCH Guidance*, Feb. 2021.

99 Notoriously, he had also authored: J. Sweeney and B. Law, "Gene Find Casts Doubt on Double 'Cot Death' Murders," *Observer*, July 15, 2001.

100 Identified examples of FDIA: P. Ferrara et al., "Factitious Disorders and Munchausen Syndrome: The Tip of the Iceberg," *Journal of Child Health Care* 17, no. 4 (2013): 366–74.

100 In managing these feelings: S. Freud, "Criminals from a Sense of Guilt," in *Some Character Types Met With in Psychoanalytic Work*, Standard Edition (1916; London: Vintage, 2001), 14:332–33.

CHAPTER 6 DOLORES LOVED TO DEATH

107 Fleming apparently believed: At the time of the murders, it was determined that Yates suffered from postpartum depression, postpartum psychosis, and schizophrenia. Had she been in the UK, she might have been considered under the Infanticide Act, at least for her youngest child. A. Hammer and S. Cohen, " 'Killer Mom' Asked for Mercy in Social Media Post Just Hours Before 'Stabbing Two Sons to Death and Hiding Them in Bathtub,' " *Daily Mail*, Nov. 27, 2022, www.dailymail.co.uk.

112 As the forensic psychotherapist: E. V. Welldon, *Mother, Madonna, Whore: The Idealisation and Denigration of Motherhood* (London: Free Association Books, 1988).

114 "Mature object love": D. Pines, *A Woman's Unconscious Use of Her Body: A Psychoanalytical Perspective* (London: Virago Press, 1993), 86.

CHAPTER 7 AMBER POWER AND PERVERSION

128 a famous 1949 paper: D. W. Winnicott, "Hate in the Counter-transference," *International Journal of Psycho-analysis* 30 (1949): 69–74.

137 "sado-masochistic relationship": E. V. Welldon, *Playing with Dynamite: A Personal Approach to the Psychoanalytic Understanding of Perversions, Violence, and Criminality* (London: Karnac Books, 2011).

141 I have learned that: F. Cortoni, K. M. Babchishin, and C. Rat, "The Proportion of Sexual Offenders Who Are Female Is Higher Than Thought:
A Meta-analysis," *Criminal Justice and Behavior* 44, no. 2 (2017): 145–62,
doi:10:1177/0093854816658923.

149 "I have been a legal practitioner": H. Kennedy, *Misogyny: A Human Rights
Issue,* Scottish Government Independent Publications, March 8, 2022,
www.gov.scot/publications/misogyny-human-rights-issue.

CHAPTER 8 TANIA TRAUMA AND REVENGE

157 As the psychiatrist: B. van der Kolk, *The Body Keeps the Score: Mind, Brain,
and Body in the Transformation of Trauma* (London: Penguin, 2014).

162 She had never experienced: W. R. Bion, "The K Link," in *Learning from
Experience* (London: Heinemann, 1962; reprinted by Karnac, 1984), 89–94.

CHAPTER 9 MAJA OBJECTS OF OBSESSION

171 This was apparently confirmed: T. Turner, "Erotomania and Queen Victoria: Or Love Among the Assassins?," *Psychiatric Bulletin* 14 (1990): 224–27.

185 As the cases of Rachel Bellesen: Bellesen shot and killed her ex-partner
after he attacked her and tried to rape her. What followed was a public
trial that would test the lengths necessary to prove self-defense, even after
a lifetime of domestic abuse.

185 In her statement, Heard: C. Grady, "Johnny Depp, Amber Heard, and
Their $50 Million Defamation Suit, Explained," *Vox,* June 1, 2022, www
.vox.com.

CHAPTER 10 LILLIAN BREAKING POINT

203 Baroness Kennedy has: H. Kennedy, *Eve Was Shamed: How British Justice
Is Failing Women* (London: Chatto and Windus, 2018).

CONCLUSION

211 With echoes of: Jeremy Gauh.

211 "What I did?": "'What I did?' NYC Mom Accused of Hiding Murdered
Sons in Tub Ranted Outside Shelter," *New York Post,* Nov. 27, 2022.

212 As Jessica Winter described: J. Winter, "What We Still Don't Understand
About Postpartum Psychosis," *The New Yorker,* March 14, 2023.

213 recent report on Youth Risk Behavior: *Youth Risk Behavior Survey: Data
Summary and Trends Report, 2011–2021,* Division of Adolescent and School
Health, U.S. Centers for Disease Control and Prevention.

214 The escalation of risky behaviors: The particular vulnerability of women is highlighted in the CDC report: "Several experiences of violence are increasing, especially for certain groups of youth. These data show increases in the proportion of youth who did not go to school because of safety concerns, increases among female students experiencing sexual violence by anyone and being forced to have sex, and increases among male students experiencing electronic bullying," ibid., 2.

215 Faced with an unplanned pregnancy: Human Rights Watch, "Human Rights Crisis: Abortion in the United States After Dobbs," April 18, 2023, https://www.hrw.org/news/2023/04/18/human-rights-crisis-abortion -united-states-after-dobbs. The recent report on the impact of *Dobbs v. Jackson Women's Health Organization* on human rights describes the consequences of this ruling and also warms that it "violates principles of equality and non-discrimination; they fall disproportionately on marginalized populations including Black, indigenous, and people of color; people with disabilities; immigrants; and those living in poverty." This case overturned fifty years of precedent of the right to an abortion, established by *Roe v. Wade*, where Roe held that abortion right is part of a right to privacy, springing from the First, Fourth, Fifth, Ninth and Fourteenth Amendments to the Constitution. Center for Reproductive Rights, "Dobbs v. Jackson Women's Health Organization," https://reproductiverights.org /case/scotus-mississippi-abortion-ban.

216 These, in turn, are: Unfortunately, almost all other indicators of health and well-being in the CDC report, including protective sexual behaviors (i.e., condom use, sexually transmitted disease [STD] testing, and HIV testing), experiences of violence, mental health, and suicidal thoughts and behaviors, worsened significantly.

216 In the United States women: "Nationally, one of every 39 Black women in prison is serving life without parole compared with one of every 59 imprisoned white women." A. Nellis, *In the Extreme: Women Serving Life Without Parole and Death Sentences in the United States,* The Sentencing Project, Sept. 2021, 7.

217 According to a 2021 report: Ibid.

220 Initiatives within female prisons: M. Petrillo, " 'We've All Got a Big Story': Experiences of a Trauma-Informed Intervention in Prison," *Howard Journal of Crime and Justice* 60: 232–50, doi.org/10.1111/hojo.12408.

221 The situation in the United States: A. Nellis, *In the Extreme,* 2021; Vera Institute of Justice, "Gender and Justice in America," www.vera.org. Between 1980 and 2021, the number of incarcerated women increased by more than 525 percent, rising from a total of 26,326 in 1980 to 168,449 in 2021. While 2020 saw a substantial downsizing due to the COVID-19 pandemic, this trend reversed with a 10 percent increase in 2021. N. Monazzam and

K. M. Budd, "Incarcerated Women and Girls: Fact Sheet," The Sentencing project, www.sentencingproject.org.

221 some of whom face the death sentence: The U.S. does not accept the Infanticide Law, in which a woman who kills her baby within the first year of life, and can be found to suffer from disturbance of mind due to pregnancy or lactation, can be spared a murder charge. As one of the leading experts in perinatal illness in the United States, Margaret Spinelli describes, "Maternal infanticide, or the murder of a child in the first year of life by its mother, is a subject both compelling and repulsive. The victim is innocent, but the perpetrator may be a victim too. In the USA, mentally ill women who commit infanticide may receive long prison sentences or even the death penalty. England, Canada, Australia, and more than 20 European countries have 'infanticide laws,' which provide more humane treatment and psychiatric care for mentally ill mothers who kill. One of the reasons for the sentences in the USA lies in our archaic insanity defense. In addition, the psychiatric community does not recognize perinatal illness as a formal diagnosis. Furthermore, general forensic psychiatrists who testify in the courtroom have little knowledge of perinatal illness." M. Spinelli, "Infanticide and American Criminal Justice (1980–2018)," *Archives of Women's Mental Health* 22, no. 1 (2019), 173–77, doi: 10.1007/s00737-018-0873-7; F. Wilson et al., "Neonaticides in the United States 2008–2017," *Academic Forensic Pathology* 12, no. 1 (2022), doi: 10.1177/19253621221077870. Classifications of the motivations for maternal killing of their newborns or infants under the age of one are offered in a recent study: K. Greenwood et al., "Content Analysis of Infanticide and Neonaticide Cases in the UK," *Journal of Investigative Psychology and Offender Profiling* 20, no. 2 (2023), 121–34, https://doi.org/10.1002/jip.1612. For further reading, see A. Motz, *The Psychology of Female Violence: Crimes Against the Body* (London: Routledge, 2008).

221 Recent reports: This report, *In the Extreme,* describes the experiences of women awaiting execution in the United States, including two women whose crimes were committed when they were under age eighteen. The increasing incarceration of girls and women in the United States is also described by the Vera Institute of Justice. Vera Institute of Justice, "Gender and Justice in America," www.vera.org/news/gender-and-justice-in-america.

Index

factors driving, 60, 213–14
full spectrum of, 209
generational cycles of, xx
ignorance and denial about, xi–xiv,
    xviii
impact of, on professional treating,
    xvii–xviii
importance of attending to, xix–xx,
    212
link between motherhood and, 61
male coercion and, xiii
medical professionals as target of, 38
perpetrators as victims of, 219, 221
rise in sexual abuse of young women
    and girls and, 213–14, 233n
risk factors and, 216
romantic partners and, 150
self-harm as starting point to
    understand, 60
social attitudes and, xiii, 213–18, 222
stereotypes of, xii–xiv
unplanned pregnancies and, 215
femininity, 44–45, 59, 106, 115, 117,
    142, 222
feminism, 188
fetal alcohol syndrome, 84
filming of crime, 160–61
Fleming, Dimone, 107, 211–12, 231n
Florida, 82
forensic psychotherapy, xi, 4–5, 6,
    7, 19–20, 37, 39–40, 94, 99–100,
    112–13, 168, 221
forgiveness, 207
foster care, 10–12, 17–18, 29, 59, 70, 78,
    125, 147, 151, 156, 158
fragility, 180
Freud, Sigmund, 30, 179, 230n
full care order, 78

gaslighting, 196, 204
gender roles, reversal of, 45
George V, King, 171
gifts, 167

Grace, 85, 86–106, 144–45, 148, 220,
    222
grandchildren, 57–59
grief
    after killing child, 120, 211
    legacies of, 3, 16–19
    self-harm and, 31
    unresolved mourning and, 181
guardian *ad litem*, 75, 77, 79, 81, 83
guilt
    bulimia and, 156
    child abuse victim and, 30, 41, 161,
        164
    child murderer and, 111, 120
    child sexual abuse victim and, 8, 41
    domestic violence victim and, 204–7
    loss of child and, 11
    reducing sense of, 18, 164, 166
    self-harm and, 30
    sexual assault victim and, 158

halfway house, 153
harassment, 168–69, 174
Harris, Jean, 188–89
hatred
    for coercive mother, 164
    love and, 167
    therapists' feelings of, 128–29
health-care system, 222
Heard, Amber, 185
Hearst, Patty, xiv–xv
help
    humiliation of asking for, 43
    self-harm as cry for, 30–31
helplessness, 160, 180
    learned, 203
Hindley, Myra, xii
histrionic personality disorder, 72, 101
Hitler, Adolf, 54–55
HIV, 213, 216, 233n
Holocaust, xv, 124–25
Holofernes (biblical figure), xii
home, prison as, 34, 36

mother's and, 42, 65–66, 68
as outlet for pain, 59–60
rejection triggering, 40
roots of, 74–75, 221–22
social factors and, 221
therapy and, 157
underground, 211
volatile behavior, 48, 66, 69, 73, 79
vulnerability, 43, 48, 218

weakness, 41, 44–45
Welldon, Estela, 5, 112–13, 137
Wesleyan University, 124
whole system approach, 26
Winnicott, Donald, 69, 128–29
Winter, Jessica, 212
womanhood, idealization of, xii, 81, 84, 212–13, 220
women
  denial of potential as perpetrators of violence, 149
  desensitized to harming child, 148

idealization of, xii, 60, 84, 122, 142
imprisoned, xiii, 5, 25
involved with sexual offenders, xii
in mixed wards with men, 5
as perpetrators of violence, 149
recognizing agency and complexity of, xvii–xviii, 212–13
roles of, xiv
silencing of, 149–50
traumas ignored and untreated, 149
victim stereotype and, 49
vilification of, 149, 212–13
women of color, xviii, 216, 233n
Women's Mental Health Program, Mount Sinai, 212
worthlessness, 11, 41–43, 61, 137, 165
Wuornos, Aileen, xii

Yates, Andrea, xii, 107, 115, 212, 239n
young offenders' institute, 29
Youth Risk Behavior report (CDC), 213, 216

A NOTE ON THE TYPE

This book was set in Adobe Garamond. Designed for the Adobe Corporation by Robert Slimbach, the fonts are based on types first cut by Claude Garamond (ca. 1480–1561). Garamond was a pupil of Geoffroy Tory and is believed to have followed the Venetian models, although he introduced a number of important differences, and it is to him that we owe the letter we now know as "old style." He gave to his letters a certain elegance and feeling of movement that won their creator an immediate reputation and the patronage of Francis I of France.

Typeset by Scribe,
Philadelphia, Pennsylvania

Printed and bound by Berryville Graphics,
Berryville, Virginia